Hacking Point of Sale

Hacking Point of Sale

Payment Application Secrets,
Threats, and Solutions

Slava Gomzin

WILEY

Hacking Point of Sale: Payment Application Secrets, Threats, and Solutions

Published by
John Wiley & Sons, Inc.
10475 Crosspoint Boulevard
Indianapolis, IN 46256
www.wiley.com

Copyright © 2014 by John Wiley & Sons, Inc., Indianapolis, Indiana
Published simultaneously in Canada

ISBN: 978-1-118-81011-8
ISBN: 978-1-118-81010-1 (ebk)
ISBN: 978-1-118-81007-1 (ebk)

Manufactured in the United States of America
10 9 8 7 6 5 4 3 2 1

For general information on our other products and services please contact our Customer Care Department within the United States at (877) 762-2974, outside the United States at (317) 572-3993 or fax (317) 572-4002.

Wiley publishes in a variety of print and electronic formats and by print-on-demand. Some material included with standard print versions of this book may not be included in e-books or in print-on-demand. If this book refers to media such as a CD or DVD that is not included in the version you purchased, you may download this material at http://booksupport.wiley.com. For more information about Wiley products, visit www.wiley.com.

Library of Congress Control Number: 2013954096

To all of us who pay and get paid with plastic.

About the Author

Slava Gomzin is a Security and Payments Technologist at Hewlett-Packard, where he helps create products that are integrated into modern payment processing ecosystems using the latest security and payments technologies. Prior to joining Hewlett-Packard, Slava was a security architect, corporate product security officer, R & D and application security manager, and development team leader at Retalix, a Division of NCR Retail. As PCI ISA, he focused on security and PA-DSS, PCI DSS, and PCI P2PE compliance of POS systems, payment applications, and gateways. Before moving into security, Slava worked in R & D on design and implementation of new products including next-generation POS systems and various interfaces to payment gateways and processors. He currently holds CISSP, PCIP, ECSP, and Security+ certifications. Slava blogs about payment and technology security at www.gomzin.com.

About the Technical Editor

Rob Shimonski (www.shimonski.com) is an experienced entrepreneur and an active participant in the business community. Rob is a best-selling author and editor with over 15 years of experience developing, producing, and distributing print media in the form of books, magazines, and periodicals. To date, Rob has successfully created over 100 books that are currently in circulation. Rob has worked for countless companies including CompTIA, Wiley, Microsoft, McGraw-Hill Education, Elsevier, Cisco, the National Security Agency, and Digidesign. Rob has over 20 years of experience working in IT, networking, systems, and security. He is a veteran of the U.S. military and has been entrenched in security topics for his entire professional career. Rob has an extremely diverse background in security and networking and has successfully helped over a dozen major companies get on track with PCI.

Credits

Executive Editor
Carol Long

Senior Project Editor
Adaobi Obi Tulton

Technical Editor
Rob Shimonski

Production Editor
Daniel Scribner

Copy Editor
Christina Haviland

Editorial Manager
Mary Beth Wakefield

Freelancer Editorial Manager
Rosemarie Graham

Associate Director of Marketing
David Mayhew

Marketing Manager
Ashley Zurcher

Business Manager
Amy Knies

Vice President and Executive Group Publisher
Richard Swadley

Associate Publisher
Jim Minatel

Project Coordinator, Cover
Katie Crocker

Proofreader
Sarah Kaikini, Word One

Indexer
Robert Swanson

Cover Designer
Ryan Sneed/Wiley

Cover Image
© defun/iStockphoto.com

Acknowledgments

First, I would like to thank Wiley for providing me with this unique authorship opportunity. Thanks to my editor, Adaobi Obi Tulton, for her patience, attention, and support throughout the entire publishing process. Special thanks to Carol Long who believed in this book and made it possible. Thanks also to my first editor, Jeannette de Beauvoir, who helped me to polish and promote my book proposal.

Writing a book like this wouldn't be possible without gaining experience and learning from other professionals over the years. I would like to thank my former coworkers. Special thanks to Shmuel Witman, Doug McClellan, Sagi Zagagi, and Ofer Nimtsovich, who influenced me at different stages of my career by sharing their knowledge and vision, and helped me to survive in this industry and develop myself professionally.

Finally, special credit goes to my wife, Svetlana, and my daughters, Alona, Aliza, and Arina, for understanding the reasons for my absence from their lives on countless weekends and evenings while I was working on this book.

Contents at a Glance

Contents

Introduction

False facts are highly injurious to the progress of science, for they often long endure; but false views, if supported by some evidence, do little harm, as everyone takes a salutary pleasure in providing their falseness; and when this is done, one path towards error is closed and the road to truth is often at the same time opened.

—Charles Darwin

Nearly five million point-of-sale (POS) terminals process about 1,500 credit and debit card transactions every second in the United States alone.[1, 2, 3] Most of these systems, regardless of their formal compliance with industry security standards, potentially expose millions of credit card records—including those being processed in memory, transmitted between internal servers, sent for authorization or settlement, and accumulated on hard drives. This sensitive data is often weakly protected or not protected at all. It is just a matter of time before someone comes along and takes it away. Valuable cardholder information can be stolen from many places in a merchant's POS system, such as unprotected memory, unencrypted network transmission, poorly encrypted disk storage, card reader interface, or compromised pinpad device.

There are more than one billion active credit and debit card accounts in the United States.[4] It is not surprising that such cards have become an attractive target for hackers. In 2011, payment card information was involved in 48% of security breaches—more than any other data type.[5] In 2012, POS terminals and payment data were record breakers in three different categories: The variety of compromised assets, the variety of compromised data, and the breach count by data variety.[6]

Information about breaches and new types of malware aimed specifically at payment systems is popping up in the mass media almost every day, and yet we're seeing only the tip of the iceberg since many incidents aren't reported to the public. In such a critical situation, it's very important to assess the balance of power between offensive and defensive sides in order to decide what to do next.

PCI standards provide a great security baseline, but they still don't protect electronic payments adequately. Once merchants and software vendors achieve

PCI compliance, they should continue securing their systems beyond the basics in order to reach a reasonable level of protection.

This book summarizes, systemizes, and shares knowledge about payment application security. All the aspects of card payment processing—from the structure of magnetic stripe to architecture and deployment models to communication protocols— are reviewed from the security viewpoint. Usually, information security takes care of three major subjects: confidentiality, integrity, and availability. All three are very important. When we talk about security of payment applications, all three subjects are still applicable: the payment data should be protected from disclosure at all times, it should not be altered, and the payment service should be ready to use 100% of the time. However, as we know, the greatest threat related to electronic payments is stealing sensitive authentication data, specifically Track 1, Track 2, or PAN. Therefore, payment application security is naturally focused on the first information security principle, confidentiality, and its associated threat, information disclosure. This fact explains why security standards related to payments, such as PCI, primarily talk about controls which take care of confidentiality.

Speaking of POS and electronic payments, we certainly are not thinking of just traditional brick and mortar stores. Online payments are another huge field which probably deserves no less attention. Since both of these areas are equally huge, they would not fit properly into the framework of a single book. Discussion about online payments requires at least an overview of special topics such as security of data centers and, obviously, web application security. At the same time, some very important subjects, such as POI devices, are not applicable when talking about e-commerce security. This book is dedicated to in-store payment systems and all the aspects of their security. Perhaps online payments will be a great topic for my next book.

Before we dive into the details of vulnerabilities and attack vectors, let's define the scope of the threats. It is important to understand that while we are talking about threats to POS systems, most of the attacks are performed on *payment applications* which can be either an internal part of the POS system or a completely separate module. Payment application is a desired target because in most cases it is a piece of software running under a Windows operating system on PC-based devices connected to a local network or even directly to the Internet. In combination with the fact that it accepts, processes, stores, and transmits sensitive payment card information, this opens various possibilities to steal the money remotely. From this point forward when we say "point of sale" it means "payment application" and vice versa.

Author's Note

In the spring of 2011, I was urgently called to my then employer's corporate headquarters in Israel to work on a special project. I was asked to lead the design and development of a new payment system for one of the largest supermarket chains in Europe (name withheld for privacy). I had been working full time on security and PCI compliance rather than development, but my 10 years of experience in the development of payment interfaces gave them some hope of saving the project after several previous failures. I was given substantial resources, but the schedule was very tight for a project of such magnitude: we had two months to release a working version. In addition, the solution needed to be designed using the latest technology and security standards.

The development team I was given was made up of the best possible programmers. Almost immediately, however, I ran into an unexpected problem: Since the product was new, no one in the group had a clue about payment interfaces—despite the fact that they already had experience in POS development. Of course, there was no question about security or PCI compliance.

The first few days and even weeks were spent explaining electronic payments in general, the details of the architecture of payment applications, and security standards in this area. Everyone knew what a credit card was and how to swipe it, but that was it! I thought it would be useful to have a guide to introduce new architects and programmers to the field, but I knew that such a guide didn't exist. My own knowledge in this area was accumulated through many years of work on a variety of payment systems and studying the application security. That's when the idea for this book was born.

Eventually, the payment solution was successfully delivered on time and I returned to the United States to continue with my regular job. But I couldn't stop thinking about the book. Since then, the idea was slightly transformed to reflect the latest developments in the industry. For example, the widespread introduction of PCI standards has led to a shift in attack vectors, from data storage to memory. Also, newborn P2PE standards brought high hopes for merchants and great challenges for software developers and hardware manufacturers. However, the essential goal remained the same: Create a guide for developers, security professionals, users of payment systems, and executives, to help them understand the incredible blending of architecture principles, industry standards, software vulnerabilities, attack vectors, and cryptographic techniques that together make up payment application security.

Who This Book Is For

There are several types of users that will benefit from reading and using the information in this book.

Point of Sale and Payment Application Developers, Development Managers, and *Software Architects* working for software vendors and service providers will learn the basics of payment applications and how to protect their products from security threats. There are a few code samples provided for this group at the end of the book. (I know, hackers do not code in C#, but they know to translate it to C when needed.)

QA Analysts and *Managers* will get some ideas on how to create and conduct security penetration testing of payment software.

Security Architects, Managers, Consultants, and *Executives* working for merchants will learn what questions they should ask payment application vendors and service providers in order to determine the level of protection of their software and hardware.

Solutions Architects, Project and *Product Managers,* and *Executives* working for both vendors and merchants will learn about areas of potential vulnerabilities in order to be able to estimate the risks associated with implementing payment solutions and efforts necessary to mitigate them.

Pros and Cons of Security Through Obscurity

I was thinking about this issue when I started writing the book and was noticing a significant amount of sensitive information I potentially disclose to "bad guys." I am sure there will be people asking "Why are you talking about these issues in the first place? We are putting so much effort into achieving PCI compliance, and you are saying it is not enough and showing how to hack PCI compliant applications! You are ruining our work! Let's keep these vulnerabilities secret until the PCI Council notices them, admits their importance, develops countermeasures, includes them into the next version of standards, and requires us to implement them!" Well, it sounds already too complicated to do in a reasonable period of time. And what if the bad guys already learned some of this stuff? They won't tell you about their knowledge. They will also keep it secret until the day they break your system.

There are two "clubs" in this game—hackers and developers. Both are closed clubs and both are trying to keep their secrets from each other. The problem begins when hackers become developers, or developers become hackers. In the first case, you get an "insider"—someone who knows your application's secret tricks, back doors, and weaknesses. This information can be disclosed to third parties, or used directly by that person. In the second case, you have "secret" information that went with the person who left the company and was then free to use it or sell it to others. Both cases are bad if application security is mostly achieved through obscurity.

As Bruce Schneier said, "Disclosed vulnerability is one that—at least in most cases—is patched. And a patched vulnerability makes us all more secure. Minimize the number of secrets in your security system. To the extent that you can accomplish that, you increase the robustness of your security. To the extent you can't, you increase its fragility. Obscuring system details is a separate decision from making your system secure regardless of publication; it depends on the availability of a community that can evaluate those details and the relative communities of "good guys" and "bad guys" that can make use of those details to secure other systems".[7, 8] I am sure there is a community that is ready for this publication.

What This Book Is Not

This book is not about payment card fraud protection. Those controls only protect the cardholder and the merchant before the card is swiped. However, they do not secure the sensitive cardholder data once it is entered into the system. Examples of such security measures are using CVV or ZIP code verification during authorization.

Although there is an entire chapter about PCI, as well as multiple references to the standards which became an essential part of the payment industry, this book is not a guide on PCI compliance. There are publications and training courses that will teach you about PCI. Rather, this book looks beyond PCI and provides practical recommendations on how to implement real application security controls. Neither is it about security of payment processing from the point of view of credit card brands. PCI standards help to secure only selected fragments of the big picture. However, the entire process, including implementation and deployment of payment applications, is vulnerable by design, and responsibility for its security is delegated to merchants, payment processors, software/hardware vendors, and service providers.

Security of payment processing data centers is also outside the scope of this book because it requires much more than just a single chapter. This book is focused on the retail store which is more vulnerable than any other electronic payment flow players.

How This Book Is Structured

Good programmers follow coding conventions and best practices. One of the basic development principles is dividing the code into small, relatively independent pieces—several lines of code in size—which can be easily read and understood. The same approach was implemented in this book to minimize the size of each single section. The text is structured in a manner similar to professional technical documents, with a detailed table of contents that makes it simple to quickly locate and read specific pieces of information.

The book is divided into three main parts:

1. Technology overview

2. Description of attacks and vulnerabilities

3. Solutions for the problems (mitigations and protection measures)

Part I, "Anatomy of Payment Application Vulnerabilities" (Chapters 1, 2, and 3), sets the scene for Parts II and III by explaining the technological background of electronic payments. Even though it's an introduction to the world of cards and payment applications, all their components are reviewed from a security point of view.

Chapter 1, "Processing Payment Transactions," covers the basics of payment processing: How different organizations—players in the plastic game—participate in the transaction flow, their responsibilities and challenges, and the differences between various payment transaction types, with detailed explanations of exception and error-handling scenarios.

Chapter 2, "Payment Applications Architecture," introduces basic design concepts, compares different deployment models, and explains the main functional modules of payment application divided into two groups—interfaces and processors. It also explains the types of connectivity and differences between communication and message protocols.

Chapter 3, "PCI," describes security standards that regulate the industry employing payment applications, and shows how they protect the sensitive cardholder data from being stolen. This chapter explains the difference between PCI DSS and PA-DSS from both merchant and software vendor perspectives. There is a description of standards (such as ISO and FIPS) that indirectly affect payment application security. The chapter introduces the PCI P2PE standard (the technical details of P2PE implementation are also explained in Chapter 8).

Part II, "Attacks on Point-of-sale Systems" (Chapters 4, 5, and 6) explains how card data can be stolen from POS machines, and why particular areas of payment applications are more vulnerable than others.

Chapter 4, "Turning 40 Digits Into Gold," explains what is inside the payment card and how this knowledge helps the bad guys use stolen cards to get cash.

The goal of this chapter is to demonstrate the ease and simplicity of the credit card fraud by providing a step-by-step explanation of the process, from obtaining the "dump" to getting the cash. There's a detailed description of the carding that includes hidden and small but important tricks of encoding, embossing, and tipping fake cards.

Chapter 5, "Penetrating Security Free Zones," describes payment application vulnerabilities not addressed by existing PCI security regulations. Although PCI defines a great security baseline, many areas of payment applications are covered by neither PCI nor other standards. This chapter also contains "bonus" sections about non-software attacks that are not directly related to payment applications but aimed at other areas of POS, such as the physical security of pinpad devices and design flaws in POS payment processes.

Chapter 6, "Breaking into PCI-protected Areas," covers payment application vulnerabilities in areas that are supposed to be protected by current PCI security standards. Even though PCI standards require encryption on "data at rest," there are various vulnerabilities associated with data storage, such as weak encryption mechanisms and poor key management.

Part III, "Defense" (Chapters 7, 8, and 9), addresses the issues described in the previous part. It describes how to prevent attacks on payment applications by employing powerful cryptographic tools for protecting the cardholder data and payment application code.

Chapter 7, "Cryptography in Payment Applications," explains the basics of cryptography in the context of payment application security, which provides necessary foundations for implementing protection controls defined in subsequent chapters. Information in this chapter includes a description of main cryptographic principles and applications such as symmetric and asymmetric encryption, digital signatures, and cryptographic standards. It provides the reader with knowledge needed for understanding and designing powerful protection mechanisms such as sensitive cardholder data encryption, digital signing, and point-to-point encryption.

Chapter 8, "Protecting Cardholder Data," explains how the power of modern cryptography can be utilized in order to protect sensitive cardholder information from the moment of swiping the card at the POS to the transaction settlement. The chapter describes various methods of data encryption at any possible state—in memory, in transit, and at rest—including an introduction to the latest industry trend—a technology capable of protecting them all called point-to-point encryption. The chapter defines the different types of point-to-point encryption implementation—hardware, software, and hybrid—and how they affect security. It also explains the essentials of typical P2PE solutions such as DUKPT key management scheme.

Chapter 9, "Securing Application Code," explains how to protect the payment application itself from attacks in the hazardous environment of retail stores. Attacks on sensitive data in memory, in transit, and at rest are not the only ways to penetrate POS systems. This chapter explains how to protect the application itself by utilizing client and server certificates, digital signatures, and code obfuscation.

Appendix A, "POS Vulnerability Rank Calculator," is a handy tool for merchants, software vendors, and security assessors. The questionnaire will assist in security risk assessment by evaluating the availability and quality of payment application security controls.

Appendix B, "Glossary of Terms and Abbreviations" deciphers the acronyms and defines the terminology used by payment application security professionals.

Notes

1. "Point-of-sale terminals (per 100,000 adults)," The World Bank, 2008 – 2012, http://data.worldbank.org/indicator/FB.POS.TOTL.P5

2. "Table 26. Age Distribution of the Population by Sex and Generation: 2011," United States Census Bureau, http://www.census.gov/population/age/data/2011comp.html

3. "The 2007 Federal Reserve Payments Study," Federal Reserve System (2007), http://www.frbservices.org/files/communications/pdf/research/2007_payments_study.pdf

4. "Credit card statistics, industry facts, debt statistics," CreditCards.com, http://www.creditcards.com/credit-card-news/credit-card-industry-facts-personal-debt-statistics-1276.php#Circulation

5. *2012 Data Breach Investigations Report*, Verizon, http://www.verizonenterprise.com/resources/reports/rp_data-breach-investigations-report-2012-ebk_en_xg.pdf

6. *2013 Data Breach Investigations Report*, Verizon, http://www.verizonenterprise.com/DBIR/2013/

7. Bruce Schneier, "Secrecy, Security, and Obscurity," *Crypto-Gram Newsletter* (May 2002), http://www.schneier.com/crypto-gram-0205.html#1

8. Bruce Schneier, "The Vulnerabilities Market and the Future of Security," *Crypto-Gram Newsletter* (June 2012), http://www.schneier.com/crypto-gram-1206.html#1

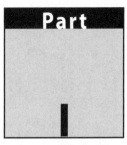

Anatomy of Payment Application Vulnerabilities

Science in the service of humanity is technology, but lack of wisdom may make the service harmful.
—Isaac Asimov

In This Part

Processing Payment Transactions

Because people have no thoughts to deal in, they deal cards, and try and win one another's money. Idiots!

—Arthur Schopenhauer

In order to understand the vulnerability points of point-of-sale and payment applications, it is necessary to know the basics—how, when, and why sensitive cardholder data moves between different peers during the payment transaction cycle:

- Why (the reason): Is it really necessary to hold, store, and transmit this data throughout the entire process?
- How (the location and the routes): What are the areas with a concentration of sensitive records?
- When (the timing): How long is this information available in those areas?

Payment Cards

The use of payment cards is obviously one of the main subjects of this book. There are several main types of payment cards commonly used for payments:

The credit card was the first payment card and it is still very common. By paying with a credit card, customers use their available credit and pay the bill afterwards. Credit cards are not usually protected by a Personal Identification Number (PIN), which allows them to be used for online purchases.

The debit (ATM, Cash) card is a relatively new method of payment. It is different from a credit card because the debit cardholder pays with the money available in their bank account, which is debited immediately in real time. A debit card seems to be more dangerous compared to a credit card because the debit card is directly linked to the bank checking account and usually allows ATM cash withdrawals. On the other hand, it is more protected by the required two-factor authentication (PIN number plus card itself). The real dangerous element of many branded debit cards is that they can be processed as credit cards, without entering the PIN.

The gift card is similar to a debit card but usually does not have the protection provided by a PIN. The gift card is not linked to a bank account and normally "contains" fixed amounts of funds. The card itself does not hold any financial information—the point-of-sale (POS) terminal communicates with the gift card provider during payment transactions in order to get authorization. Gift cards are less dangerous than credit and debit cards because only fixed, often very limited, amounts of money can be stolen.

The fleet (or proprietary) card is similar to a credit card but can be used only at particular locations (usually gas stations and convenience stores) and for purchasing only limited types of merchandise (such as fuel and other automobile items). Fleet cards, even though often issued by major card brands, are less interesting to "bad guys" because they cannot be used for ATM withdrawal, online shopping, or purchases in department or grocery stores.

Table 1-1 shows a list of major payment card types and their main features.

Table 1-1: Payment Card Types

CARD TYPE	ISSUED	PURCHASE POWER, $$	ACCEPTANCE	PROTECTED ACCORDING TO PCI DATA SECURITY STANDARDS?
Credit	By banks under payment brands (such as Visa) or directly by payment brands (such as American Express)	Several thousand	Virtually any brick-and-mortar or online merchant.	Yes
Debit	By banks with or without payment brands	Several thousand	Virtually any brick-and-mortar or online merchant; bank ATM.	Only if issued under payment brand

Continues

Table 1-1 *(continued)*

CARD TYPE	ISSUED	PURCHASE POWER, $$	ACCEPTANCE	PROTECTED ACCORDING TO PCI DATA SECURITY STANDARDS?
Gift	By payment brands or proprietary providers	Several hundred	If branded, virtually any brick-and-mortar or online merchant. If proprietary, only particular merchants.	Only if issued under payment brand
Fleet	By banks, payment brands, or proprietary providers	Several hundred	Particular merchants (usually gas stations and c-stores) and limited merchandise types (usually fuel).	Only if issued under payment brand

PCI: Payment Card Industry

Card Entry Methods

There are two main methods used to enter the card data into the POS in order to start a payment transaction: *swipe* and *manual entry*.

MSR

The first method uses a *Magnetic Stripe Reader,* or MSR, which is a device that reads the magnetic stripe on payment cards. Modern MSR devices have encryption capabilities and can be used in point-to-point encryption (P2PE) solutions (see Chapter 8 for more details). The easiest way to enter the card data into the POS is to just swipe the card in the MSR so it can read the magnetic stripe and automatically enter all the necessary information. However, if the magnetic stripe is damaged, the customer or cashier can manually enter the account number and expiration date embossed on the front of the card.

Some MSR devices emulate keyboard input, so swiping the card is equivalent to simply typing numbers and letters on the computer keyboard. Stealing the track data in this case is as simple as sniffing the MSR input by installing a *keystroke logger.*[1]

Pinpad

The second method uses a pinpad. A pinpad, or Point of Interaction (POI) with a built-in MSR, is a more sophisticated device because it has firmware which can be customized for various functions including protection of the card's sensitive data. Most pinpads also have hardware encryption capabilities implemented as TRSM (Tamper-Resistant Security Module). In addition to MSR, POI also includes other peripherals, such as a customer display and keyboard (in addition to the pinpad), for better direct interaction with the customer throughout the payment process.

Key Players

According to Visa, there are five key players in the card payment processing game: *Consumers, Merchants, Acquirers, Issuers,* and *Card Brands.*[2] However, in practice, there are usually more participants. In addition to Consumers, Merchants, Acquirers, Issuers, and Card Brands, there are also *Gateways, Processors, Software Vendors,* and *Hardware Manufacturers* who facilitate the payment transaction processing.

Before diving into the details of these players, I would like to remind you that the scope of this book is security of POS and associated payment applications which are located in brick-and-mortar stores. Despite the fact that merchants account for a relatively small percentage of the overall payment processing life cycle, their portion of responsibility and risk is incomparably larger than anyone else's share. There are several reasons for this:

1. First, merchants have a very distributed structure compared to others—a typical retail chain may consist of dozens to thousands of stores. Compare this to a processor who may have a few enterprise-scale data centers where it is much easier to organize the security measures.

2. Second, retail stores are public places with all the ensuing consequences for security.

3. Third, most merchants rely on hardware and software vendors as their technology providers (including security) and simply are not ready to accept the fact that they have a technology which is vulnerable by design. When the PC and Internet revolution in the late 1990s started replacing the old cash registers and standalone credit terminals with complex POS systems with integrated payment applications, it also began bringing countless system and network security flaws and eventually made them an inescapable day-to-day nightmare reality for millions of retailers around the world.

Consumer (Cardholder)

It's us. We go to stores, swipe the cards, and pay the bills.

Ideally, consumers are not supposed to care about security beyond keeping their PIN a secret. If the card is lost or stolen, the consumer just wants to call the bank and get a new one. When our card is swiped, our private information is shared with the merchant, whose POS system is supposed to protect our information throughout the process. We rely on modern high-end technologies to protect our plastic money.

In practice, unfortunately, it's not happening. Not all the cards are protected by a PIN. So if the card is lost or stolen, and this fact went unnoticed, the consumer's money can be easily stolen. And when the card is swiped at the POS, the data is not being kept confidential 100 percent of the time, so the bill arriving at the end of month might contain surprising charges.

Merchant

Merchants, such as supermarkets, convenience stores, restaurants, or hotels, are central figures in the process. They make a lot of decisions, both business and technical: what types of payments to accept—credit, debit, or both; what brands to accept; what bank to open a merchant account with; what kind of POS and payment terminal hardware and software to purchase (or lease); and, finally, how to protect the cardholder data. This last decision might sound different and irrelevant compared to others, but this is the reality—merchants must take care of payment data security because other players often fail to do so.

Nevertheless, merchants still take card payments because they want to sell their goods and services. Their POS hardware and software accepts and processes the card information, sends it to their payment processor for authorization and settlement, and eventually receives money on their merchant account.

Acquirer

Acquirers, or Acquiring Banks, authorize the payment transactions and settle them with the card issuers. Payment processors route transactions, based on transaction and card type, to a corresponding acquirer for authorization and settlement. Acquirers regulate the basic merchant discount rates (the fees that a merchant pays for each processed payment transaction).

Issuer

Issuers, or Issuing Banks, maintain the customer accounts and issue the cards to customers. They bill the customers for their transactions and send money back to acquirers so they can pay the merchants. Issuers manufacture the cards and so are responsible for physical security features.

Card Brands

Card Brands, or Card Networks, facilitate the entire process of payment authorization and settlement. Networks, such as VisaNet, maintain connections between acquirers and issuers. Some card brands, such as Visa and MasterCard, do not participate directly in acquiring and issuing, but rather delegate those functions to third-party independent organizations.[3] Other brands, such as American Express, issue cards and acquire payment transactions themselves.

Card brands regulate the payment processing but do not intervene directly in most cases, including security of sensitive cardholder data in the stores. The various card brands founded the PCI Security Standards Council (PCI SSC) which creates and maintains security standards in order to make merchants responsible for payment data protection.

More Players

In addition to the main players in the payment processing game, there are "man-in-the-middle" participants who provide a lot of "extras" to merchants. Theoretically, a merchant might be able to accept electronic payments without these additional organizations by communicating directly with acquirers. In practice, however, given the complexity of the payment processing schemes and the enormous amount of different payment cards and methods, such implementation would be almost impossible without involvement of payment processors and gateways.

Payment Processor

Payment Processors handle the payment transactions between the merchant and multiple acquirers. They also maintain *merchant accounts* where merchants actually receive their money paid by the cardholders for their goods or services.

Processors route payment transactions to the appropriate acquirer based on the payment type and card brand, such as credit, debit, gift, or fleet cards issued by Visa, MasterCard, American Express, or others. Payment processors create financial (transaction) reports for merchants. There are many other helpful functions that payment processors provide. In many cases, however, they cannot provide payment data security to merchants simply because they have no presence at their stores.

Processors may offer extra functions such as tokenization and even point-to-point encryption. However, this often does not resolve the security problems entirely as many merchants use third-party hardware and software to support more than one payment processor. Moreover, tokenization features provided by many processors do not resolve the card data security problem.

CROSS-REFERENCE   See Chapter 3 for more details on PCI.

In the example shown in Figure 1-1, the merchant may process all credit transactions with processor B, but send gift card transactions to processor C.

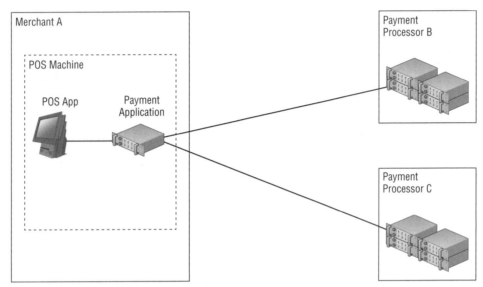

Figure 1-1: Merchant connected to payment processor

Unlike acquirers, payment processors support various payment card types and methods, such as gift cards, fleet cards, Electronic Benefit Transfers (EBTs), and more. They are not limited to credit and debit cards only.

Payment Gateway

In many cases, a merchant's POS payment system talks directly to the payment processor. Sometimes, however, in-between the merchant and payment processor there is another "man in the middle" called Payment Gateway (or Payment Switch). Its primary function is providing *gateway*, or *routing*, services to merchants.

Imagine the situation when merchant A has a service agreement with payment processor B which takes $0.30 plus a 2 percent fee for each processed transaction. Everything is great until the merchant sees a commercial for payment processor C which promises to charge $0.29 plus a 1.9 percent fee per transaction. This apparently small difference could save a lot of money for merchant A who makes thousands of transactions every day. However, in order to switch from payment processor B to C, merchant A must pay the POS software vendor $200,000 for making changes in its payment application so it would be able to communicate with processor C; because originally it was designed to only work with processor B. Figure 1-2 shows that if merchant A were using a payment gateway, such a change would be transparent for its POS software because the routing would be done at the payment gateway's switch that runs in a data center.

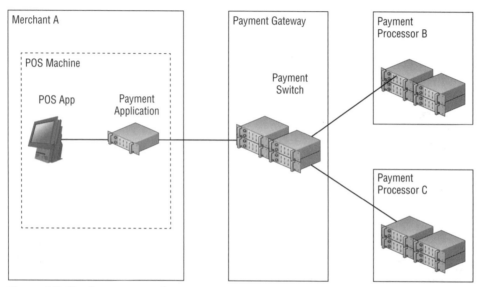

Figure 1-2: Merchant connected to payment gateway

Payment gateways might provide additional convenient services, such as point-to-point encryption, centralized reporting, POI device management, tokenization, and more.

The main difference between a payment processor and a gateway is that the processors, in addition to the switch functions provided by gateways, also maintain merchant accounts and facilitate settlement processes.

Another important role that a payment gateway might play is providing a piece of software that runs at the store and talks with the POS/payment application on one end, and the gateway's switch (server running in the data center) on the other end. In this way, the payment gateway might influence the security of the merchant's payment infrastructure. It can either improve it (for example, by providing P2PE functionality) or damage it (by implanting its insecure component into a previously secure POS system). In most cases, the merchant is still responsible for the security of the gateway's client application running at the store.

Even More Players

Even though the key players such as issuers, acquirers, and card brands are necessary elements in payment processing, the reality is that they have minimal to no influence on security of the payment data in the merchant stores because their part of the process happens "up in the clouds," far away from the dangerous surface of the retail environment. Processors and gateways are a bit closer to reality because they communicate directly with the stores and sometimes even provide their piece of software running at the POS. However, they still have no control over the situation because their interfaces are just a single fragment of a complex integrated payment environment, and there are other players in the payment processing game who are located right at the front line: payment software vendors and hardware manufacturers.

Payment Software Vendors

Third-party software vendors develop POS and payment applications for merchants. These applications handle (process, transmit, and store) the sensitive data during the entire payment cycle in the retail store, from the moment of card swipe to the settlement. If you take a look at the information brochures provided by payment brands, you will not find software vendors in the list of payment-process players. This is wrong. Software vendors create applications which are installed at the stores and, among other things, are supposed to protect the cardholder data from being stolen. Unlike merchants, application developers are in a good position to invent and implement complex security technologies. If a POS system, which is usually created by a third-party software vendor and not by the merchant itself, fails to protect the cardholder data, the entire payment security fails because retail stores are the main target of hacker attacks.

Payment application vendors are obligated to obey the PCI PA-DSS (Payment Application Data Security Standard), which is not strong and effective enough to protect sensitive data (see Chapter 3 for more about PA-DSS).

Hardware Manufacturers

Hardware manufacturers are another example of misrepresentation of the payment-processing cycle. They create the peripheral devices necessary for transaction processing, such as MSR and pinpads (see more information about these devices later in this chapter). These devices are located at the front line of the payment data security because they accept, process, and transmit the sensitive authorization data, in the form of magnetic stripe swipe or manual entry, at the very first phase of the payment cycle. Pinpad devices must be PCI PTS compliant in order to be allowed to process debit transactions. Both MSR and pinpad devices must be PCI PIN Transaction Security (PTS) compliant in order to be included in P2PE solutions. For all that, their manufacturers are often still not mentioned while describing the payment-processing flow.

Payment Stages

Card payment transactions go through the stages starting with the initial swipe at the POS and ending by the bill being sent to the cardholder. From the entire payment system perspective, there are two main stages of payment processing: *authorization* and *settlement*. From the POS and payment application viewpoints, however, there is more granularity behind these two phases.

Authorization

The very first step in a card payment process is called *authorization*. It is necessary in order to check the cardholder's credit or, in the case of a debit card, check whether the cardholder's bank account has enough funds to process the payment. The authorization flow is shown in Figure 1-3.

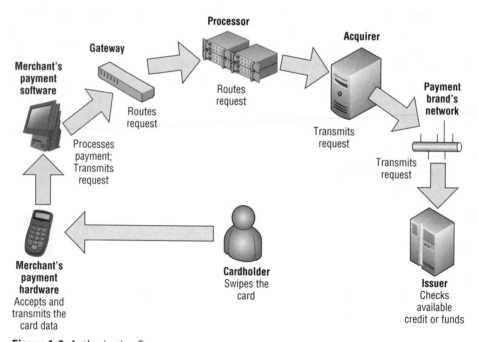

Figure 1-3: Authorization flow

In a retail store, for example, as soon as the cashier finishes scanning the items selected by the customer, he hits the subtotal button which usually switches the POS to payment mode. The customer is then prompted to select the method of payment and, if it is a credit, debit, gift, or EBT card, swipes the card at the card reader, which can be either a simple MSR or a sophisticated POI device. The payment application analyzes the card data and initiates the payment transaction according to card type and Bank Identification Number (*BIN*) *range* (more details about BIN range are discussed in Chapter 4). The next "station" for the payment transaction is either payment gateway or payment processor. The transaction data is routed to the appropriate acquirer which then communicates with the issuer in order to get an *approval*. The issuer is the one who maintains the database with the information about the cardholder's account and checks its status in real time.

If a credit transaction is being performed, the issuer will check the amount of credit and compare it with the transaction amount. If the customer has enough credit to cover the full payment transaction amount, the issuer will return an approval response to the acquirer which returns it to the payment processor and so on back to the POS. In the case of a debit card, the issuer will check the cardholder's bank checking account to make sure the account has enough funds. A similar checkup is performed for gift cards with the only difference that a gift card has no bank account associated with it. Instead, each gift card is linked to a special database record maintained by the gift card provider. In any case, if the customer does not have appropriate credit or enough funds in their bank account or gift card record, the transaction will be *declined* by the issuer, and the decline response will be returned all the way back to the POS, which will display an appropriate message prompting the customer to use a different method of payment.

The authorization stage is most important from a data security viewpoint because it requires sending all available sensitive authentication data (Track 1 or Track 2 or both) from the POS throughout the entire system to the acquirer. Most of the attacks on card data occur at this stage.

Settlement

Once authorization is obtained and the transaction is finalized by the POS system, the payment must be *settled*, which means that the payment is *reconciled* between the merchant, its acquirer, and the issuer. During the settlement, the merchant (or more precisely, its payment system) sends the transaction data to the processor which forwards it to the acquirer. The acquirer or the processor credits the merchant's account, and sends the data to the issuer who posts the transaction to the cardholder's account. Figure 1-4 shows the settlement flow.

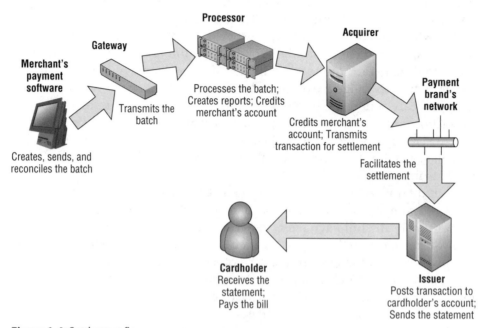

Figure 1-4: Settlement flow

From a security viewpoint, settlement is less dangerous than the authorization stage because it usually does not operate with full sensitive authentication data (Tracks 1 and 2). On the other hand, the settlement process requires accumulation of multiple transactions in batches as well as storage of the Primary Account Number (PAN), while authorization data is normally destroyed as soon as approval is received by the POS (Table 1-2). Therefore, in the case of a security breach associated with data storage, information about multiple transactions stored in the batches and awaiting settlement can be "sucked out" in a short period of time. Stealing an equivalent amount of card data during the authorization stage would require long term "listening" to the system.

Table 1-2: Participation in Authorization and Settlement Processing

INVOLVED PARTY	AUTHORIZATION	SETTLEMENT
Cardholder	Swipes the card or keys the account number at POS.	Pays the bill!
Merchant (personnel, network and server infrastructure)	Accepts, processes, and transmits the sensitive authentication data.	Stores and transmits the sensitive cardholder data.
Merchant's hardware (MSR, pin-pad devices)	Accepts, processes, and transmits the sensitive authentication data to the payment application.	N/A
Merchant's software (POS, payment application)	Processes the payment transaction; Routes transaction to appropriate payment gateway or processor.	Stores transaction batches; Initiates and processes the settlement through the payment gateway or processor.
Payment gateway	Routes the request to appropriate payment processor or acquirer.	Stores transaction batches; Initiates and processes the settlement through appropriate processor or acquirer.
Payment processor	Sends the request to appropriate acquirer.	Stores transaction batches; Initiates and processes the settlement; Credits the merchant's account
Acquirer	Sends the request to the payment brand's network or issuer.	Credits the merchant's account.
Payment brand	Passes the request from acquirer to issuer.	Facilitates settlement.
Issuer	Checks the cardholder's available credit (credit card) or funds (debit, gift cards); Provides online response.	Posts transaction on cardholder's account; Sends the bill to the cardholder.

Payment Transactions

Each payment transaction has two parameters: *authorization amount* and *transaction amount*. At the authorization stage, the acquirer authorizes the merchant to charge the cardholder for the amount of money which is less or equal to the *authorization amount*. Once the payment is finalized, the merchant sends the transaction to the acquirer for the settlement with the *transaction amount* which cannot exceed the *authorization amount*.

Sale vs. PreAuth/Completion

Depending on transaction and merchant type, authorization can be requested for a particular payment amount or for an abstract *limit amount*. For example, if you purchase groceries in the local supermarket, the POS will likely obtain authorization for the exact amount of your purchase. This "plain" transaction is called *Sale*.

However, if you pay for fuel at the gas station, the payment application first obtains pre-authorization *(PreAuth)* for some predefined "limit" amount which can be either dictated by the card brand or set by the merchant. This is because the POS system does not know exactly how much fuel will be pumped into the tank. Once the fueling is finished, the POS at the fuel pump will calculate and send the exact amount of the payment. Such an additional step in payment processing is called *completion*.

An important difference from a security viewpoint between Sale, PreAuth, and Completion messages is that both Sale and PreAuth contain sensitive authentication information (full track data or PAN), while a Completion message usually contains only the PAN or no card data at all because the transaction was already initiated so Completion can be linked with the original PreAuth using other forms of identification, such as transaction number or token.

Void and Return

It's fair to say that *Void* and *Return* are just the opposite of Sale or PreAuth/Completion. If the payment is done by mistake, or the customer wants to return the merchandise and get their money back, the cashier can initiate a Void or Return payment transaction. There is a difference between Void and Return though. Void is usually triggered when the customer or merchant wants to cancel the entire transaction which might include several items and payment methods. Return, or *Refund*, is normally used when the customer returns a single item and the merchant needs to return only a partial amount rather than the entire payment.

Another important difference (from a security viewpoint) between Void and Return is that Void cannot be performed without a link to the original Sale transaction, while Return can be initiated any time. Void is just a cancellation of a previously existing payment, while Return is placing the money into the cardholder's account without any connection to previous activity. In other words, it is much easier to use Return to steal money from a merchant's account and put it into the bad guy's account. Also, Void transactions (if implemented correctly by payment application vendor and processor) do not necessarily contain sensitive information because the original transaction record already contains the card data.

Fallback Processing

Fallback processing (also referred as *Stand-In*, or *Store & Forward*, or *Offline Authorization*) is a very important function for a merchant's business continuity. It provides the ability to accept card payments "offline" when the network connectivity or payment-processing hosts are down for any reason. If a payment application cannot obtain online authorization from the acquirer, under some circumstances (depending on card type, transaction amount, and other parameters) it is allowed to generate internal approval and store transactions for further processing. Fallback authorization can be almost transparent for untutored cashiers and customers. In many cases, however, some evidence of offline authorization is present and can be recognized:

- Transaction processing time for offline approval can be noticeably longer compared to online authorization because a payment application can be programmed to wait for *response timeout* before it is allowed to approve the payment internally. Response timeout values are defined by payment processors as part of the *message protocol* and may vary significantly depending on connectivity and communication type. However, in most cases the value can be set to several seconds, which is distinctly longer than the several milliseconds required for online processing on fast networks.

  Failover processing (such as *dial-up fallback*) can be another reason for significant delay in obtaining offline approval. Some processors require the payment application to switch to a backup host or different communication line in order to attempt online authorization if the main connection or host is down.

- When a payment application receives online approval for a payment transaction, the host response contains an authorization code generated by the acquirer's software. This code is often printed on the *payment slip* of the transaction receipt. If the POS goes to the offline mode, the payment application generates its own authorization code while approving the transaction offline. Such a code can be generated using a different algorithm (sometimes simply running a counter or current timestamp) and, therefore, it can be easily distinguished by the cashier or customer from the code created by the host. For example:

  Authorization code returned by the host: FVIKP0.

  Offline authorization code generated by payment application: LA1234.

A very important feature of fallback processing is the fact that the POS must store sensitive cardholder data on disk for the entire period of network outage, which may vary from a few seconds to several days. Such a need to accumulate sensitive information in potentially very large amounts opens an obvious opportunity for the bad guys. Normally, if the system is properly designed, the cardholder data is no longer stored at the POS machine after the authorization phase is done. However, in the case of Store & Forward (S&F), the authorization cannot be technically done because there is no communication with the authorization host.

Timeout Reversals

Timeout Reversal, or TOR, is a mechanism that prevents duplicate charges, which is described in more detail in Chapter 2. TOR is another example (after S&F) of a situation when the POS must store locally (even if only temporarily and in encrypted form) the sensitive authentication data which could then be retrieved by an attacker.

Special Transaction Types

There are less common POS transaction types (Table 1-3) that are mostly used either in exceptional situations or when handling special card types. Examples of such transactions are gift card balance inquiry and recharge. *Balance inquiry* is used to check the remaining balance of the gift card, and the resulting transaction data may contain full track data. *Recharge* is used to add funds to a gift card using another method of payment (such as cash or credit card), thus containing sensitive card data information.

Table 1-3: Payment Transaction Types

TRANSACTION TYPE	SYNONYM	FUNCTION	SECURITY CONCERNS
Sale	Purchase	Regular payment transaction (mostly used)	Contains full sensitive authentication data (magnetic Tracks 1 and 2)
PreAuth	Authorization	Checks available balance and obtains authorization	Contains full sensitive authentication data (magnetic Tracks 1 and 2)
Complete	Completion	Finalizes the payment initiated by PreAuth	May contain PAN
Void	Post Void	Cancels previously processed payment	Requires a link to the original transaction; May contain full sensitive authentication data
Return	Refund	Credits cardholder's account (opposite to Sale)	Contains full sensitive authentication data (magnetic Tracks 1 and 2); Can be used to move money out of merchant's account
TOR	Reversal	Attempts to cancel transaction of any type when no response was received from the host	Contains full sensitive authentication data (magnetic Tracks 1 and 2)
Balance Inquiry	Check Balance	Checks available balance on gift card account	Contains full sensitive authentication data (magnetic Tracks 1 and 2)
Recharge	Reload	Adds funds to gift card account	Contains full sensitive authentication data (magnetic Tracks 1 and 2)

Key Areas of Payment Application Vulnerabilities

There are several ways to attack a POS system and its associated payment application in order to steal sensitive card data. Such methods are often called *Attack Vectors* in information security theory. An attack vector usually includes a scenario of the attack—a description about the performed steps and tools used. If you know that a particular invasion is possible, at least theoretically, the particular scenario (for example, penetration methods, specific instructions, and tools used during the attack) is not so important when discussing the application security controls (protection measures). Therefore, instead of attack vectors, there will be a focus on *Vulnerability Areas* of the attacks throughout this book.

Assuming that in the context of this research the target (object) of the attack is always sensitive payment data (or cardholder information), and the environment (subject) is a brick-and-mortar merchant POS and payment application, vulnerability area usually describes the location (both physical and logical) of the data in the application at the moment of the attack. There are three such locations, or states of the data, in any software program including a payment application:

1. **Data in Memory**—When the payment application processes an authorization or settlement, it performs various manipulations with the payment card data in the memory of the hosting computer (usually the RAM of the POS machine).

2. **Data at Rest**—The payment application stores data, either temporarily or for long term, on the hard drive.

3. **Data in Transit**—The payment application sends and receives data to and from other applications and devices.

With the exception of data in memory, other data states have sub-areas determined by a difference in technology around them. For instance, data at rest can be stored in database or log files, and data in transit can be sent via a LAN or serial connection.

Another key vulnerability area is payment *Application Code* itself and its *Configuration* (config). The code or config do not contain any cardholder information by themselves, but can be *tampered* with (modified) by an attacker or malicious software in order to gain unauthorized access to the data in other key vulnerability areas.

With that said, there are four key vulnerability areas of payment applications which are shown in Figure 1-5:

1. Data in memory

2. Data at rest

3. Data in transit

4. Application code and configuration

Table 1-4 lists the key vulnerability areas with all sub-areas. These terms will be used in the discussions about payment application threats and mitigations throughout this book. More details about vulnerability areas and their examples can be found in Chapter 2.

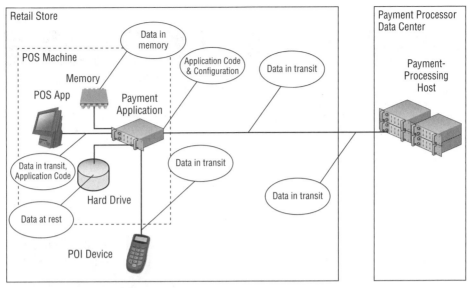

Figure 1-5: Key vulnerability areas

Table 1-4: Vulnerability Areas of Payment Applications

KEY AREA	SUB-AREA	EXAMPLES	TYPICAL DATA	USUALLY PROTECTED?
Data in memory			Full	No
Data at rest	Temporary storage	S&F, TOR, active transaction databases	Full	Yes
	Long-term storage	Batch, settle-ment, archive records	PAN	Yes
	Log files		Random	
Data in transit	Local communication	LAN between application modules	Full	No
	Communication between POI device and POS		Full	No
	Communication to processors	Host links	Full	No

Continues

Table 1-4 *(continued)*

KEY AREA	SUB-AREA	EXAMPLES	TYPICAL DATA	USUALLY PROTECTED?
Application code and configuration	Application code		N/A	No
	Application configuration		N/A	No

Summary

There are several main types of payment cards: credit, debit, gift, and fleet. Credit and debit cards are the most vulnerable because they are widely accepted and carry significant amounts of money.

There are several participants or "players" in electronic payment processing: cardholder, merchant, software vendor, hardware manufacturer, gateway, processor, acquirer, card brand, and issuer. The merchant is the most vulnerable element in this chain because it faces the public directly, and its interaction with the customers has a significant surface: multiple stores and POS.

The process of payment by plastic card consists of two main stages: authorization and settlement. The authorization phase is more dangerous because it requires transmission of sensitive authentication data, which is often unencrypted, throughout multiple systems. Such data can be intercepted by an attacker and used to produce counterfeit cards.

There are several key vulnerability areas of a POS system and its associated payment application:

- Data in memory
- Data at rest
- Data in transit
- Application code and configuration

Each of these vulnerability areas has its specifics and can be attacked using different methods at different times throughout the payment processing cycle.

Notes

1. USB Keystroke Loggers, Amazon.com, `http://www.amazon.com/s/ref=nb_sb_noss?url=search-alias%3Daps&field-keywords=USB%20keystroke%20Logger`

2. Card Acceptance Guidelines for Visa Merchants, Visa, `http://usa.visa.com/download/merchants/card-acceptance-guidelines-for-visa-merchants.pdf`

3. Merchant Acquirer List, Visa, `http://usa.visa.com/merchants/new-acceptance/merchant-acquirer-list.html`

Payment Application Architecture

No fathers or mothers think their own children ugly; and this self-deceit is yet stronger with respect to the offspring of the mind.

—*Miguel de Cervantes*

In order to understand all of the different types of threats that may break the payment application (PA), it is first necessary to learn about the internal structure of these systems. The details of concrete implementations may vary from vendor to vendor, but the main design principles remain closely similar due to the narrow specialization of such applications.

Essential Payment Application Blocks

Typical payment application architecture, shown in Figure 2-1, consists of external interfaces and processing modules. Interfaces are the bridges to the outer world. Processing modules drive the flow of the payment transaction.

Interfaces

All systems need to communicate with the outside world of peripheral hardware and external software, so *device* and *application interfaces* are essential parts of any payment application. There are three types of *external interfaces* that connect the PA with devices and applications:

1. POI device interface
2. POS API
3. Payment processor link

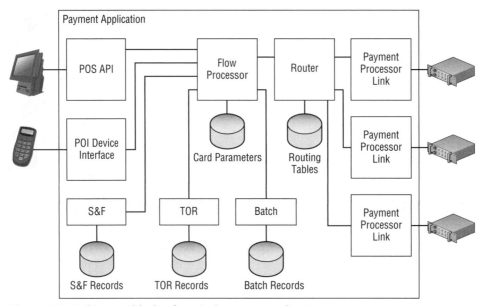

Figure 2-1: Architecture blocks of a typical payment application

A single payment application may have several implemented interfaces of any type, depending on the required number of supported peripherals, POS models, and authorization networks.

POI Device Interface

The POI Device Interface is in charge of the data exchange with the pinpad or standalone MSR devices. This interface includes implementation of device-specific communication and message protocol (or several protocols if the application supports multiple peripheral types). Typical communication is done either through a serial (COM) port or using TCP/IP over LAN. However, message protocols vary, and vendors implement their own "languages." Recent models allow the use of encryption methods such as Secure Socket Layer (SSL) or data payload encryption, as well as authentication with certificates for added security.

A common "feature" of many POI devices' communication and message protocols is a lack of built-in communication security mechanisms for cardholder data protection. Default communication implementations don't require any encryption of sensitive data or device authentication by the payment application, which means that sensitive data can be easily eavesdropped or the device can be altered.

POS API

The Point-of-Sale Application Programming Interface (POS API) is responsible for communication with the POS application to handle the payment transaction flow, which includes receiving transaction parameters, processing cashier and customer prompts, and returning the results. This type of communication can be done in different ways depending on the particular application design of POS and PA, from an in-process memory data exchange to a remote TCP/IP or HTTP connection. It is typically called an API because a single PA can support different POS applications, and the integration is done by POS developers using API specifications provided by the PA vendor.

Security concerns remain the same as those for device interfaces: there are no standard security mechanisms. Specific issues depend on the type of connectivity. If POS and PA run under the same OS process, the memory of the process can be scanned using RAM scraping in order to retrieve sensitive data. In the case of remote communication interfaces based on network protocols such as TCP/IP (or higher in OSI Model protocol stack HTTP and Web Services), the vulnerabilities are the same as those for any network communication (see Chapter 5 for details).

PA vendors may state that communication between POS and PA doesn't carry sensitive data because PA handles all the aspects of any payment transaction and only returns the *masked* results to the POS at the end without exposing the details of the magnetic stripe. Such statements can be only partially true due to the following concerns. First, in the case of manual entry, when the MSR fails to read the magnetic stripe, the PAN is usually entered by the cashier at the POS and sent to the PA along with additional sensitive data such as expiration date, CVV, or ZIP code. Second, the PA interface may expose methods that return an unmasked PAN or even whole tracks in clear text. Such API methods, if not protected by access controls, can be manipulated by malicious software.

Payment Processor Link

The processor link supports two main functions:

1. It converts transaction parameters from the application internal representation to a special format according to the payment processor *message protocol*.

2. It communicates with the authorization host using a *communication protocol* supported by the payment processor.

Each processor link is hard-coded to communicate with a particular processor. However, the location of the processor's server is usually soft-coded (configured). For example, a host configuration may contain the IP address and server port for TCP/IP-based communication protocols on private networks, or the URL for HTTP-based protocols over the Internet.

If the configuration isn't protected and there is no authentication between client and server, those parameters can be tampered with so the payment application may end up communicating with a bogus host. Such modification is invisible to the payment system because the fake host may just log all the traffic (in order to extract and steal all sensitive cardholder information) and then reroute it to the legitimate processor (so the intrusion will remain undisclosed).

Special links can be created for development testing or in-house applications. Such "dummy" links do not necessarily communicate with the outside world in order to obtain authorization, but can be programmed to simply return automatic "approval" responses based on minimal or no conditions. If regular card transactions are routed to such a link (see the upcoming "Router" section of this chapter), the payment will be processed by the POS without any actual transaction being recorded.

Processing Modules

The second group of payment application blocks consists of flow-processing modules that drive the payment process from the moment of swiping the card to getting the merchant paid and the cardholder's account charged. The main processing modules include:

- Router
- S&F (Store and Forward)
- TOR (Timeout Reversal)
- Batch

Router

The router module is intended to send ("route") the payment transaction for authorization, completion, or settlement to a particular payment processor link based on the card BIN range, card type, transaction type, or other predefined system parameters. Usually, PA has more than one payment processor link implemented on different levels—POS, store, or data center switch—depending on the particular system architecture. For example, credit card payments can be routed to a standard payment processor; PIN transactions can be sent to a particular debit network; and gift cards can be sent to a proprietary ("closed loop") switch. In order to make decisions, the router uses a *routing table* that contains (at least) PAN range records with pointers to particular payment processor links. For example, according to the configuration defined in Table 2-1, all transactions made with Visa cards will be sent for authorization to Bank of America, while American Express card transactions will be routed for processing directly to American Express Bank.

Table 2-1: Example of PAN Range Routing Table

PAN FROM	PAN TO	LINK ID
4000000000000000	4999999999999999	BOA
340000000000000	349999999999999	AMEX
370000000000000	379999999999999	AMEX

Routing decisions can also be made based on other criteria, such as transaction type. For example, all gift card activations, reloads, and balance inquiries can be set up to be routed to a gift card processing network regardless of the card's PAN.

A person familiar with the payment application design (such as an intruder or a former employee) may be able to play with the routing configuration (if it isn't protected from tampering) and force the system to forward transactions with fake cards from predefined PAN ranges to "dummy" processor links. Such transactions will obtain legitimate approval without recording the actual payment in the processor's database.

S&F: Store and Forward

The S&F module implements a very important *fallback* function that allows merchants to support business continuity by the uninterrupted acceptance of electronic payments.

> **NOTE** See the "Fallback Processing" section in Chapter 1 for more details. Do not confuse this type of fallback with *dial-up fallback*, which is described in the "Physical Connections" section of this chapter.

When the authorization network is down and the transaction fits the offline processing criteria defined by the payment processor, the S&F module generates offline approval and stores the transaction in the S&F database. As soon as the authorization network becomes available again, S&F forwards the stored transactions to the host. Another option is forwarding stored transactions as part of the end-of-day process for settlement (see the upcoming "Batch" discussion for details about the *Settlement* process).

The most notable feature of S&F, from a security point of view, is that offline transaction records can be stuck on a POS or BO machine for periods of time ranging from seconds to days, depending on the scale of the network outage. Such records often include full track data necessary for host processing. PCI DSS and PA-DSS standards don't allow full track data storage, as noted in these references:

> *Sensitive authentication data must not be stored after authorization (even if encrypted)*[1, 2]

However, "after authorization" is the key word in this sentence. When applied to fallback processing, this requirement means that track data can be stored for S&F, and in reality almost all payment applications do so.

TOR: Timeout Reversal

Timeout reversal is the error-control mechanism that prevents duplicate charges on the cardholder account. Duplicate charges occur when the POS doesn't receive an authorization response from the host (called *response timeout*) when the transaction is actually approved and recorded by the processor. In this case, the transaction doesn't appear to be finalized from the POS, cashier, and customer viewpoints, but the customer's account is charged. If the cashier swipes the card again and receives approval, the customer account will be charged twice. In order to prevent such situations, when the payment application doesn't receive a host response (or, in other words, receives a response timeout), it generates and sends the *timeout reversal* (TOR) message instructing the host to cancel the transaction—whether it was approved or not. If the TOR module cannot communicate with the host (expected behavior in this situation, due to the same reason that caused the original response timeout), it accumulates timeout reversal messages in the *TOR database* and forwards them to the server as soon as the network comes back online again. This process is very similar to the S&F mechanism. The main security concern about TOR is also similar to the one with S&F: sensitive authentication data storage.

Thanks to S&F and TOR features, the exposure of sensitive authentication data is expanded to new media (disk storage instead of just memory handling) and extended for longer periods of time (from minutes to hours to days, instead of just the several milliseconds required for online processing).

Batch

The Batch Module (also called *Close Batch*, *Close Shift*, *End of Day*, or *Settlement Module*) is responsible for the recording and settlement of payment transactions processed during a specific period, usually one business day.

The word *batch* is inherited from the days when credit cards were processed manually by imprinting the card using a special manual imprinter device. The imprint left traces of PAN, expiration date, and cardholder name (embossed on the front of the plastic card) on the transaction slip. During the workday, those pieces of paper were stocked in *batches* and sent to the credit companies for settlement. Nowadays, the settlement process in general remains the same with the only difference being that it's performed automatically by computers.

There are a couple of details about the batch closing process that may require your attention. First, some processors still require sending full PAN during the settlement, which means that large amounts of account numbers are accumulated by the PA during the day to send later for settlement. As you can imagine, this fact didn't go unnoticed by the concerned party. However, some payment processors have already changed their interfaces so they don't require sending PAN on settlement anymore.

The second issue is much more serious because there's still no solution. It has to do with reconciliation and chargebacks. Some protocols require resending transaction records at the end of the day if the total dollar amount of processed payments at the host doesn't match the total calculated by the store payment system. This error-correction process is called reconciliation. During the end-of-day settlement and reconciliation, transactions can be rejected by the processor for any reason. For example, a payment may have been approved offline and processed by the S&F module. Such a rejection is called a *chargeback*. The problem with both reconciliation and chargeback is that they require the full PAN to be re-sent to the host, which means that all account numbers should be archived for at least several days. This "feature" of the batch processing module is very attractive for some individuals.

Data Storage

Besides the "data in transit" which is mostly associated with communication interfaces and protocols, another possible state of sensitive cardholder information is "data at rest," a term used to describe any form of hard-drive storage such as database, flat-data file, or log file. There are multiple use cases for data storage in payment applications: TOR, S&F, batch records, and application log files. Even single-payment applications can utilize different technologies (and protection mechanisms) for different modules. For example, TOR, S&F, and batch may use a database such as the MS SQL Server, while application logs can be stored as simple flat files. In this case, the payment application may implement separate encryption schemes for databases and flat files.

Unlike communication and message protocols, there have been no attempts to establish standards for payment-application data storage. Available technologies are diverse, and software vendors are free to pick whichever one they like. In most situations, there is no standard approach to the encryption of data at rest. Therefore, developers "invent" proprietary encryption and key management solutions often assumed to use strong encryption algorithms approved by industry standards. In practice, it means that the application calls a standard cryptographic library such as .NET's System.Security.Cryptography or Java's JCE—which is great, because the more a crypto library is used, the more it is secure. However, the overall implementation of the encryption mechanism in those applications is still proprietary which means its vulnerability level is undetermined.

The point is that the code of any encryption algorithm is only one side of the entire cryptographic mechanism. Even the strongest cryptography will fail if it's surrounded by weak authentication and poor key management. DUKPT used for debit PIN protection is a notable exception and an example of a standardized technology that defines not only an encryption algorithm (3DES) but also key management and even the physical environment around it (see Chapter 8 for more details about DUKPT).

Using multiple data storage technologies may require the use of different cryptographic protection mechanisms, which increases application vulnerability. The lack of standard security technology for payment application data storage results in various vulnerabilities associated with data at rest. Those vulnerabilities are reviewed in Chapter 6.

Typical Payment Transaction Flow

In order to understand how the modules just described communicate with each other, let's review a simple best-case scenario of a payment transaction to see how sensitive authentication data flows between different payment application modules.

Figure 2-2 shows that even the simplest flow is divided into three relatively independent sub-flows, and the entire process is event-driven.

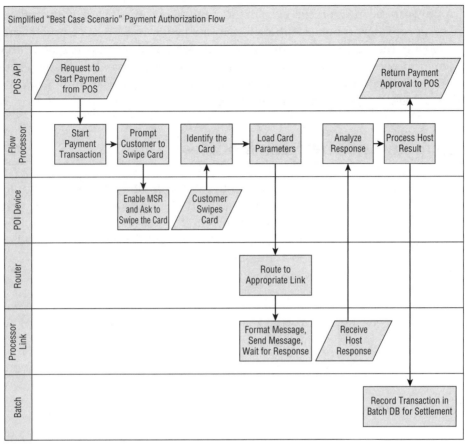

Figure 2-2: Typical Payment Transaction Flow

From a payment application point of view, everything starts when the cashier finishes scanning the items and hits the "payment" button (various POS models call it by different names, but the idea is always the same), which switches control from the POS to the payment application. The customer is prompted to swipe the card. As soon as the card is swiped, it is identified and an authorization request message is created and routed to the appropriate payment processor link (based on card type and other parameters loaded from the configuration database). The processor link formats the message according to message protocol rules, establishes a connection with the host, and sends the message for authorization using the communication protocol. In this best-case scenario, everything works well, so the application quickly receives an approval response from the host, records the results in the batch database, and signals to the POS that payment is done.

As you can see in Figure 2-2, even in the simplest optimistic case (with straight online approval, without exceptions, customer prompts, S&F, TOR, and before settlement), the cardholder information is present at almost every step of the payment process. In a single transaction lifetime, sensitive data is squeezed (more than once) through all possible states: in memory, at rest, and in transit. There are endless possibilities for hacking.

Communication Between Modules

In addition to external API and device interfaces, different PA modules should communicate with each other using some kind of *internal message protocol* that defines a proprietary format for commands and messages. At first glance this communication is unnoticeable, especially if the modules are either compiled into a single binary or located at the same machine.

There is a significant risk of sniffing and tampering if:

- The modules reside on different computers, or
- They are located on the same machine but can be easily distinguished by their function and have their own API

The following sections present more details about internal PA communication.

Physical Connections

The first credit card payment terminals communicated with their payment networks over regular telephone lines using *dial-up modems*. A modem is a device that translates serial communication signals from computers to electric waves (similar to voice) that can be transmitted over regular ground-phone wires. This communication was extremely slow because it took a long time for a modem to establish the connection ("dial up") to the server even before the message could be sent. There were, however, some advantages, one of which was that sensitive information couldn't be captured remotely using traditional network sniffers.

Some merchants still use dial-up modems, while many use them as a failover mechanism to be used in case the main network connection through the leased line, frame relay, or Internet is down for any reason. In those cases, the payment application automatically switches to the *dial-up fallback* line so the payment processing continues uninterrupted. As soon as the network connection comes back online, the payment application switches back to the main channel.

Leased line and *frame relay* systems are used by merchants as an underlying connection for traditional network communication. They are common forms of connectivity between retail stores and their headquarters or payment processors.

The obvious security advantage of WAN—its isolation from public networks such as the Internet—is at the same time problematic: PCI security standards don't require encryption on these networks.

Serial connections through RS232 are used primarily between the POI device and the computer hosting the POS and payment applications. Dial-up modems also use serial COM ports for communication with their hosting computer. Even though the serial port isn't vulnerable to traditional network sniffing, it can be eavesdropped upon using special serial sniffers.

Communication Protocols

The message exchange between sender and recipient is done using *communication protocols* that live at the high levels of the Open System Interconnect (OSI) stack (as shown in Table 2-2). A payment application module implementing this communication protocol is responsible for establishing connection, delivery of the message bits from the sender to the recipient, and error control. High-level communication protocols can utilize several OSI stack levels[3], which is usually transparent for the payment application as it communicates with the tip of the iceberg on application level 7 of the OSI stack.

Web Services is one example of a complex protocol associated with security challenges on different OSI stack levels.[4]

Table 2-2: Payment Application Communication and OSI Stack

LAYER NUMBER	LAYER NAME	PAYMENT APPLICATION COMMUNICATION	EXAMPLES
Layer 7	Application	Communication Protocols	HTTP, SOAP
Layer 6	Presentation	Communication Protocols	SSL
Layer 5	Session	Communication Protocols	Named Pipes, RPC, Full Duplex
Layer 4	Transport	Communication Protocols	TCP
Layer 3	Network		IP
Layer 2	Data Link	Physical Connections	Ethernet (LAN), Frame Relay (WAN)
Layer 1	Physical	Physical Connections	DSL, RS-232, 10BASE

Local Communication

Internal interfaces and POS APIs use communication protocols such as DLL API or Windows COM. DLL APIs and In-Process COM calls are used if both client (for example, POS application) and server (EPS) are running under the same OS process (in the same *address space*). Out-of-Process COM can be used for communication between different processes when the POS and EPS (or two internal PA modules) are separate executable applications.

Local (inter-process or in-process) in-memory communication is not exposed to remote sniffing because there's no network communication involved. However, such communication is exposed to RAM scraping (see Chapter 5 for details).

Message Protocols

When talking about payment-application communication, it's necessary to distinguish between two different types of protocols—*message* and *communication*—that are important from a security viewpoint.

Message protocols work on the application software level above the OSI stack. Message protocols provide two main functions:

1. Conversion, using a special *message format*, of transaction parameters (such as dollar amount, Track 2, and PAN) from their internal application representation into a different form understandable by the other peer of the communication channel. This conversion process is usually called *message serialization*. Once the transaction message is serialized by the sender, it can be sent using a *communication protocol* to the recipient, who performs the opposite transformation—*deserialization*—to convert the data back into a format readable by the receiving application (not necessarily the same as the one used by the sender).

2. Definition and implementation of *message processing rules* such as response timeouts, number of resend attempts, fallback, and many other exception and error-handling rules.

3. Figure 2-3 demonstrates the implementation of message protocol by the payment application's processor link module.

Standard versus Proprietary Message Protocols

As a rule, message protocols for any data exchange between the payment application and the processor are developed by the latter. While there's a solid standardization and regulation of the payment card format (such as physical characteristics of the magnetic stripe and format of magnetic tracks), there is a clear lack of similar standards in the message-protocols area. Despite the fact that a formal industry standard exists for financial transaction messages

(ISO 8583[5]), the majority of processors have created their own proprietary protocols, in some cases just mutated versions of ISO 8583 but often having completely different formats and rules. There are a few publicly available examples of proprietary message protocols (mostly outdated) that can be found online.[6, 7, 8]

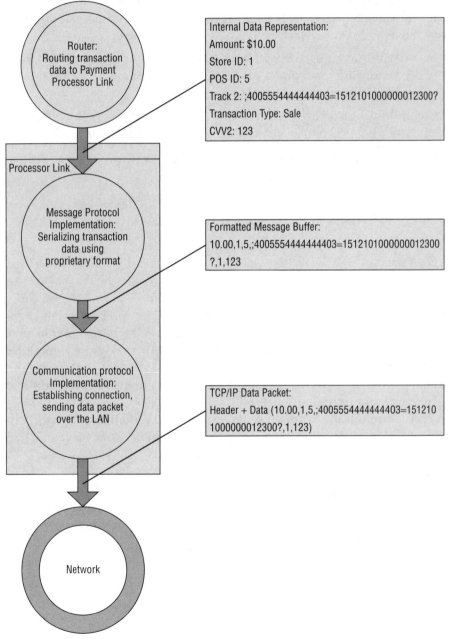

Figure 2-3: Interaction between protocols in processor link

The fact that many payment processors still keep their specifications confidential is a shining example of *security through obscurity*.[9]

Many message protocols were designed in the 1990s, and most of them were created without security in mind. The only concerns back then were reliability and scalability. There was no built-in functionality to protect data confidentiality and integrity (such as encryption, cryptographic authentication, or digital signing). When it comes to security, the processors and payment application vendors mostly rely on two factors:

1. **Security through obscurity** which is based on assuming that many links to processors are maintained via leased lines that aren't supposed to be accessed by unauthorized parties.

2. **Communication security** which is provided by the network infrastructure (such as VPN or IPSec) instead of the payment software or hardware.

The obvious disadvantage of both approaches is that sensitive data is transmitted in clear text and can be easily wiretapped.

Internal Protocols

As covered earlier in this chapter, there are three main types of payment-application interfaces: POS API, Payment Processor Link, and POI Device Interface. All three are external communication interfaces. However, the PA may have a distributed architecture in which separate modules are deployed at physically separate locations (see the "Hybrid POS/Store System" section later in this chapter). In this case, there is also an internal communication interface that transmits data (including sensitive cardholder information) between different modules of the entire payment application. Such an internal channel usually employs proprietary, often undocumented, message and communication protocols that are different from external protocols.

Internal communication can be even more vulnerable than its external counterpart because it usually lives on an unprotected local network, since PCI DSS and PA-DSS don't require encrypting LAN traffic.

Communication Summary

Table 2-3 shows how different types of PA interfaces use various types of connectivity, communication, and message protocols.

Table 2-3: Summary of Payment-Application Interfaces and Protocols

PAYMENT APPLICATION INTERFACE	CONNECTION	COMMUNICATION PROTOCOLS	MESSAGE PROTOCOLS	MANDATORY DATA ENCRYPTION	MANDATORY CLIENT AUTHENTICATION
Payment Processor Link	Dial-up	Serial	Proprietary	-	-
	LAN, WAN	TCP/IP, HTTP, WS	ISO 8583, Proprietary	-	-
	Internet	TCP/IP, HTTP, WS	ISO 8583, Proprietary	●	-
POI Device	COM, USB	Serial	Proprietary	-	-
	LAN	TCP/IP	Proprietary	-	-
POS API, Internal	Memory	DLL API, COM	Proprietary	-	-
	LAN	TCP/IP, HTTP, WS	Proprietary	-	-

There are a couple of common trends of PA communication that can be observed in the Table 2-3:

- Most interfaces use proprietary message protocols, which usually results in a lack of security.
- Only one type of connection (over the Internet) has mandatory encryption (PCI DSS/PA-DSS requirement).

Deployment of Payment Applications

Payment application modules can be distributed (*deployed*) between different physical locations. For example, on POS and BO machines in the store, and even remote servers running in data centers. The deployment model determines the level of vulnerability of the payment system. This section explains how various design approaches affect the security of the entire system.

The Concept of EPS

EPS stands for Electronic Payment System. Sometimes, the third letter of this abbreviation is interpreted as "Server" or "Service," which doesn't change the meaning of the term significantly. The main purpose of EPS is isolating the electronic payment processing application from the rest of the point-of-sale functions. Many experts think that payment processing is a separate and self-sufficient business domain. At the same time, there's no doubt that payment is an integral part of the point-of-sale transaction flow.

Despite the fact that there's no clear "academic" definition of EPS, and the border between generic POS functionality and payment processing is vague, there are obvious benefits to such a separation from a security viewpoint. Vendors who create EPS software are subject experts in payment technologies (including security), whereas POS developers have to be experts in many fields (taxation, inventory, and others) so they cannot be fully focused on security. A logical (and often physical) separation of the POS and payment system allows "removing POS from the scope" (security auditors terminology meaning that security standard requirements like PCI are not applicable to a particular application or machine).

Placing the POS application or machine "out of scope" saves a lot of development and implementation work for both software manufacturers and consumers. However, EPS isn't a silver bullet solution and there are many other factors, such as deployment model and encryption schemes, affecting the overall system security.

Payment Switch

There are at least two functional types of computers in a typical retail store: POS and BO. The payment application modules can be distributed between these two types depending on the particular design of the software vendor or sometimes the requirements of the merchant's payment processor. In fact, there is another (third) possible location outside the store.

Many payment software vendors or merchants have their own processing host that consolidates transaction messages from multiple stores and forwards them to the appropriate payment processors. This host is usually called the *payment switch*. Its primary function is to separate the payment application from jobs that can be done better in a central location, for example, routing a transaction to the appropriate processor based on its BIN range or card type (see Figure 2-4).

At first glance, the deployment model with a proprietary payment switch appears more secure, because it is easy to protect an application in a data center that isn't exposed to the kind of hazardous environment one finds in a retail store. However, the payment application is still there—something has to talk to the pinpad, POS, and the switch, handle cashier and customer prompts, process and store S&F and TOR messages, and perform many other necessary functions that can't be exported to a remote location.

Although implementing a proprietary payment switch helps reduce the exposure of sensitive data at some points (such as long-term cardholder data storage of settlement records), it does not significantly improve the overall security level of the store.

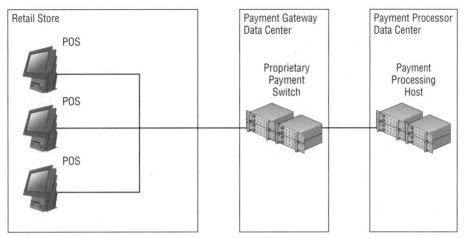

Figure 2-4: Payment switch

Comparing Deployment Models

In order to compare the risks associated with different architecture and deployment models, I suggest using the following method of vulnerability score calculation by counting points of exposure to security threats.

Calculating Vulnerability Score

Let's assume we have a hypothetical store with a single POS machine and a BOS (back office server) computer used as the store server. In practice, most stores have more than just one register; a typical grocery retailer, for example, maintains dozens of lanes. However, the number of POS machines doesn't directly affect the vulnerability of the system. All the lanes have the same or very similar hardware, software, and configuration. As soon as the store network and first POS machine are penetrated, it's easy to "export" the breach to other machines.

The store server is a different story, because usually it is more protected, at least from a physical point of view—it's located at the "back" of the store and isn't exposed directly to customers. Also, it is much easier to harden a single machine than dozens of POS machines.

On the other hand, the store server may consolidate sensitive data from all the lanes in the store, so once it's broken, there's no need to penetrate any of the POS machines. Therefore, the store server should be weighted the same as multiple POS machines when calculating the vulnerability score, and the overall store score should be calculated as follows:

Vulnerability Score = POS Score + Server Score

For a deployment model with a payment switch, when long-term data storage (settlement data and transaction history for chargeback processing containing primary account numbers) is taken outside the store and implemented in the data center, it is common practice to subtract one point from the overall vulnerability score. However, I would not recommend doing so because hidden, often undocumented data can still be there (see Chapter 6 for more details about hidden data).

The score for each PA component (machine) is calculated based on the factors (*exposure areas*) derived from the key vulnerability areas of payment applications defined in Chapter 1:

- Data in memory
- Data at rest
- Data in transit
- Application code and configuration

Data in memory and application code & config are calculated as single exposure areas, while data at rest and data in transit are divided to several sub-categories (Table 2-4).

Table 2-4: Vulnerability Score Factors

EXPOSURE AREA	KEY VULNERABILITY AREA
Memory	Data in memory
Temporary data storage	Data at rest
Settlement records	Data at rest
Application code & config	Application code & config
Connection to POI	Data in transit
Internal communication	Data in transit
Host links	Data in transit

If a particular exposure area is not covered by PCIDSS and PA-DSS requirements, the score is multiplied by 2 in order to accommodate a risk associated with lack of regulation.

Store EPS Deployment Model

In a store EPS deployment model, payment processing is done by the EPS in a central location at the store server, as depicted in Figure 2-5. The EPS is maintaining direct communication with all POS and POI devices. The EPS is handling everything from card-entry flow to processing payment transactions, therefore, no sensitive data is transferred between the POS and the EPS.

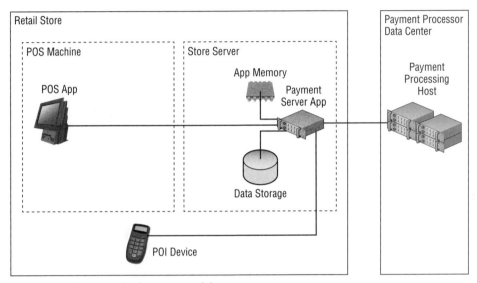

Figure 2-5: Store EPS deployment model

Some of the security pros and cons of this model are:

- **Pro**—The POS machine isn't exposed to sensitive data because it doesn't communicate with POI devices.
- **Pro**—Communication between the POS and the store server machines doesn't contain sensitive data, so there's no need to encrypt this traffic.
- **Con**—Communication between POI devices and the store server is implemented through the store LAN (usually TCP/IP packets), exposing sensitive cardholder information to the network.

The input data and results of vulnerability score calculation for the store EPS deployment model are listed in Table 2-5.

Table 2-5: Vulnerability Score of Store EPS Deployment Model

EXPOSURE AREA	NO MANDATORY APPLICATION PROTECTION (X2)	VULNERABILITY AT POS MACHINE (+1)	VULNERABILITY AT STORE SERVER (+1)	SCORE
Memory	●	-	●	2
Temporary data storage	-	-	●	1
Settlement records	-	-	●	1
Application code & config	●	-	●	2
Connection to POI	●	-	●	2
Internal communication	●	-	-	0
Host links	●	-	●	2
Vulnerability Score				**10**

POS EPS Deployment Model

In a POS EPS deployment model, payment-processing is done by an EPS located at each POS machine, as depicted in Figure 2-6. The EPS is maintaining direct communication with POS and POI devices and is handling everything from card entry flow to processing payment transaction; therefore, no sensitive data is transferred between the POS and the EPS. The EPS is maintaining a direct connection with the payment processor's switch located outside the store.

Some of the security pros and cons of this model are:

- **Pro**—There's no central location in the store that accumulates all the sensitive data in memory, disk storage, or network traffic. It is easier (and less expensive!) to protect a single machine and application instance; however, once it is broken, all the store data is gone.

- **Pro**—POS application (code) is not handling sensitive data because all payment functionality is delegated to a separate EPS application.

- **Con**—All POS machines (memory, data storage) at the store are exposed to sensitive data as well as communication between the POS machine and the payment host.

The input data and results of vulnerability score calculation for the POS EPS deployment model are listed in Table 2-6.

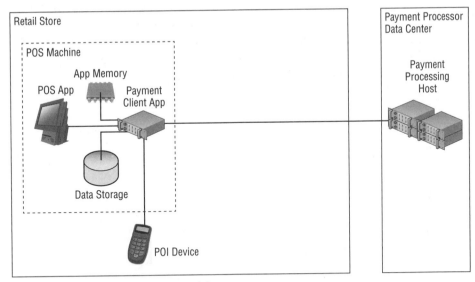

Figure 2-6: POS EPS deployment model

Table 2-6: Vulnerability Score of POS EPS Deployment Model

EXPOSURE AREA	NO MANDATORY APPLICATION PROTECTION (X2)	VULNERABILITY AT POS MACHINE (+1)	VULNERABILITY AT STORE SERVER (+1)	SCORE
Memory	●	●	-	2
Temporary data storage	-	●	-	1
Settlement records	-	●	-	1
Application code & config	●	●	-	2
Connection to POI	●	●	-	2
Internal communication	●	-	-	0
Host links	●	●	-	2
Vulnerability Score				**10**

Hybrid POS/Store Deployment Model

The hybrid POS/Store deployment model is the most vulnerable solution because the PA modules are spread across different physical machines. As depicted in Figure 2-7, initial payment processing (such as interfacing with POI and handling payment transaction flow) is done at the POS machine, which also communicates with the server module at the store level. The links to the payment switch or processors are implemented from the store server.

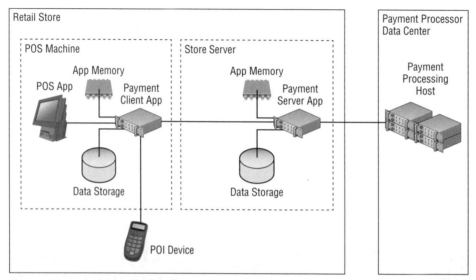

Figure 2-7: Hybrid POS/Store deployment model

There are no security pros associated with this model. The security con is that both the POS and the store server machines and almost all their components (memory, data storage, application code, and communication lines) are entirely vulnerable.

The input data and results of vulnerability score calculation for the Hybrid POS/Store EPS deployment model are listed in Table 2-7.

Gas Station Payment Systems

Deployment of a payment system at a gas station looks different from that of a regular retail store because it involves additional pieces of hardware and software: the *fueling pump* and the *forecourt controller*. As with POS and POI hardware, there are many pump models that are manufactured by several different vendors. From the viewpoint of payment security, they can be divided into at least two groups: *Dispenser Payment Terminals* (DPT) and *Island Payment Terminals* (IPT).

Table 2-7: Vulnerability Score of Hybrid POS/Store Deployment Model

EXPOSURE AREA	NO MANDATORY APPLICATION PROTECTION (X2)	VULNERABILITY AT POS MACHINE (+1)	VULNERABILITY AT STORE SERVER (+1)	SCORE
Memory	●	●	●	4
Temporary data storage	-	●	●	2
Settlement records	-	-	●	1
Application code & config	●	●	●	4
Connection to POI	●	●	-	2
Internal communication	●	●	●	4
Host links	●	-	●	2
Vulnerability Score				**19**

The difference between the two is simple—the former has MSR and pinpad devices built into the pump, while the latter has independent POI devices logically isolated from the pump and controller (there are models of DPT, however, that are logically isolated from the pump). Obviously, the second type is more secure because it allows implementing the EPS concept with a complete separation between the POS and payment flows.

The first group—the integrated payment terminal—is vulnerable for two reasons:

1. Sensitive cardholder data is exposed in additional areas of software and hardware, such as the fuel pump controller and related communication lines.

2. Most built-in card readers and fuel pump controllers currently do not support Hardware P2PE (see Chapter 8 for details about P2PE).

In addition, fueling pumps are often unattended, which obviously does not contribute to the security of their pinpads and opens a Pandora's box of skimming.[10]

The bottom line is that gas station payment applications can be even more dangerous than their counterparts in regular retail stores.

Mobile Payments

When speaking nowadays about electronic payments, it is impossible not to mention the most promising industry trend—mobile payments. Even though paying with a cell phone in brick-and-mortar stores is not yet a common trend in the United States, it might be just a matter of a few years before it becomes a common behavior. Many payment processors, payment software vendors, cellular communication providers, banks, payment brands, startup companies, and even Internet search engines[11, 12, 13] are fighting for the right to be the first to accept mobile payments and become the standard in this fast-rising sector. As always, the new technology brings new security challenges.

Currently, there are two main types of mobile payment technology:

1. Near Field Communication (NFC)-based

2. Anything else

Both approaches have the same issues associated with specifics of mobile and web application security. NFC-based payment applications, however, have additional vulnerabilities associated with the way a mobile device communicates with the merchant's POS. Let's review the architecture and deployment model of typical mobile payment solutions for retail stores.

NFC-based Mobile Payment Technology

The common feature of this group of mobile payment solutions is utilizing Near Field Communication (NFC) technology, which allows exchanging information between electronic devices within very close proximity using high frequency (13.56 MHz) radio communication. NFC, which is essentially a collection of several protocols and standards[14, 15, 16], is employed by different applications including proximity cards, NFC Tags, and, most recently, mobile payments. There are mobile payment solutions, such as Google Wallet, that utilize unique NFC features (Table 2.8) such as short maximum range (less than a few inches) and very fast connection setup time (<0.1s).

Table 2-8: Comparing NFC with Other Contactless Communication Technologies

TECHNOLOGY	TYPICAL RANGE	CONNECTION SETUP TIME	OUT-OF-THE-BOX ENCRYPTION
NFC	~ 1 inch	less than 0.1 second	No
Bluetooth	30 ft.	less than 6 seconds	Yes
WiFi	120 ft.	several seconds	Yes

In such solutions[17, 18], a mobile phone equipped with an NFC device emulates a contactless payment card which can be read by an NFC-enabled POI (see Figure 2-8).

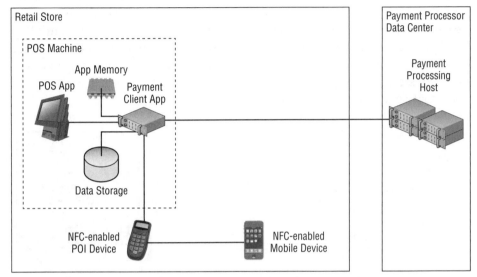

Figure 2-8: Architecture and deployment of an NFC-based payment solution

The payment card authentication data (the content of plastic cards' magnetic stripes) can either be stored on the mobile device or downloaded from the cloud.

In any case, the sensitive data should be transmitted from the mobile to the POI device in order to initiate payment transaction, which opens the door to potential attacks and raises security concerns[19, 20, 21]. These security concerns are discussed in Chapter 8.

Non-NFC Mobile Payment Solutions

There are many "alternative" mobile payment solutions that are not NFC-based. Such applications have strong advantages over the NFC-based products because they do not require NFC equipment. This is an advantage because:

- Many popular mobile phones, such as the Apple iPhone, are not equipped with an NFC transmitter.

- Only limited numbers of merchants have deployed POI devices with NFC readers.

An example of "Non-NFC" mobile payment applications is Starbucks' Mobile App which shows the card number as well as a barcode on the phone's display. In order to start the payment, the card number is entered manually or the barcode is scanned by a cashier, and the payment is processed as a typical card payment from this point.

If a mobile payment application is designed with security in mind, instead of storing the card number in the device and showing it on the screen, the randomly generated one-time token is displayed (and encoded into the barcode) in order to establish the link between the customer's mobile device and merchant's POS (see Figure 2-9). The actual authentication data (such as PAN and expiration date) is transferred "in the cloud" between the mobile solution's and payment processor's data centers (or even inside the same data center if the payment processor is also the mobile payment solution provider).

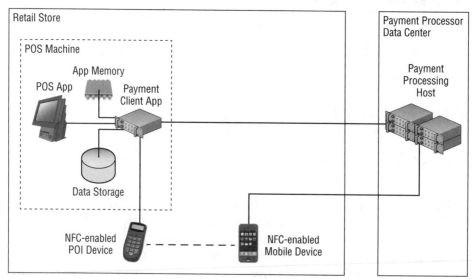

Figure 2-9: Secure architecture and deployment of mobile payments without NFC

In a well-designed "non-NFC" mobile payment solution, sensitive authentication data never touches the mobile device and POS payment application, which is a huge security benefit compared to contactless/NFC models which require transmission of actual card data through the mobile device to the POS.

Summary

Typical payment applications consist of several interfaces and processing modules:

- Interfaces
  - POI Device
  - POS API
  - Payment Processor Link

- Processing Modules
  - Router
  - S&F
  - TOR
  - Batch

Interfaces communicate with the outside world using various types of connectivity, communication technologies, and message protocols. Processing modules execute the workflows and store the sensitive cardholder data on hard drives. There is no standard security (encryption) technology defined for either interface protocols (data in transit) or processing modules (data at rest) of payment applications.

There are three main payment application deployment models:

1. Store EPS
2. POS EPS
3. Hybrid Store/POS

Each model has its own security advantages and disadvantages. However, the Hybrid Store/POS model is the most vulnerable.

Mobile payment solutions are divided into two major groups:

1. NFC-based
2. Non-NFC

NFC-based applications are potentially more vulnerable because they store and/or transmit sensitive cardholder data.

Notes

1. *PCI DSS Requirements and Security Assessment Procedures Version 2.0*, PCI SSC (October 2010), `https://www.pcisecuritystandards.org/documents/ pci_dss_v2.pdf`

2. *PCI PA-DSS Requirements and Security Assessment Procedures Version 2.0*, PCI SSC (October 2010), `https://www.pcisecuritystandards.org/documents/ pa-dss_v2.pdf`

3. *INTERNATIONAL STANDARD ISO/IEC 7498-1, Information Technology – Open Systems Interconnection – Basic Reference Model: The Basic Model*, ISO/IEC (1996), `http://www.ecma-international.org/activities/ Communications/TG11/s020269e.pdf`

4. Mark O'Neil, *Web Services Security*, (New York: McGraw-Hill/Osborne, 2003).

5. *ISO 8583-1:2003, Financial transaction card originated messages – Interchange message specifications – Part 1: Messages, data elements and code values*, ISO. (2003), `http://www.iso.org/iso/iso_catalogue/catalogue_tc/catalogue_detail.htm?csnumber=31628`

6. *Online Processing, Technical Specification*, Paymentech. (2001), `http://www.chasepaymentech.com/library/pdf/Online_5.0.pdf`

7. *Orbital Gateway Interface Specification*, Chase Paymentech. (2008), `http://rafeekphp.files.wordpress.com/2009/04/orbital-gateway-interface-specification-43.pdf`

8. *Technical Reference Guide, Open Terminal Requirement Specification - Book 1*, Nets (2012), `http://www.nets.eu/dk-da/Service/verifikation-af-betalingsloesninger/Documents/ct-trg-otrs-en.pdf`

9. Bruce Schneier, "Secrecy, Security, and Obscurity," *Crypto-Gram Newsletter*, (May 2002), `http://www.schneier.com/crypto-gram-0205.html#1`

10. *Credit Card Skimmers Found On Walnut Creek*, CBS, (May 2013), `http://sanfrancisco.cbslocal.com/2013/05/17/credit-card-skimmers-found-on-walnut-creek-gas-station-pumps/`

11. Google Wallet, `http://www.google.com/wallet/buy-in-store/`

12. Starbucks Mobile Apps, `http://www.starbucks.com/coffeehouse/mobile-apps`

13. Square Wallet, `https://squareup.com/wallet`

14. *ISO/IEC 18000-3, Information technology – Radio frequency identification for item management – Part 3: Parameters for air interface communications at 13,56 MHz*, ISO/IEC (2004), `http://www.iso.org/iso/home/store/catalogue_tc/catalogue_detail.htm?csnumber=53424`

15. *ISO/IEC 14443-1, Identification cards – Contactless integrated circuit cards – Proximity cards – Part 1: Physical characteristics*, ISO/IEC (2008), `http://www.iso.org/iso/iso_catalogue/catalogue_ics/catalogue_detail_ics.htm?csnumber=39693`

16. *ISO/IEC 13157-1, Information technology – Telecommunications and information exchange between systems – NFC Security – Part 1: NFC-SEC NFCIP-1 security services and protocol*, ISO/IEC, (2010), `http://www.iso.org/iso/home/store/catalogue_tc/catalogue_detail.htm?csnumber=53430`

17. Barclaycard PayTag, `http://www.barclaycard.co.uk/personal/pay-with-barclaycard/what-is-paytag`

18. Isis, `https://www.paywithisis.com/`

19. Charlie Miller, *Don't stand so close to me: an analysis of NFC attack surface*, DefCon 20, (2012), `https://media.blackhat.com/bh-us-12/Briefings/C_Miller/BH_US_12_Miller_NFC_attack_surface_Slides.pdf`

20. Kristin Paget, *Credit Card Fraud: The Contactless Generation*, ShmooCon, (2012), `http://www.shmoocon.org/2012/presentations/Paget_shmoocon2012-credit-cards.pdf`

21. Eddie Lee, *NFC Hacking: The Easy Way*, (DefCon 20, 2012), `http://black-winghq.com/assets/labs/presentations/EddieLeeDefcon20.pdf`

PCI

If a lot of cures are suggested for a disease, it means that disease is incurable.

—Anton Chekhov

Standards are an interesting phenomenon, especially in the information technology field. On the one hand, they create bureaucracy, kill creativity, and scare away many talented people. On the other hand, standards save resources, provide reliability, and allow totally different people and organizations to speak to each other using the same language.

In the payment card industry (PCI), this phenomenon is even more interesting. There are established security standards without underlying technology standards. Simply put, most security standards for payment applications tell you what to protect without explaining how to do it. This in no way means that the technology does not exist. It's just not defined and not standardized enough.

These days, whenever there is a discussion about security standards regulating payment applications, the first thing that comes to mind is *PCI*. Such an instinct is unsurprising today because, since 2004, PCI standards have been filling the niche that was empty for a long time. However, it does not mean that PCI rules are the only ones regulating payments. There are other standards which influence the industry, especially these days when new promising technologies such as P2PE come to the arena and bring with them a new wave of hitherto unknown hardware and software requirements. This chapter reviews "known" PCI standards. Other standards that influence payment application security (cryptographic and coding) are reviewed in subsequent chapters.

> **NOTE** Although PCI stands for *payment card industry*, it is common to say PCI when talking about a set of standards developed to regulate the security of various electronic payment systems.

Although this might be the most boring chapter in the book, I recommend at least browsing through it in order to understand what standards should be followed and what shouldn't be used if you care about real security.

What is PCI?

PCI is a great invention. It helps to make payment systems much more secure. The problem with PCI standards is that they came out too late, when the (insecure) technologies around payment card processing had already been established and widely deployed. Any deviation from current technologies (which is necessary in order to provide real security) would require rebuilding the entire system from scratch, which would cost millions of dollars if implemented worldwide. As a result, instead of offering a new secure technology, the main method of PCI security standards is compensating for the vulnerability (by design) of electronic payment systems by building up several extra layers of security controls around existing technologies. This makes the end users (payment processors, service providers, hardware/software vendors, and finally merchants who often have no clue about security) responsible for their implementation. Therefore, the payment systems are often insecure even if they are PCI compliant.

Figure 3-1 shows the number of data breaches in the United States (retail/merchant sector only) officially registered by the Privacy Rights Clearinghouse since 2005, the same year when PCI Data Security Standards (DSS) were first introduced to the world (December 2004 to be more precise).

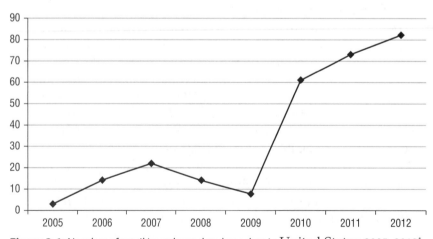

Figure 3-1: Number of retail/merchant data breaches in United States, 2005–2012[1]

Unfortunately, there are no statistics on the number of PCI compliant merchants, but let's assume this number has been growing since 2005. The number of breaches decreased in 2008–2009 and then started climbing again in 2010. Such "strange" behavior can be easily explained. The 2008–2009 reduction was the result of more and more merchants implementing PCI DSS requirements. However, hackers adapted to the new rules relatively quickly, which resulted in significant protection in only one area—data at rest—as they learned to exploit the remaining unprotected key vulnerabilities of payment applications—memory, data in transit, and application code and configuration—as well as physical weaknesses of POI devices. This caused the 2010 jump in the number of breaches.

Since 2010, the situation has continued to worsen so that today we are in the same position as several years ago with no significant barriers that could stop the bad guys from doing their job. Even if these numbers are not precise, we know from the media that payment card data breaches still occur and in even greater numbers, despite the eight years of PCI.

Don't get me wrong—criticism of PCI security standards is not a goal of this book. PCI is a necessary security baseline, a starting point for further improvements, especially for service providers and large merchants. What I am trying to achieve is making it clear that "PCI compliance" is not equal to "security," especially when applied to POS systems and payment applications deployed by small- and mid-size merchants. Nothing helps the attackers more than a false sense of security on the part of the merchant.

PCI Standards

PCI standards cover several different aspects of the electronic payment life cycle. The first and most famous piece is PCI Data Security Standard (PCI DSS) which tells merchants (such as retailers) and service providers (such as payment processors and gateways) how to protect sensitive cardholder information. The second and most important piece for payment software vendors is Payment Application Data Security Standard (PA-DSS) which tells the payment application developers how they should design their products to be compliant with PCI DSS. The third piece is PTS, which takes care of hardware devices, such as POI and HSM (hardware security modules), and their cryptographic modules and firmware. And finally, the newbie—P2PE—which had absorbed the complications of the previous three pieces and added new hitherto unknown challenges in the form of extra software and hardware validation requirements. Table 3-1 shows the applicability of the four PCI standards.

Table 3-1: Applicability of PCI standards

PCI STANDARD	OBJECTS	OBJECTIVES	SUBJECTS
PCI DSS	Environment	Payment transaction processing environment such as retail stores and payment processing data centers	Merchants, service providers (payment processors, gateways, banks)
PA-DSS	Software	Payment applications	Software vendors
PTS	Hardware	SCD (including firmware): POI, HSM	Hardware manufacturers
P2PE	Environment, Hardware, Software	P2PE solutions, P2PE applications	P2PE solution providers, P2PE software vendors

Since there is always confusion and many questions about the applicability of particular PCI standards, let's look (Table 3-2) at this issue from different angles: if you are _____, what standards should you comply with?

Table 3-2: Compliance with PCI standards

IF YOU ...	YOU SHOULD COMPLY WITH ...
develop and sell payment applications	PA-DSS
buy and use payment applications	PCI DSS
resell and install payment applications	-
develop payment application for single customer	-
develop and use payment applications	PCI DSS
provide payment application as a service	PA-DSS and/or PCI DSS
process payment transactions	PCI DSS
manufacture POI device	PTS
manufacture HSM device	PTS
develop and sell P2PE payment applications	P2PE
develop and provide P2PE solution as a service	P2PE
hack payment applications	your own moral standards

PA-DSS vs. PCI DSS

The real difference between PCI DSS and PA-DSS is not objects, objectives, or subjects, but responsibility: who compensates for the lack of credit card security and mitigates the attack vectors? Such responsibility is shared between the merchant and software vendors without any reasonable proportion, with the main burden put on merchants. Table 3-3 reviews the high-level attack vectors and responsibility for their mitigation as defined by PCI DSS and PA-DSS.

Table 3-3: Responsibility for Implementing Security Controls According to PCI

VULNERABILITY AREA	ADDRESSED IN	RESPONSIBLE FOR MITIGATION
Payment application memory	PCI DSS	Merchant
Communication over local network	PCI DSS	Merchant
Communication over public network	PA-DSS, PCI DSS	PA Vendor, Merchant
Communication between PA and POI	PCI DSS	Merchant
Link to payment processor (if not via public network)	PCI DSS	Merchant
Application code	PCI DSS, PA-DSS	Merchant
Application Configuration	PCI DSS	Merchant
POI device (physical)	PCI DSS	Merchant
Encryption key management	PCI DSS, PA-DSS	Merchant
Sensitive data storage	PA-DSS, PCI DSS	PA Vendor, Merchant
Overall responsibility for card data breach	PCI DSS	Merchant

As you can see in Table 3-3, even protection of areas such as memory or application code, which are natively associated with software, fall under user (merchant) responsibility. PA-DSS does not require application developers to encrypt the sensitive data in memory or obfuscate their compiled code. Merchants must protect the payment applications by implementing all sorts of work-arounds, such as firewalls and file integrity monitoring. It is not surprising that those controls often fail because the end users aren't the ones trained to care about the security of their applications.

PA-DSS

The Payment Application Data Security Standard (PA-DSS) was created as a validation program for POS software vendors who sell their products to multiple customers. It provides the buyers with assurance that their new purchase will not violate the PCI DSS rules. PA-DSS is the only one of the PCI family of standards that directly takes care of payment *application* security.

Validation Process

In a nutshell, the validation process consists of going through the list of testing procedures (168 in PA-DSS) and putting the "V" in the right column: "In place" or "Not in place." The assessment begins as soon as the PA vendor selects the Qualified Security Assessor (QSA) from the list published on the PCI SSC website[2] and signs the non-disclosure and statement of work agreements (and pays the bill, of course). Currently, 80 companies are listed as PA-QSA (not to be confused with QSA companies which are authorized to perform PCI DSS assessments only, although the same company or person can be both QSA and PA-QSA).

The validation process is not too complicated and is usually comprised of the following steps:

1. Initial meeting (can be onsite or phone call)—PA developers and PA-QSA review the scope of the project, the time lines, and the high-level application design, and discuss the lab and documentation requirements.

2. On-site assessment—Includes two steps:

    a. Testing the actual application in the vendor's lab—The auditor, PA-QSA, is instructed by the developers because this is the first (and maybe also the last) time he/she is seeing the system. Penetration testing is conducted by running all possible types of transactions and cards to make sure there is no sensitive data written to the hard drive. They may do some network sniffing to make sure no credentials are sent in clear text. No catchy tools or techniques are needed, and no one tries to actually break the system because QSA is not a professional penetration tester. In most cases, if the application does not store (or pretends it does not store) the sensitive data in clear text, it passes the test.

    b. Interview with the personnel—This is a formality. The auditors have to ask a few questions and record the names of the developers and QA team for the report.

3. Reviewing implemented processes, documentation, and evidences—This step is mostly paperwork. The most painful part (especially, for the first-timer) is creating the PCI Implementation Guide—the document that

each PA vendor must provide to the customers (the users of the payment software). The content of this document is mostly technical disclaimers that remind the merchants that credit card acceptance is a dangerous business and it is the merchant's responsibility to fix the security design flaws of payment card processing.

4. Creating Report of Validation (ROV)—This document is prepared by PA-QSA and it is sent to the PCI Council for acceptance. This step may take time as the Council might reject any statement in the report and return it to QSA. Then QSA rewrites all rejected portions in a more secure way and resubmits the document. Once the ROV is accepted (approved) by the Council, the invoice is issued to the vendor and the validated application is listed (as long as the bill is paid).

NOTE   ROV is not required for revalidation (self-validation of a minor release without major changes). In this case, the process is even simpler: the attestation of validation (AOV) letter is created by the vendor (without QSA) and sent directly to the Council along with payment, which automatically renews the listing.

List of Validated Payment Applications

The PCI Council maintains the List of Validated Payment Applications on its website.[3] Before purchasing new payment software or installing a new version, the merchant should check the website to make sure the product is validated and eligible for new deployment. Revalidation is required for every new release of a payment application, or at least annually. Obviously, no software vendor can afford to revalidate each and every patch version, which would be unfeasible (validation process eats human resources) and economically unprofitable (each revalidation and listing costs money). Therefore, since it is unlikely that the list reflects the real picture (exact versions of software that run at stores), it is symbolic, yet still an important tool for merchants.

The 13 Requirements and POS Security

Table 3-4 reviews how 13 of the PA-DSS requirements help developers protect the main vulnerability areas of payment applications. Note that this review is not a generic assessment of the entire standard, but particularly applies to the POS and payment applications primarily deployed in brick-and-mortar business locations, such as retail stores or gas stations.

Table 3-4: PA-DSS Requirements and Payment Application Key Vulnerability Areas

	PA-DSS REQUIREMENT	DATA IN MEMORY	DATA IN TRANSIT	DATA AT REST	PA CODE & CONFIG
1	Do not retain full magnetic stripe, card verification code or value (CAV2, CID, CVC2, CVV2), or PIN block data	-	-	○	-
2	Protect stored cardholder data	-	-	●	-
3	Provide secure authentication features	-	-	-	-
4	Log payment application activity	-	-	-	-
5	Develop secure payment applications	-	-	-	○
6	Protect wireless transmissions	-	○	-	-
7	Test payment applications to address vulnerabilities	-	-	-	○
8	Facilitate secure network implementation	-	-	-	-
9	Cardholder data must never be stored on a server connected to the Internet	-	-	-	-
10	Facilitate secure remote access to payment application	-	-	-	-
11	Encrypt sensitive traffic over public networks	-	○	-	-
12	Encrypt all non-console administrative access	-	-	-	-
13	Maintain instructional documentation and training programs for customers, resellers, and integrators	-	-	-	-

● – provides an adequate, full protection if implemented correctly

○– provides only limited or selective protection

- – provides no direct protection

As you can see in the Table 3-4, these 13 requirements, even if fanatically followed, will probably not protect cardholder data from being stolen in one way or another. The only full coverage PA-DSS provides is for the data at rest, as historically that was the first and easiest data from which to steal the magnetic tracks (during the "before PCI" era developers did not care to encrypt anything, so the hacker's job was as simple as choosing which merchant to rob first). However, Chapter 6 shows how even the strongest PA-DSS requirement can easily be rendered useless.

Now let's go through these 13 PA-DSS requirements again in more detail to see why they are mostly helpless as explicit application security controls.

Requirement 1: Do Not Retain Full Magnetic Stripe, Card Verification Code or Value (CAV2, CID, CVC2, CVV2), or PIN Block Data

The most important sub-requirement here is 1.1:

Do not store sensitive authentication data after authorization (even if encrypted)[4]

The keyword here is *"after authorization."* This means that any sensitive data (such as Tracks 1 and 2, PAN, CVV2) is allowed to be stored before the transaction is approved by the processor. If the processor is unreachable for any reason (for example, the network is down), such a transaction goes to S&F and/or TOR databases, usually along with all sensitive data, and can be stored there for seconds, minutes, hours, or even days until the connectivity comes back. If the network is down for a significant period of time, the local POS database might end up containing thousands of records of sensitive data.

So what exactly does this requirement secure? If the information is properly encrypted, no matter how many records are stored at any given time, no one will be able to decrypt them. On the other hand, if information is not reliably protected, nothing will stop someone who wants to steal the temporary records *before the authorization* just by pulling them out one after the other as POS is processing more and more transactions.

Conclusion: This requirement is concerned with the magnitude of the potential data breach—the less data stored, the less damage is caused once the breach occurs.

Requirement 2: Protect Stored Cardholder Data

It is important to admit that this requirement is the most significant achievement of the PCI. If it is implemented correctly (for example, using hardware-based strong cryptography and key management) it provides a real data protection mechanism. However, there are two issues here. First, it is rarely implemented correctly (and it is not necessarily developers who are to blame for it). Second, data storage is only one target from several other vulnerability areas. Even if the data storage is completely sealed, other application surfaces (memory, data in transit, and application code and configuration) are still welcoming strangers.

Requirement 3: Provide Secure Authentication Features

This requirement is divorced from reality if applied to POS. Normally, a payment application does not allow any access to cardholder data at the POS machine, and often not even at the store level. There is simply no need for the cashier to see the tracks or PAN. This requirement might be relevant to server systems but not to the POS. Therefore, any efforts to enforce POS authentication management are helpless.

Requirement 4: Log Payment Application Activity

Implementation of this requirement does not protect anything. Logs belong to *reactive security controls*[5] which are supposed to help computer forensic investigators trace the origins of the attack. Usually it happens several months after the first records are leaked through the data breach.

Requirement 5: Develop Secure Payment Applications

This requirement contains several recommendations regarding good practices for secure coding, which are supposed to help protect the application code, such as sub-requirement 5.2:

> *Develop all payment applications (internal and external, and including web administrative access to product) based on secure coding guidelines. Cover prevention of common coding vulnerabilities in software development processes.*[6]

Unfortunately, there is a small problem with these recommendations: they are mostly useless for POS systems running in brick-and-mortar stores where hackers use *other* applications' and operating systems' vulnerabilities to break in. Indeed, what is the point of exploiting a payment application's buffer overflow vulnerability in order to steal the card data, if all you need to do is sniff the local network connection or scan the POS machine memory? However, without doubt, the guidelines about some vulnerabilities (such as SQL injection) would be helpful for e-commerce developers. More details about secure coding guidelines can be found in Chapter 9.

Requirement 6: Protect Wireless Transmissions

This requirement is confusing. It sends the wrong message to payment application developers. Instead of taking care of ANY kind of communication, they either rely on end users by instructing them to enable the built-in wireless encryption (which can be weak because it is implemented by people who are not supposed to deal with cryptography), or simply declare that this requirement is not applicable because their product does not require wireless.

Requirement 7: Test Payment Applications to Address Vulnerabilities

Beyond all doubt, risk assessment and integrity protection, which are being promoted by this requirement, are necessary attributes of secure development processes. However, they do not directly help to defend against any particular threat. As already explained for Requirement 5, vulnerabilities of the payment application code itself are rarely exploited in order to gain access to sensitive data. It is rather the vulnerable design of the entire payment system that is exploited by the hackers. It is not the buffer overflow in the payment application code, but clear text Track 2 data in POS machine memory and store LAN (both are allowed by PCI standards!) that cause the security breach.

Requirement 8: Facilitate Secure Network Implementation

This is the shortest and funniest one: "Payment application cannot interfere with antivirus protection, firewall configurations, or any other device, application, or configuration required for PCI DSS compliance." Programmers—does anyone know how to write an application that interferes with antivirus? Oh, by the way, don't forget to test your application with all known brands of antiviruses and firewalls! Perhaps the authors had a really bad experience with some free antivirus program.

Requirement 9: Cardholder Data Must Never be Stored on a Server Connected to the Internet.

I would agree! However, does the fact that *"the payment application stores cardholder data in the internal network"* (Requirement 9.1.a) prevent that data from being stolen? Unfortunately, no.

Requirement 10: Facilitate Secure Remote Access to Payment Application

This requirement basically admits that the security of payment systems relies on the security of its perimeter and the honesty of its operators. With such an approach, once the perimeter is broken (or penetrated from inside!), the data is gone! Note that *two-factor authentication*, which is promoted in Requirement 10.1, is not the same as *dual control* or *split knowledge*. Two-factor authentication is a really great feature, but it is intended for a different kind of security and cannot protect the system from bad users and insiders. More about split knowledge can be found in the "Point-to-Point Encryption" section of Chapter 8.

Requirement 11: Encrypt Sensitive Traffic Over Public Networks

This requirement raises three more questions:

1. How significant is the difference between public and private network security?

2. Since when are private networks considered secure?

3. If payment application vendors are capable, according to PCI requirements, of encrypting communication on public networks, wouldn't it be better to do the same on ALL networks and connections?

The following testing procedure is especially alarming:

11.1.b If the payment application allows data transmission over public networks, examine the PA-DSS Implementation Guide prepared by the vendor, and verify the vendor includes directions for customers and resellers/integrators to use strong cryptography and security protocols.[7]

Does this really say that the payment application developers should delegate implementation of "strong cryptography and security protocols" to "customers and resellers/integrators"?

Requirement 12: Encrypt All Non-console Administrative Access

This requirement is laconic and self-explanatory: "Instruct customers to encrypt all non-console administrative access with strong cryptography." This seems like an attempt to transfer the responsibility for designing secure systems from software vendors to the end users. Instead of a request to develop secure payment-processing technology so that merchants can operate their computers and networks without a constant risk of data breach, the standard wants to require the merchants' employees to study secure protocols "such as SSH, VPN, or SSL/TLS."

Requirement 13: Maintain Instructional Documentation and Training Programs for Customers, Resellers, and Integrators

Documentation is the most powerful application security mechanism... on paper.

PA-DSS and Merchants

Merchants (actually, their IT and security experts and managers) must understand PA-DSS because they should be able to identify "lawful" payment application vulnerabilities. They should be ready to ask developers the right questions about their applications' security controls beyond just PCI. Merchants must learn the weaknesses of PA-DSS in order to make sure their applications have adequate protection mechanisms that compensate for lack of environmental security (and vice versa—they have access, network, and physical controls strong enough to compensate for payment application vulnerabilities). There are multiple examples of this.

For instance, PCI DSS allows a payment application to send sensitive data unencrypted on local networks, which is a great exposure area. In this case, the merchant should verify whether or not its payment application is compliant with the standards (i.e., sends sensitive cardholder data over the local network in clear text). If it is, the network should be protected by different methods, for example, encrypted tunnel with IPSec (see Chapter 8 for more details). Such multiple "misunderstandings" may cause a situation when neither the PA vendor nor the merchant protect the data. The PA vendor thinks the merchant protects the network according to PCI DSS requirements, while the merchant relies on the security expertise of software developers.

PCI DSS

Unlike PA-DSS where the process of compliance status achievement is called *validation*, the similar PCI DSS process is called *assessment*. Perhaps, because of the difference between their objectives: single payment application in PA-DSS, versus the entire payment-processing environment in PCI DSS.

Even though technically the PCI DSS assessment process is the same as PA-DSS validation—putting "V" in the right column of the testing procedures list and creating the report—there are significant differences:

> **The scope of the PCI DSS assessment is too wide** (even physically – it may include multiple locations such as retail stores, offices, and data centers), which consumes a lot of resources from both the auditor and the merchant, and does not allow them to concentrate on any particular topic or conduct any thorough testing. There are 310 testing procedures in PCI DSS, almost twice as many as PA-DSS's 168 tests, so the cycle is longer and requires more evidence (read: paperwork). Indeed, even assuming that addressing each testing procedure requires only 30 minutes (in practice, it can be even more because it includes explaining the requirement, interviewing the employees, reviewing the evidence, testing the environment, and writing down the report), the assessment takes almost a month of full-time work days! It can be even worse for large multi-store chains because the efforts would be multiplied by the number of stores and/or data centers because some evidences require samples from more than just one instance.

> By the time the audit is ended and a report is written and accepted, the actual picture at the starting point of the assessment might already be

different because the subject is not a particular version of software or hardware, but a constantly changing environment.

PCI DSS is a double standard. The form and scale of the assessment vary significantly depending on the size of the merchant or service provider. The merchants are divided into several levels based on the amount of card transactions they process each year. Every payment brand has its own definition rules and requirements for those levels, so different rules from different brands should be correlated in order to get a clear picture of the certification path. Depending on the level, the merchants might be required to either hire the QSA or complete the self-assessment questionnaire (SAQ).

Large merchants such as well-known big supermarket chains definitely go through the most difficult path with a third-party auditor, while smaller merchants just complete the paperwork themselves. Even without going into the details, it is clear that the same POS system may have different security levels depending on its owner, simply because many deployments are never tested by third-party auditors.

The PCI Council does not maintain the list of PCI DSS certified organizations as it does for PA-DSS validations. The compliance status of service providers such as payment gateways and processors can be verified at the Visa website in the Global Registry of Service Providers.[8] However, there is no such information about merchants available for consumers. When you swipe your card in a store, there is no way to know whether, at least formally, your sensitive account data are secure. According to Visa, 1,700 U.S.-based merchants processing more than 20,000 transactions annually are still not PCI compliant.[9] Statistics for the smaller stores (processing less than 20,000 transactions) do not exist.

The 12 Requirements and Payment Application Security

Let's go through the list of PCI protection measures and try to understand why hackers constantly manage to steal the payment card data despite the almost 10-year old merchants' PCI compliance.

Table 3-5 shows how the user (merchant) of the software (payment application) is tasked with implementing the security controls which, logically, should be present out of the box. It also shows which requirements are really effective when applied to the POS payment application running in a store, which will be explained in more detail after review of Table 3-5.

Table 3-5: PCI DSS Requirements and Payment Application Key Vulnerability Areas

	PCI DSS REQUIREMENT	DATA IN MEMORY	DATA IN TRANSIT	DATA AT REST	PA CODE & CONFIG
1	Install and maintain a firewall configuration to protect cardholder data	○	○	○	○
2	Do not use vendor-supplied defaults for system passwords and other security parameters	-	○	○	-
3	Protect stored cardholder data	-	-	●	-
4	Encrypt transmission of cardholder data across open, public networks	-	○	-	-
5	Use and regularly update antivirus software or programs	○	-	○	○
6	Develop and maintain secure systems and applications	○	○	○	○
7	Restrict access to cardholder data by business' need to know	-	-	-	-
8	Assign a unique ID to each person with computer access	○	○	○	○
9	Restrict physical access to cardholder data	-	-	-	-
10	Track and monitor all access to network resources and cardholder data	-	-	-	-
11	Regularly test security systems and processes	-	-	-	-
12	Maintain a policy that addresses information security for all personnel	-	-	-	-

● – provides an adequate, full protection if implemented correctly

○ – provides only limited or selective protection

- – provides no direct protection

You probably noticed that only about 50% of the requirements are somewhat effective in practice to restrain the attacks of hackers. In fact, only one requirement (#3: Protect stored cardholder data) contains a concrete measure that adequately (more or less, depending on interpretation and implementation) covers only one vulnerability area. Let's review each of the 12 PCI DSS requirements that payment brands created for merchants so they could plug the gaps in leaking payment software.

Requirement 1: Install and Maintain a Firewall Configuration to Protect Cardholder Data

The idea behind this requirement is to create a barrier between the area where payments live (sensitive cardholder data in clear text) and the rest of the world (where hackers live, in networking terms). This is a really great idea which was probably based on the sterile conditions of data centers. In a decent data center, all the servers are physically secured and logical access to them is very limited (for instance, normally no one is browsing the Internet on the domain controller). The network is the only bridge that allows access to this space. In such an almost ideal environment, perhaps, a properly set up firewall might be capable of creating a decent secure zone isolated from the outer world. Qualified network engineers will make sure the firewall is configured correctly to filter out any alien data coming in and confidential information going out.

Now, imagine an average retail store. The POS computer and POI device is on the counter, and all network and serial connections are totally exposed, both physically and logically. Anyone can either physically touch or logically access both open and "protected" sides of the network. In such a hazardous environment, where exactly are the outer and the inner zones? Someone can just plug a flash drive into the hosting POS computer, or check e-mail and click on attachment in the back office store server, and the malware is installed right in the heart of the payment system!

Another question: Are there people qualified to properly set up the firewall—not just one but thousands and thousands of them—in each and every shop?

Requirement 2: Do Not Use Vendor-supplied Defaults for System Passwords and Other Security Parameters

This is the right requirement from a generic security point of view, but doesn't it sound too basic to be placed as a separate rule? Isn't it supposed to be part of the education for the people who are supposed to implement other pretty sophisticated requirements, such as firewall configurations (Requirement 1), or installation and configuration of antiviruses and software patches (Requirements 5 and 6)? Isn't it supposed to be an obvious rule for in-store security experts who are going to "track and monitor all access to network resources" and "regularly test security systems and processes" (Requirements 10 and 11)?

Requirement 3: Protect Stored Cardholder Data

From the beginning of the PCI era, this requirement has been in primary focus. That's because the very first vectors of attacks against payment systems were very simple: penetrate the environment and take the sensitive card data which was always stored in clear text. So Requirement #3 was introduced in order to stop this particular trend. The goal has been accomplished, although only partially:

- First, many merchants still are not PCI compliant.
- Second, even those who are still might have the clear text data they don't know about, for example, error messages in log files.
- Finally, payment applications often use weak encryption algorithms or poorly implemented key management.

Another issue with this security measure is that it only protects 1 out of 4 key vulnerability areas (see Table 3-5).

Requirement 4: Encrypt Transmission of Cardholder Data Across Open Public Networks

Even though this measure is one of the few that recall the real application security controls, its scope is too limited. In today's reality when networks are easily penetrated from both outside and inside, everyone (not just security experts) knows that a message must be encrypted when sent via a wireless network or the Internet. It's true that it wasn't obvious for many people 10 years ago, exactly the same way it is not obvious to everyone that *everything* must be encrypted while transmitted through wires, no matter whether it is Internet, LAN, or serial cable between pinpad and POS machine.

Heartland Payment Systems, one of the largest payment processors, experienced a data breach in 2008:

> *The source of the breach: a piece of malicious software planted on the company's payment-processing network that **recorded payment card data as it was being sent** for processing to Heartland by thousands of the company's retail clients.*[10]

Requirement 5: Use and Regularly Update Antivirus Software or Programs.

There is something irrational in this requirement. It sounds like a cry for help and disengagement at the same time. "There is nothing we can offer to protect your customers' data. Please ask someone else to come and try to do something!"

There is nothing wrong with having antivirus on a POS machine. In fact, every PC is running antivirus today as a security precaution measure. It is wrong, however, to rely on antivirus as a protective measure against payment card data fraud. A regular cardholder might ask: Does the security of my private information depend on antivirus vendors? Are the AV vendors aware of their responsibility for protecting sensitive cardholder data? Are they familiar with architecture, vulnerabilities, and threats of POS and payment systems?

During a four-month long cyberattack by Chinese hackers on The New York Times, *the company's antivirus software missed 44 of the 45 pieces of malware installed by attackers on the network.*[11]

The malware created for stealing credit card data is often the zero-day software which is crafted for a specific task, usually customized for a particular payment application and masked as part of that application or operating system. It is not the same as a generic virus or worm which are created to infect as many computers as possible. Antivirus programs can be helpful only when such malware become very common "off the shelf" products.

Another issue with using antivirus is that it requires continuous updates (downloads) of virus signature databases in order to be efficient. Such updates can either be provided by a centralized system created by corporate IT or direct download from the Internet. Large retailers might be able to create their own update systems. However, most merchants still use the direct download which requires maintaining a constant Internet connection. Yes, the firewall can be configured to allow only specific protocols, port numbers, and servers, but you cannot expect the average user to do it right.

Requirement 6: Develop and Maintain Secure Systems and Applications

This is a reasonable requirement that may provide protection from many exploits. It works perfectly with software equipped with automatic, invisible for the user, update mechanisms like Windows or Google Chrome. Unfortunately, many software vendors, including those who develop payment applications, still do not have such automated systems in place, so their update processes require human intervention, which makes them ineffective.

In addition, even totally up-to-date software is not a silver bullet. Many vulnerability areas such as exposed sensitive data in memory are difficult, if not impossible, for mitigation in software, and therefore their presence in payment applications is legalized by PCI security standards.

Requirement 7: Restrict Access to Cardholder Data by Business Need-to-know

This sounds obvious even for non-experts and provides some protection, mostly against particular threats such as insiders, although it does not eliminate them completely. The problem is that even if the payment applications and environments are fully PCI compliant, the data in clear text is still present in the system in one form or another, and there are always people having full access to it—system admins, network engineers, customer-support personnel, technicians, security analysts, and sometimes even developers. There must be highly trusted employees who are allowed to touch the most intimate parts of the system in order to perform maintenance or troubleshooting. Those people are not necessarily bad guys (even though sometimes they are!) but their credentials can be stolen with Trojans and key loggers or social engineering and used by hackers to gain the same highest level of access.

Requirement 8: Assign a Unique ID to Each Person with Computer Access

Unique identification is not a security mechanism that would protect against any specific threat in any payment application vulnerability area. Rather, this is a forensic tool that is helpful in post-mortem investigation of data breach for tracing the hackers. Some security experts may say this can be qualified as deterrent security control (an access control that discourages violation of security policy).[12] However, it is difficult to imagine that traceability would scare away the bad guys sitting somewhere in Russia or China.

Nevertheless, Requirement 8 contains a couple of important sub-requirements:

8.3 Incorporate two-factor authentication for remote access (network-level access originating from outside the network) to the network by employees, administrators, and third parties.

8.4 Render all passwords unreadable during transmission and storage on all system components using strong cryptography.[13]

Those are right and somewhat effective measures if implemented correctly, although they still cover only limited areas of potential threats (attempts to access the network from outside in Requirement 8.3, and network sniffing in Requirement 8.4), and do not provide total protection in any particular area of payment application vulnerabilities.

Requirement 9: Restrict Physical Access to Cardholder Data

This is the right requirement for service providers such as banks, payment processors, and gateways who store and process their data in data centers. It is also an easy one for them to implement because decent data centers mostly have the necessary physical security controls already in place.

This requirement is nonsense and totally useless, however, for merchants and their payment applications running in the stores. Imagine customers "authorized before entering" a retail store and "given a physical token (for example, a badge or access device) that expires and that identifies the visitors as not on-site personnel" (Requirements 9.3.1 and 9.3.2). The retail store environment is fully exposed to strangers, and software developers must accept this fact as a given condition and understand that they cannot fully rely on any physical security controls when designing protection mechanisms for payment applications.

Requirement 10: Track and Monitor All Access to Network Resources and Cardholder Data

In general, this requirement has the same issue as the previous requirement. It makes sense for data centers of payment processors and headquarters of large retailers, but it does not fit the field conditions of retail stores and therefore cannot make much contribution to payment application security.

This requirement is focused on total logging that is supposed to provide two main functions: tracking and monitoring. The first part is irrelevant to the payment application and data protection because it only provides "post-mortem" services (similar to Requirement 8) which are helpful only when investigating the data breach after the fact. The second part, theoretically, may help to recognize the intrusion, but it still cannot prevent it.

In addition, those monitoring activities are infeasible in retail store environments, especially in situations where small merchants do not have dedicated IT personnel able to "review logs for all system components at least daily" (Requirement 10.6).

Requirement 11: Regularly Test Security Systems and Processes

This is another instance of security control which is good in theory but ineffective in practice. Let's take, for example, Requirement 11.3:

> *Perform external and internal penetration testing at least once a year and after any significant infrastructure or application upgrade or modification (such as an operating system upgrade, a sub-network added to the environment, or a web server added to the environment).*[14]

Good penetration testing conducted by true experts is not cheap. The chances are very small that all of the millions and millions of stores out there will go through really thorough penetration testing after any changes. Now, imagine the situation where the successful penetration testing was done on January 1. On January 2, there was a change made in a firewall configuration which left the payment network segment with POS machines open for outside access. During the next penetration testing on January 1 of the next year the vulnerability will be found, reported, and then probably fixed on January 2. The hackers will have a one-year window for scanning the network, finding the hole, penetrating the environment, and planting the malware.

Another example is Requirement 11.5:

> *Deploy file-integrity monitoring tools to alert personnel to unauthorized modification of critical system files, configuration files, or content files; and configure the software to perform critical file comparisons at least weekly.*[15]

First, small merchants are unable to implement this due to lack of in-house expertise. Both large and small merchants can purchase and install good file integrity monitoring tools. However, it's not the presence of a tool in the system but its proper configuration and usage that defines whether or not it will be able to detect an intrusion. Many users will either partially disable the detection functionality (for example, to allow silent automatic updates from payment application vendors) or ignore the notification messages (if the system does not block new files immediately but instead just creates and sends warnings).

Requirement 12: Maintain a Policy That Addresses Information Security for All Personnel

This is the most exciting one of the 12 requirements. Unfortunately, this is also probably the least effective one from an application security perspective. Indeed, it is hard to imagine how a bunch of paper can protect, for instance, a Track 2 data traveling in clear text from the pinpad device to the POS machine, or unencrypted PAN and CVV2 remaining in a volatile memory of a payment application process after a manual transaction. Seriously, do you know anyone, at least in the retail and payment industry, who ever reads their security policies—except of course the poor people who write them, security auditors (once a year), and lawyers (after a security breach occurs)?

It does not mean, however, that Requirement 12 is incorrect in general when applied to the right organization. In fact, some sub-requirements such as 12.1.2,

> *Establish, publish, maintain, and disseminate a security policy that ... includes an annual process that identifies threats, and vulnerabilities, and results in a formal risk assessment.*[16]

are very useful as a common security best practice (again, the same as for many previous requirements: for large organizations only). The problem is that the cardholders cannot rely on ephemeral policies and procedures as a strong security control that is supposed to be capable of preventing the disclosure of their private information. No one can vouch for the fact that these policies and procedures are executed in reality, and even if they are actually carried out, no one knows how frequently and what their real efficiency is.

The programmers say that documentation does not fail, it's the code that does. I would rephrase it this way: policy does not leak, the payment application does.

PCI DSS and Small Merchants

As you probably noticed in previous sections that reviewed the 12 PCI DSS requirements, there are many cases when the effectiveness of a particular requirement was linked to the size of the merchant. Some security measures, such as firewall configuration, can be efficient with large retailers who have IT and security resources, but they are almost completely useless for small merchants who fully rely on security provided by their payment hardware, application vendors, and payment processors.

In addition, most of the merchants (normally those with less than 6 million annual transactions) don't even pass the third-party assessment by QSA and just fill in the SAQ, which questions the quality and even the fact of implementation of many controls.[17] Let's go through the 12 requirements one more time (see Table 3-6) and see what level of protection they carry depending on the size of the merchant.

Table 3-6: Efficiency of PCI DSS Requirements Depending on Merchant Size

	PCI DSS REQUIREMENT	LARGE MERCHANTS	SMALL MERCHANTS
1	Install and maintain a firewall configuration to protect cardholder data	●	-
2	Do not use vendor-supplied defaults for system passwords and other security parameters	●	-
3	Protect stored cardholder data	○	○
4	Encrypt transmission of cardholder data across open, public networks	●	○
5	Use and regularly update antivirus software or programs	●	●
6	Develop and maintain secure systems and applications	○	-
7	Restrict access to cardholder data by business need-to-know	●	-
8	Assign a unique ID to each person with computer access	●	-
9	Restrict physical access to cardholder data	-	-
10	Track and monitor all access to network resources and cardholder data	●	-
11	Regularly test security systems and processes	●	-
12	Maintain a policy that addresses information security for all personnel	●	-

● – can be implemented by merchant

○ – merchant relies on payment application vendor

- – it is unrealistic to expect a proper implementation from merchant as it requires special expertise and/or extra (expensive) resources

As you can see from the data in Table 3-6, small merchants cannot be adequately protected from data breach by PCI DSS because they are unable to implement effectively most of the controls required by the standard.

PCI DSS and PA Developers

Unlike PA-DSS, which implicitly takes care of payment application, PCI DSS is focused on the entire operation environment rather than particular software products. It is valid to say that PA-DSS is a subset of the more pervasive PCI DSS. Does it mean that the payment application developer can ignore PCI DSS? Probably not. PA-DSS was created to support more sophisticated PCI DSS requirements in payment software. PA developers must understand the potential hazards of the environment where PA lives through learning PCI DSS. They should realize that PA does not run in a vacuum, but in a retail store environment that is insecure by definition.

Not all payment applications pass PA-DSS validation. There are rules defining the scope of the PA-DSS assessment applicability. The following groups of payment applications are not eligible for PA-DSS audit, but their developers should still follow the requirements of either PCI DSS or PA-DSS.

- Payment applications developed in-house by merchants.
- Payment applications developed by software vendors for single customers.
- Payment applications that are sold "off the shelf" without much customization required after installation (this is rarely used, so is a strange exception).

The idea behind the "exceptions" is that such applications are going through the PCI DSS audit of their owner anyway. In this case, the application should be "PA-DSS ready," meaning that it does not formally pass through the PA-DSS audit but complies with the PA-DSS requirements. The PCI DSS auditor is supposed to do the assessment instead of the PA-DSS auditor, according to corresponding PCI DSS standard requirements. Thus, the people responsible for such an application's security design and development should be familiar with PA-DSS or PCI DSS or both.

Comparing PA-DSS and PCI DSS Requirements

PCI DSS is big, having 12 requirements with 211 sub-requirements containing a total of 310 testing procedures. Although PA-DSS has more high-level requirements (13), the numbers of sub-requirements (90) and testing procedures (168) are significantly lower than PCI DSS. Reviewing and commenting on each and every sub-requirement and testing procedure would be the topic for an entirely separate book. Therefore, our goal can be narrowed by filtering, focusing on whatever is directly relevant to the payment application. If you look closely at the

12 PCI DSS requirements, you immediately notice that some of them duplicate the PA-DSS requirements (or vice versa).

Table 3-7 compares the two standards and shows that the overlapping requirements make a bit more sense, so it might be helpful to distinguish them from a few standalone requirements that are often useless from an application security point of view.

Table 3-7: Comparing PA-DSS and PCI DSS Requirements

PA-DSS REQUIREMENT	PCI DSS REQUIREMENT	GUARANTEES STRONG PROTECTION OF:	FACILITATES CASUAL PROTECTION OF:
1. Do not retain full magnetic stripe, card verification code or value (CAV2, CID, CVC2, CVV2), or PIN block data	3.2 Do not store sensitive authentication data after authorization (even if encrypted)	None	Data at rest
2. Protect stored cardholder data	3. Protect stored cardholder data	Data at rest	Data at rest
3. Provide secure authentication features	8. Assign a unique ID to each person with computer access	None	Data at rest
4. Log payment application activity	10. Track and monitor all access to network resources and cardholder data	None	None
5. Develop secure payment applications	6. Develop and maintain secure systems and applications	None	Application code
6. Protect wireless transmissions	4. Encrypt transmission of cardholder data across open, public networks	None	Data in transit
7. Test payment applications to address vulnerabilities	6. Develop and maintain secure systems and applications	None	Application code
8. Facilitate secure network implementation		None	None

Continues

Table 3-7 *(continued)*

PA-DSS REQUIREMENT	PCI DSS REQUIREMENT	GUARANTEES STRONG PROTECTION OF:	FACILITATES CASUAL PROTECTION OF:
9. Cardholder data must never be stored on a server connected to the Internet	1.3.7 Place system components that store cardholder data (such as a database) in an internal network zone, segregated from the DMZ and other untrusted networks	None	Data at rest
10. Facilitate secure remote access to payment application	8.3 Incorporate two-factor authentication for remote access (network-level access originating from outside the network) to the network by employees, administrators, and third parties	None	None
11. Encrypt sensitive traffic over public networks	4. Encrypt transmission of cardholder data across open, public networks	None	Data in transit
12. Encrypt all non-console administrative access	2.3 Encrypt all non-console administrative access using strong cryptography. Use technologies such as SSH, VPN, or SSL/TLS for web-based management and other non-console administrative access	None	Data in transit, Data at rest
13. Maintain instructional documentation and training programs for customers, resellers, and integrators		None	None
	5. Use and regularly update antivirus software or programs	None	Data at rest, Data in memory, Application code
	7. Restrict access to cardholder data by business need to know	None	None

Continues

Table 3-7 *(continued)*

PA-DSS REQUIREMENT	PCI DSS REQUIREMENT	GUARANTEES STRONG PROTECTION OF:	FACILITATES CASUAL PROTECTION OF:
	9. Restrict physical access to cardholder data	None	None
	11. Regularly test security systems and processes	None	None
	12. Maintain a policy that addresses information security for all personnel	None	None

PTS

PIN Transaction Security (PTS) isn't so important for payment application vendors unless their application runs on a pinpad device. In integrated POS solutions, the PIN Entry Devices (PED) or POI devices, which are the main objects of the PTS assessment, take care of debit PIN security using well known Triple DES encryption and DUKPT key management mechanisms. If the same scheme was used by payment terminals for card data protection, it would eliminate most of the payment application security problems.

However, before the era of almost universal acceptance of PIN cards, POS machines were not equipped with PED or integrated with POI devices. Regular MSR devices, which were used for swiping credit cards, did not have cryptographic capabilities that would allow them to implement DUKPT (now some of them do). Therefore, unfortunately, PTS provides no direct protection to sensitive payment data, although there is an exception: when a PTS-validated device is part of a P2PE solution. PA developers just started hearing about PTS after P2PE standards entered the scene, and some PA vendors became a P2PE solution provider which requires loose integration between various software and hardware components and standards. More information about P2PE standard requirements can be found in the next section.

Recently, HSM manufacturers also began validating their products with a special version of PTS created for HSM.[18] The list of PTS validated pinpads, HSM, and other devices is published on the PCI SSC website.[19]

P2PE

The PCI SSC provides a vague definition of the P2PE standard:

Detailed security requirements and testing procedures for application vendors and providers of P2PE solutions to ensure that their solutions can meet the necessary requirements for the protection of payment card data.[20]

However, P2PE is a huge jump from existing PCI standards which tried to build the secure payment system from physically, logically, and organizationally separated, poorly protected blocks of compliance, that were untrusting and trying to blame each other: merchants, POS and PA software vendors, hardware manufacturers, and payment processors. PCI P2PE is the first serious attempt to create a really secure single system built from the pinpad device to the POS to the bulletproof (from the merchant's store environment perspective) data center of a payment gateway or processor. In addition, security of P2PE systems is designed to be solely dependent on strong cryptography protected by hardware rather than the odd ephemeral controls and naked, home-brewed, software-based cryptography usually offered by software vendors and backed by PCI DSS and PA-DSS.

Before we start the review of P2PE, it is important to note that there are different types of point-to-point encryption: *hardware*, *software*, and *hybrid* (more details about implementation of each version can be found in the Point-to-Point Encryption section of Chapter 8). Currently available versions of the standard only cover Hardware[21] and Hardware/Hybrid[22] P2PE solutions. Software P2PE requirements are planned for the future, but no specific dates have yet been provided. Only Hardware P2PE has a real capability to provide maximal protection to cardholder data. Any software implementation of cryptography on the store level is vulnerable in one way or another.

The PCI P2PE standard is huge, even compared to the pretty heavy PCI DSS: 6 domains having 491 requirements and total of 648(!) testing procedures. The good news is that not all domains are applicable to all solutions. For example, domains 2 and 4 can be excluded from the scope of assessment for many Hardware P2PE solutions.

The fact that P2PE covers the entire payment processing cycle also dictates the structure of the standard, which consists of six domains:

- **Domain 1: Encryption Device Management** is about security of POI devices. In order to be allowed as part of a P2PE solution, the device must be PCI PTS validated[23], with SRED (secure reading and exchange of data) listed as a "function provided."

- **Domain 2: Application Security** is not applicable to a solution with a payment application that does not touch sensitive data in clear text. It is applicable only if the POI device's firmware takes care of all key management and cryptographic operations and sends only encrypted data to the PA hosted by POS.

- **Domain 3: Encryption Environment** takes care of POI device deployment and environment issues such as secure transportation procedures, maintenance, and key injections.

- **Domain 4: Segmentation between Encryption and Decryption Environments**, according to PCI P2PE, "has no applicable requirements for hardware/hardware solutions since the account data is encrypted for transmission by the PCI-approved POI device before the data leaves the device, and the merchant has no access to the decryption environment or the cryptographic keys."

- **Domain 5: Decryption Environment and Device Management** is about security of the payment processor's data center environment. All key management and decryption operations must be done in HSM certified with FIPS 140-2 and/or PCI PTS. In addition, the entire environment must be PCI DSS compliant.

- **Domain 6: P2PE Cryptographic Key Operations** is all about cryptographic keys: secure generation, rotation, and injection. It takes care of the key management in both encrypting Secure Cryptographic Device (SCD) of the POI and decrypting HSM in the data centers. In addition, it contains a set of requirements to KIF (Key Injection Facilities) which inject the encryption keys into the SCD of POI devices. Such facilities should also be validated by P2PE QSA in order to be included in the P2PE solution.

The list of validated P2PE solutions is supposed to be published on the PCI SSC website[24]. However, at the time of this publication no single P2PE solution has yet been certified by the PCI Council. The list has remained empty for a relatively long time, which is not typical for other PCI standards. There are at least two reasons:

1. First, the designers of the standard took a big corporation—which would control the entire solution from the stores to the processing data centers—as a model for creating the requirements. Unfortunately, it turned out that the reality is different and there are more significant players in this complex game.

2. Second, the level of requirements set by the standard is higher than today's de facto technological and compliance status of hardware/software vendors

and merchants. In order to comply with some requirements, P2PE solution providers may need to purchase new hardware and implement new versions of software which in some cases are not yet certified with the necessary standards by other vendors.

There are obvious benefits of implementing P2PE for merchants: more security for their customers, fewer expenses on lawsuits associated with data breaches, and lower investments into PCI DSS controls. Merchants who implement P2PE are entitled to use the special P2PE Self-Assessment Questionnaire (SAQ P2PE-HW) [25, 26] which allows them to:

Reduce the scope of their PCI DSS assessments and validate to a reduced set of PCI DSS requirements.[27]

PCI Guidelines

PCI DSS and PA-DSS compliance is not required by law. However, if you have developed a POS application and want to sell it, you need to pass the PA-DSS validation in order to get some of the benefits, such as ability to sell your product to any customer. Unlike the standards, guidelines are similar to whitepapers in that they review industry trends and provide recommendations on best practices and new technologies. If you have developed a mobile POS app and want to sell it, no one can require you to follow the PCI mobile guidelines. However, there is a good chance of guidelines becoming the standard in the future.

Currently, PCI SSC offers several guidelines that are directly related to POS and payment application security.

Fallacy of Tokenization

Tokenization was introduced to the payment card industry in an attempt to ease the burden of PCI DSS compliance on merchants by replacing the original credit card account number (PAN) with a substitution called *token*. Token uniquely identifies the PAN and represents it in database queries without, however, compromising the security of the original account numbers. There are various tokenization technologies employing different methods of token generation, from hash function to randomly generated Globally Unique Identifier (GUID) to encryption schemes that imitate the original format of the card account numbers, preserving the original characteristics such as numeric format (using only characters 0-1), length (16 digits), ISO prefix (first 6 digits), and last 4 digits. Tokens can be generated at the POS by the client payment application or in the data center by the payment application server or payment processor. However and wherever the token is created, tokenization has a huge limitation which is impossible to overcome: it cannot protect the sensitive authentication data because the payment processor and acquirer have to have the original data (Track 1 or 2, or PAN and expiration date) in order to authorize the payment. Therefore, even the most secure tokenization solution is unable to provide adequate overall security to the payment system.

When the first tokenization technologies began to emerge several years ago, they attracted a lot of attention because they provided an answer to the main PCI DSS concern—data at rest. In the course of time, however, it turned out that tokenization is one of the PCI fallacies. It definitely provides some relief in particular areas, but it still does not mitigate most of the threats associated with payment applications.

Table 3-8 shows how implementation of tokenization solutions affects different areas of payment application vulnerabilities.

Table 3-8: Tokenization and Payment Application Vulnerabilities

PAYMENT APPLICATION VULNERABILITY AREA	PROTECTION PROVIDED BY TOKENIZATION TO PA AT POS
Memory	-
Temporary storage (S&F, TOR, active transactions)	-
Long-term storage (batch, settlement records)	○
Long-term storage (transaction archives)	●
Log files	○
Local communication	-
Communication between POI device and POS	-
Links to processors	-
Application code and configuration	-

● – provides an adequate, full protection if implemented correctly

○ – provides only limited or selective protection

- – provides no direct protection

PCI DSS Tokenization Guidelines[28] contain helpful recommendations on best practices for token generation as well as secure deployment and maintenance of tokenization solutions. There is a chance that those guidelines may become a standard in the future.

EMV Guidance

In October 2010, the PCI Council issued a guidance document called *PCI DSS Applicability in an EMV Environment*.[29] The 10-page paper explains why the EMV has failed to protect the confidentiality of sensitive payment data, and why merchants should still comply with PCI DSS, regardless of whether or not they process EMV cards:

> *EMV by itself does not protect the confidentiality of, or inappropriate access to sensitive authentication data and/or cardholder data.*[30]

The problem with EMV (from a payment application security viewpoint) is that originally it was not designed to provide total protection of the payment data confidentiality. The goal of EMV creation was credit card fraud protection: the EMV terminal, independently from its payment processor, is able to authenticate the cardholder and ensure the legitimacy of the payment card and transaction. It doesn't really care about security of the information it processes. Once the data is obtained as a result of conversation between the EMV chip on the card and EMV reader at the POS, it is processed, stored, and transmitted in clear text, the same way it is done for regular magnetic stripes.

There is another major issue described in the guidance:

> *Most environments processing EMV transactions today are hybrid environments, handling both EMV and non-EMV transactions.*[31]

This explains everything. Most EMV cards have a magnetic stripe in addition to the EMV chip, and vice versa—most EMV terminals are equipped with an MSR so the merchant could accept both EMV cards and also regular magnetic stripe cards. If an EMV card is processed at a regular MSR (by either an EMV or non-EMV terminal), or a regular card is swiped at an EMV-enabled terminal, such transactions are as vulnerable as any regular magnetic stripe transaction. There are several reasons to process magnetic stripe cards in an EMV-enabled environment:

- First and most obvious, the card does not have a chip (it is a regular, non-EMV card). There are still a lot of cards with magnetic stripes only, and the merchants still want to accept them.

- Technical fallback—if the chip is broken and cannot be read, some terminals will prompt to swipe the card and use its magnetic stripe as a backup source of information in order to keep the customer.

- Manual entry—if both the magnetic stripe and chip cannot be read, the terminal might prompt for manual keying of the embossed PAN (which is equivalent to entering the magnetic stripe in clear text).

▪ The merchant might process telephone orders through the same payment application (the operator will manually enter the PAN, expiration data, and CVV2 given by the customer over the phone).

Mobile Payments Guidelines for Developers

A few years ago when mobile payments began becoming a strong trend, it turned out that PCI standards were completely unfit for this new area of payment processing. Someone might say that the situation now is the opposite—it's mobile payments that do not comply with PCI standards. Such a discussion is a waste of time. Mobile payments are the current and future reality of electronic payments, and standards should be adjusted in order to define necessary technology and provide adequate security.

In 2012, in order to fill this gap, PCI SSC came up with *PCI Mobile Payment Acceptance Security Guidelines for Developers.*[32] The guidelines contain many helpful recommendations, but also have multiple problems:

▪ The guidelines do not define or recommend any particular technology that could be utilized to protect sensitive data, so if you are developer looking for practical technical advice, this is not the right source for you.

▪ Again, as in the case with PCI DSS, the responsibility for data protection is shared between five parties, including, of course, end users (merchants) and even OS developers.

▪ Even if the payment application follows all the recommendations listed in the mobile payment guidelines, it still will not be "PCI compliant":

> *No presumption should be made that meeting the guidelines and recommendations expressed in this document would cause a solution to be compliant with PA-DSS.*[33]

Summary

PA-DSS and PCI DSS, even if implemented in full, provide minimal to no protection against threats in the three (out of four) payment application key vulnerabilities: data in memory, data in transit, application code and configuration. Both PA-DSS and PCI DSS facilitate significant (but not full) protection in one of these four key vulnerability areas—data at rest—if the software vendor implements strong cryptographic mechanisms.

PCI DSS does not provide adequate protection to POS systems and payment applications deployed by small merchants who do not have significant in-house IT and security resources.

Many PA-DSS and PCI DSS requirements were designed for large organizations, data center environments, or web applications, and therefore are ineffective when applied to typical POS systems deployed by brick-and-mortar merchants.

Tokenization does not provide adequate protection for sensitive data because it is focused on the single area of payment application vulnerabilities.

EMV technology was designed to protect against credit card fraud, but it was not intended to provide confidentiality for sensitive cardholder and authentication data.

PCI mobile payment guidelines contain helpful recommendations, but they do not provide information about concrete security technologies that could be used as strong application security controls.

Notes

1. Chronology of Data Breaches: Security Breaches 2005, Present, Privacy Rights Clearinghouse, `https://www.privacyrights.org/data-breach`

2. Payment Application QSAs, PCI SSC, `https://www.pcisecuritystandards.org/approved_companies_providers/payment_application_qsas.php`

3. List of Validated Payment Applications, PCI SSC, `https://www.pcisecuritystandards.org/approved_companies_providers/validated_payment_applications.php?agree=true`

4. *PCI PA-DSS Requirements and Security Assessment Procedures Version 2.0*, PCI SSC (October 2010), `https://www.pcisecuritystandards.org/documents/pa-dss_v2.pdf`

5. James Michael Stewart, Ed Tittel, and Mike Chapple, *CISSP: Certified Information Systems Security Professional, Study Guide, 3rd Edition*, (Hoboken, NJ: Sybex, 2005), pp. 3, 461.

6. *PCI PA-DSS Requirements and Security Assessment Procedures Version 2.0*, PCI SSC (October 2010), `https://www.pcisecuritystandards.org/documents/pa-dss_v2.pdf`

7. *Ibid.*

8. Global Registry of Service Providers, Visa USA, `http://www.visa.com/splisting/`

9. U.S. PCI DSS Compliance Status, Visa (December 2012), `http://usa.visa.com/download/merchants/cisp-pcidss-compliancestats.pdf`

10. Brian Krebs, "Payment Processor Breach May Be Largest Ever," *The Washington Post* (January 2009), `http://voices.washingtonpost.com/securityfix/2009/01/payment_processor_breach_may_b.html`

11. David Goldman, "Your antivirus software probably won't prevent a cyberattack," *CNNMoney* (January 31, 2013), `http://money.cnn.com/2013/01/31/technology/security/antivirus/index.html?iid=EL`

12. Stewart, Tittel, and Chapple, *CISSP: Certified Information Systems Security Professional, Study Guide, 3rd Edition*, (Hoboken, NJ: Sybex, 2005), pp. 3, 461.

13. *PCI DSS Requirements and Security Assessment Procedures Version 2.0*, PCI SSC (October 2010). `https://www.pcisecuritystandards.org/documents/pci_dss_v2.pdf`

14. *Ibid.*

15. *Ibid.*

16. *Ibid.*

17. Merchant levels and compliance validation requirements defined, Visa USA, `http://usa.visa.com/merchants/risk_management/cisp_merchants.html`

18. *Payment Card Industry (PCI) PIN Transaction Security (PTS) Hardware Security Module (HSM) Security Requirements, Version 2.0*, PCI SSC (May 2012), `https://www.pcisecuritystandards.org/documents/PCI_HSM_Security_Requirements_v2.pdf`

19. Approved PIN Transaction Security Devices, PCI SSC, `https://www.pcisecuritystandards.org/approved_companies_providers/approved_pin_transaction_security.php`

20. *Frequently Asked Questions for PCI Point-to-Point Encryption (P2PE)*, PCI Security Standards Council (August 2012), `https://www.pcisecuritystandards.org/documents/P2PE_v1_1_FAQs_Aug2012.pdf`

21. *Payment Card Industry (PCI) Point-to-Point Encryption Solution Requirements and Testing Procedures: Encryption, Decryption, and Key Management within Secure Cryptographic Devices Version 1.1*, PCI SSC (April 2012), `https://www.pcisecuritystandards.org/documents/P2PE_%20v%201-1.pdf`

22. *Payment Card Industry (PCI) Point-to-Point Encryption Solution Requirements and Testing Procedures: Encryption and Key Management within Secure Cryptographic Devices, and Decryption of Account Data in Software (Hardware/*

Hybrid) Version 1.1, PCI SSC (December 2012), `https://www.pcisecuritystandards.org/documents/P2PE_Hybrid_v1.1.pdf`

23. Approved PIN Transaction Security Devices, PCI SSC, `https://www.pcisecuritystandards.org/approved_companies_providers/approved_pin_transaction_security.php`

24. Validated P2PE Solutions, PCI SSC, `https://www.pcisecuritystandards.org/approved_companies_providers/validated_p2pe_solutions.php`

25. *Payment Card Industry (PCI) Data Security Standard Self-Assessment Questionnaire P2PE-HW and Attestation of Compliance, Hardware Payment Terminals in a Validated P2PE Solution only, No Electronic Cardholder Data Storage, Version 2.0*, PCI SSC (June 2012), `https://www.pcisecuritystandards.org/documents/PCI_SAQ_P2PE-HW_v2.docx`

26. *Payment Card Industry (PCI) Data Security Standard Self-Assessment Questionnaire, Instructions and Guidelines, Version 2.1*, PCI SSC, (June 2012), `https://www.pcisecuritystandards.org/documents/pci_dss_SAQ_Instr_Guide_v2.1.pdf`

27. PCI Security Standards Council Releases Point-to-Point Encryption (P2PE) Resources: Program Guide and Self-Assessment Questionnaire now available, PCI SSC Press Release, (June 28, 2012), `https://www.pcisecuritystandards.org/pdfs/120627-P2PE-Program-Guide_SAQ_Update.pdf`

28. Information Supplement: PCI DSS Tokenization Guidelines, PCI SSC, (August 2011), `https://www.pcisecuritystandards.org/documents/Tokenization_Guidelines_Info_Supplement.pdf`

29. *PCI DSS Applicability in an EMV Environment, A Guidance Document, Version 1*, PCI Security Standards Council, October 2010, `https://www.pcisecuritystandards.org/documents/pci_dss_emv.pdf`

30. *Ibid*

31. *Ibid.*

32. *PCI Mobile Payment Acceptance Security Guidelines for Developers, Version: 1.0*, PCI Security Standards Council, (September 2012), `https://www.pcisecuritystandards.org/documents/Mobile_Payment_Security_Guidelines_Developers_v1.pdf`

33. *Ibid.*

Attacks on Point-of-Sale Systems

Yet across the gulf of space, minds that are to our minds as ours are to those of the beasts that perish, intellects vast and cool and unsympathetic, regarded this earth with envious eyes, and slowly and surely drew their plans against us.

—Herbert Wells

In This Part

Turning 40 Digits into Gold

*Man is pre-eminently a creative animal, predestined to strive consciously for an objective and
to engage in engineering . . . But why has he a passionate love for destruction and chaos also?*
—*Fyodor Dostoyevsky*

There is much talk about payment application security, specifically, how to
protect cardholder data from theft. But what exactly is this cardholder data and
why should it be protected at all? What is this particular piece of information
that is stolen when they talk about card data breach? And if it is stolen already,
is it really so easy to use it in order to make money? Shouldn't we first know
the answers to such questions before we even start talking about security? This
chapter will try to address these concerns.

Magic Plastic

"In a commercial sense credit is the promise to pay at a future time for valuable consideration in the present."[1] Combined with technology (I could not call
something that is already more than half a century old "modern technology"),
it produced a magnetic credit card which was the first and, up until now, very
successful implementation of a magnetic payment card.

Most of us are familiar with credit, debit (PIN), and gift cards, which represent
the biggest group of the payment cards. The basic difference between those cards
is that a credit card manipulates with money that we owe to the card issuer, a
debit card with our own money, and a gift card with money that we already
spent. From a security point of view, it looks like a debit card is the most secure
of these three types because it requires a PIN number as a second authentication factor in order to process payment.[2] However, this is not exactly true since
a PIN is not always required, so most debit cards are "dual purpose"—they

can be processed with or without PIN. Therefore, from a thief's point of view, such dual purpose cards are still useful even if no PIN number was obtained.

Physical Structure and Security Features

Before we dive into the digital jungle, let's review something that seems obvious at first glance—the physical structure of payment cards. Although this book mostly focuses on software security, we cannot forget about the real world because physical controls are an integral part of the information security discipline, and security of electronic payments is no exception. In fact, in most cases stolen credit card data is useless without creating a good looking replica of the plastic card.

There are several hallmarks that are supposed to distinguish a genuine payment card from counterfeited plastic (although it does not mean these features cannot be faked). [3, 4, 5, 6, 7]

- *Payment brand logo, background color,* and *image* distinguish the various card brands and types, and this is exactly why they cannot be relied on as strong security controls. The artwork can be easily replicated or even created from scratch (because there are no visual design standards!) using a PVC printer. There are too many issuing banks each having dozens of different card flavors. Since there is no standardization, it is virtually impossible to tell whether the artwork is authentic by just looking at the card.

- *Embossed Primary Account Number (PAN), expiration date,* and *cardholder name* (shown in Figure 4-1) are passed down from the era of manual credit card processing. In the old days, embossed information was the only way to process transactions by pressing the plastic card in an imprinter—a mechanical device that copies the embossed data from the plastic to the transaction slip made from carbon paper. Many merchants still keep them to support business continuity in events like power outages or POS software failures. Nowadays, embossed data mostly remains as an extra security feature, even though it is not a very strong security feature—an embosser can be bought online for less than $300.

- *Card Verification Value (CVV2)* is a 3- to 4-digit code printed on the front or back of the card (circled in Figure 4-2). It is rarely validated during card-presenting transactions and is mostly intended for card-not-present (online) payments (see more details in the "Card Verification Values" section of this chapter).

- *Ultraviolet (UV) marks,* which are drawn on the front of the plastic (Figure 4-3), glow when highlighted by special UV flashlight (Figure 4-4) which can be bought for less than $10.[8, 9] Cashiers can validate them just the same simple way TSA security officers check our driver's license in the airport. However, almost no one does it because such a procedure would damage the buying experience and dramatically increase transaction processing time. Also, UV marks can be relatively easily replicated by a regular inkjet printer with UV ink.[10]

Figure 4-1: Front of the plastic payment card

Figure 4-2: Back of the plastic payment card

Figure 4-3: Credit card under regular visible light

Figure 4-4: Credit card under black light showing the UV marks

▪ *Customer service phone numbers* enable one to speak with the issuer bank's customer service representative who may confirm the validity of the card, ensure it was not stolen, and has enough credit for the transaction. However, it is used only when a transaction is declined by an automatic authorization system or when a payment amount is extremely high.

▪ *Metallic tipping (optional)* is a gold or silver coating applied to the embossed numbers and letters in order to contrast them so they can be easily distinguished from the card front's background colors. This good-looking feature can be replicated with a hot foil stamping machine for less than $250.

▪ *Cardholder Signature (optional)* on the back of the card (Figure 4-2) is supposed to be compared with the cardholder's signature on the transaction receipt payment slip. In reality, have you ever signed the back of your credit card?

▪ *Cardholder photo (optional)*, which is added on the front or back of the card by some issuers, can transform the card into a photo ID. Any picture, including a photo, can be painted on a counterfeited card as part of a background image by a PVC printer.

▪ *Hologram (optional)* with the logo of the payment brand or the card issuer can be found on the front or back of the card. There is no consistency in presence, location, or content of the holograms, so cashiers are not certain what to look for or where it should be located.

▪ *Holographic magnetic stripe (optional)* is a relatively new feature which probably is not the simplest one to counterfeit, but what if it's just not there? Who knows whether it is supposed to be on the card or not?

Why Security Features Fail

There are several concerns associated with physical security controls of the payment cards:

- **Protection mechanisms are not consistent.** There are a few de facto standard features (such as embossed account number, expiration date, and cardholder name) but still there is no formal standard. For example, the card validation code has many different names (CSC, CVV, CAV, CVC, CID, CAV2, CVC2, or CVV2), different lengths (3 or 4 digits), and different locations (magnetic tracks, front or back of the card), which is confusing to inexperienced cashiers. (The "Card Verification Values" section of this chapter explains these codes in detail.)

- **Many security features are not mandatory.** For example, it was a great idea to print the cardholder's photo on the credit card. In fact, such a relatively simple feature would turn a credit card into a photo ID and could prevent regular fraud (when the cardholder's wallet is stolen). Holographic magnetic stripe is another example of a pretty strong physical protection feature that is not easy to replicate (at least, it would seriously raise the cost of counterfeit card production). However, since those features are optional and not required by any standard or law, they are not widely used and cannot be relied on.

- **Payment cards do not have physical security controls that can be validated automatically by magnetic stripe readers.** All physical protection mechanisms are designed to be recognized and validated by humans (cashiers, attendants, waiters). Therefore, unattended payment terminals such as an ATM, gas pump, or automated kiosk are the easiest fraud targets because there is no one present who could determine the authenticity of the plastic.

- **Most physical controls can be easily counterfeited.** Unlike high tech features such as EMV chips, regular physical controls can be easily replicated at home. (The "Producing Counterfeit Card" section in this chapter contains more details about required equipment.)

- **Validation of physical protection features is not mandatory and often omitted by store attendants.** Even though credit cards have some relatively strong physical security controls such as holographic magnetic stripes, cashiers rarely validate them. Many merchants, especially large chains with high turnover, do not incorporate the validation of physical controls in their transaction processing flow. Such rules would make the process of payment less attractive, but even more importantly it would seriously affect their transaction processing time, which defines how many customers each cashier can serve during the shift. The longer an average transaction time, the more cashiers merchants need to hire. Therefore, many protection mechanisms, especially physical security controls requiring human intervention, are not cost-effective. The risk of an occasional unpaid transaction is much less dangerous than periodic payment of wages for extra cashiers.

Thus, all existing non-automated protection methods of payment cards require manual validation and therefore are largely ineffective, which opens the door to one of the largest fraud monetization strategies—in-store purchases. This is discussed in more detail later in this chapter.

Inside the Magnetic Stripe

Information about the cardholder is stored on the magnetic stripe located on the back of the plastic payment card. There are 2 tracks (called Track 1 and Track 2) which are used for processing electronic payments. There is also a third track, Track 3, which is not involved in POS transactions. The data format of the magnetic tracks is defined by the ISO 7813 standard[11] and it is the same for all types of credit, debit, gift, fleet, EBT, and other payment cards. When a magnetic card is swiped at the register, the MSR device reads the tracks from the magnetic stripe and sends them to the payment processing system which parses them to several sub-elements: PAN, Expiration Date, Service Code, and additional discretional data (which is normally required only in special cases such as fleet cards processing).

"Magstripe is quite efficient but not terribly smart technology"[12], especially from a security viewpoint. Magnetic stripe can be copied (or re-created from its elements by assembling them together) and written into a blank plastic card using the Magnetic Stripe Encoder. Such devices are relatively cheap and available for purchase by anyone. Track 1 and Track 2 are the two most important elements since they are sufficient for processing most payments. Either Track 1 or Track 2 can be used to manufacture a fully functional physical payment card for brick-and-mortar store transactions or ATM cash withdrawals. The PAN (which is located on both tracks) allows online purchases.

Track 1

Track 1 contains full information about the cardholder including first and last name. The maximum length of Track 1 is 79 bytes. The first bytes are the PAN, then the cardholder name which is separated by a "^" character from the PAN on the left and Expiration Date on the right. Here is a Track 1 example, which is followed by Table 4-1 that lists the components used in the example:

%B4005554444444403^GOMZIN/SLAVA^15121010000000012300?

Table 4-1: Components of Track 1 Example

FIELD	DATA
PAN	4005554444444403
Expiration Date	1512 (December 2015)
Cardholder's first name	SLAVA
Cardholder's last name	GOMZIN
Service Code	101
CVV	123

Neither Track 1 nor 2 are protected, so the data is stored in clear text. In other words, it is possible to create a full copy of a payment card if you can obtain just 79 bytes of Track 1 (or only 40 bytes of Track 2!). Such a duplicated card can then be swiped the same way as the original at any payment terminal. Track 1 is the only track that contains alphanumeric characters—the cardholder name is not required for payment processing. Table 4-2 lists the detailed structure of Track 1.

Table 4-2: Detailed Track 1 Structure

ELEMENT	LENGTH (BYTES)	DATA TYPE AND FORMAT	DESCRIPTION
%	1	Always '%' character	Start Sentinel
B	1	Always 'B' character	Format Code
PAN	Max. 19	Digits 0–9	See PAN section for detailed structure.
^	1	Always '^' character	Separator between the PAN and Cardholder Name
Name	2 – 26	Characters	Last Name
			"/" Separator
			First Name

Continues

Table 4-2 *(continued)*

ELEMENT	LENGTH (BYTES)	DATA TYPE AND FORMAT	DESCRIPTION
^	1	Always '^' character	Separator between Cardholder Name and Expiration Date
Expiration Date	4	Digits	Usually YYMM
Service Code	3	Digits	Contains 3 sub-fields. See Service Code section for detailed structure.
Discretionary Data	Variable (but limited by total length of the Track which should not exceed 79)	Characters	Optional information depending on card type. For example, special prompt codes on fleet cards instruct the payment application to request entering driver's license number or odometer reading.
?	1	Always '?' character	End Sentinel
LRC	1	Digit	Longitudinal redundancy check defined in ISO 7811-2.[13] Normally, validated by the MSR to check the integrity of the data reading. Do not confuse with *PAN Check Digit* which is usually validated by the payment application.

Track 2

Track 2 contains minimal information required for payment processing: the PAN, Expiration Date, Service Code, and additional information which may vary depending on the card issuer and card type. Track 2 was introduced as a shorter version of Track 1 in order to improve performance of old dial up payment terminals which were using ground phone lines for communication with the authorizers.

Track 2 is still sufficient for payment processing with most payment acquirers, so Track 1 is optional in most applications.[14] The standard length of Track 2 is 40 ASCII characters (each ASCII character has a length of 1 byte). First digits (usually 16 but vary from 15 to maximum 19) are reserved for the PAN. The '=' character separates the PAN from the 4 bytes of Expiration Date followed by additional discretional data. Here is a Track 2 example, which is followed by Table 4-3 that lists the components used in the example:

;4005554444444403=15121010000000012300?

Table 4-3: Components of Track 2 Example

FIELD	DATA
PAN	4005554444444403
Expiration Date	1512 (December 2015)
Service Code	101
CVV	123

Table 4-4 lists the detailed structure of Track 2.

Table 4-4: Detailed Track 2 Structure

ELEMENT	LENGTH (BYTES)	DATA TYPE AND FORMAT	DESCRIPTION
;	1	Always ';' character	Start Sentinel
PAN	Max. 19	Digits 0–9	The same as on Track 1
=	1	Always '=' character	Separator between PAN and Expiration Date
Expiration Date	4	Digits	The same as on Track 1
Service Code	3	Digits	The same as on Track 1
Discretionary Data	Variable (but limited by total length of the Track which should not exceed 40)	Digits	See Discretionary Data on Track 1.
?	1	Always '?' character	End Sentinel
LRC	1	Digit	See LRC on Track 1.

PAN

The Primary Account Number (PAN) usually has 16 digits, with some exceptions such as American Express which uses only 15 digits. The maximum length of a PAN is 19 digits, and there are some card types having 19-digit account numbers, such as fleet cards.

PAN is embossed on the front of most payment cards which allows manual entry at the POS when the MSR fails to read the magnetic stripe for any reason (usually caused by physical damage to the card). An embossed PAN can be used for manual transaction processing when the electronic system is down. This is also the easiest and oldest way to steal money from the cardholder without any computer hacking: just write down the PAN digits and use them for phone or online purchase.

Table 4-5 shows the PAN location on magnetic tracks.

Table 4-5: PAN Location on Magnetic Tracks

TRACK	DATA
1	%B**4005554444444403**^GOMZIN/SLAVA^1512101000000012300
2	;**4005554444444403**=1512101000000012300?

Both Track 1 and Track 2 contain the same PAN, which is also constructed from several elements: ISO Prefix, account number, and check digit. Although having dumps with full Track 1 or 2 is ideal for counterfeiting the payment card, knowing only the PAN in some cases, such as card-not-present online purchases, would be sufficient for performing the fraudulent transaction.

The PAN might be sufficient for online purchases when the payment card is not swiped but is entered manually. During the online purchase, the payment application may prompt for many elements such as PAN, expiration date, cardholder's first and last name, cardholder's street address and ZIP code, phone number, or others. In fact, if CVV2 is not requested, only the PAN is validated in order to get the approval (more on that in following sections).

Expiration Date

Expiration date is encoded as four digits: two digits each for month and year. Both Track 1 and 2 contain expiration date which follows the = PAN separator on Track 2 and the second cardholder name separator "^" on Track 1 (Table 4-6). The order of month and year is defined by the ISO standard: first are the last two digits of the year and then the two digits representing the month (YYMM). For example, the card expiring on December 2015 will have the expiration date encoded as 1512.

Table 4-6: Expiration Date Location on Magnetic Tracks

TRACK	DATA
1	%B4005554444444403^GOMZIN/SLAVA^**1512**101000000012300
2	;4005554444444403=**1512**101000000012300?

The expiration date is also embossed on the front of the card. Note that the location of the month and year numbers in the embossed expiration date is opposite to the format of the date encoded in tracks, and there is a / or - separator between the month and year digits like these: MM/YY or MM-YY.

Payment applications and most payment processors and acquirers do not check the expiration date (or many or sometimes even all other elements besides the PAN). The expiration date validation procedure just ensures that the date is not past due. There is no verification of the authenticity of the expiration date, meaning that the expiration date sent for validation is not compared with the original expiration date in the card issuer's database. Therefore, virtually any randomly generated expiration date that is later than the current date would pass the validation (note that some limitations for maximum year numbers can be in place, for example, "7012" will likely be rejected by a payment application because it would interpret the card as expired in December 1970).

In addition, expiration dates—while in transit or at rest—are usually not encrypted by payment applications (PCI standards do not require it), and can be easily obtained from the memory, communication, databases, or log files.

ISO Prefix and BIN Ranges

The first 6 digits of the PAN (Table 4-7) are called the ISO Prefix, also known as *BIN* or *IIN Prefix* which is the official name.

Table 4-7: ISO Prefix Location on Magnetic Tracks

TRACK	DATA
1	%B**400555**4444444403^GOMZIN/SLAVA^1512101000000012300?
2	;**400555**4444444403=1512101000000012300?

Technically, ISO Prefix is not part of the account number because it contains generic information about the card issuer, so the real account number, which identifies the cardholder, contains only 9 digits. A 16-digit PAN would look like this:

16 (PAN) – 6 (ISO Prefix) – 1 (Check Digit – *see below*) = 9.

There are several reasons why PCI standards allow disclosure of the first six PAN digits:

- ISO Prefix is not a secret number because it does not identify the card-holder and many cardholders have the same ISO Prefix on their cards.

- ISO Prefix can be generated artificially because it contains data which is publicly known.

- Most client payment systems must know the ISO prefix of the card in order to route the transaction to the appropriate processor. Therefore, even when the sensitive card data is encrypted using P2PE encryption (see P2PE section for details), the system should still be able to see the ISO Prefix in order to process the transaction.

The fact that the first 6 and last 4 digits are almost always exposed in clear text, and "check digit" is a function that can be calculated based on PAN value, is very important for breaking the hash function of the PAN because only six digits should be brute forced.

CROSS-REFERENCE   See Chapter 6 for more details about hash function vulnerabilities.

The first digit of the ISO prefix (and PAN) is called MII (Major Industry Identifier) and, as the name implies, it identifies the industry. In practice, major payment brands have allocated MII numbers from 1 through 6 and they can be identified by the first 1 to 4 digits of the ISO Prefix (Table 4-8).

Table 4-8: BIN Ranges

MII (1ST DIGIT)	BIN RANGE	PAYMENT BRAND
1	1800xx	JCB
2	2131xx	JCB
3	34xxxx, 37xxxx	American Express
	300xxx – 305xxx, 36xxxx, 38xxxx	Diners Club
	35xxxx	JCB
4	4xxxxx	Visa

MII (1ST DIGIT)	BIN RANGE	PAYMENT BRAND
5	51xxxx – 55xxxx	MasterCard
6	6011xx, 65xxxx	Discover

This table describes only the high level division. Detailed BIN ranges can be obtained through payment brands[15], banks[16], or other online sources[17].

PAN Check Digit

The last digit of any PAN (with very rare exceptions) is called a check digit which allows distinguishing between real card account numbers and random sequences of digits when looking for PANs in memory or in files. The check digit is not really part of the account number. For example, if the PAN length is 16 digits, the account number consists of the first 15 digits, and the 16th digit is the check digit (Table 4-9). The check digit is determined by a special Mod 10 (Modulus 10) calculation (implementation is shown in the code sample below), also known as the Luhn formula invented by Hans Peter Luhn who was one of the first information scientists in America.[18] The official Mod 10 algorithm for payment cards is defined in Annex B of ISO 7812-1.[19]

Table 4-9: PAN Check Digit Location on Magnetic Tracks

TRACK	DATA
1	%B400555444444**3**^GOMZIN/SLAVA^1512101000000012300?
2	;400555444444**3**=1512101000000012300?

Check digit validation is less important in a search for full Track 1 or 2 because they can be very well distinguished by the combination of data separators (= in Track 2 or a pair of ^ in Track 1) with PAN and Expiration Date patterns. (The "Regular Expressions" section of this chapter contains more details about using check digits.)

Code Sample: Mod 10 - PAN Check Digit Verification

```
public bool LuhnTest(string cardNumber)
{
    // Clean the card number - remove dashes and spaces
    cardNumber = cardNumber.Replace("-", "").Replace(" ", "");

    // Convert card number into digits array
    int[] digits = new int[cardNumber.Length];
    for (int len = 0; len < cardNumber.Length; len++)
```

```
    {
        digits[len] = Int32.Parse(cardNumber.Substring(len, 1));
    }
    int sum = 0;
    bool alt = false;
    for (int i = digits.Length - 1; i >= 0; i--)
    {
        int curDigit = digits[i];
        if (alt)
        {
            curDigit *= 2;
            if (curDigit > 9)
            {
                curDigit -= 9;
            }
        }
        sum += curDigit;
        alt = !alt;
    }
    // If Mod 10 equals 0, the number is good and this will return true:
    return sum % 10 == 0;
}
```

Service Code

The three bytes of Service Code (Table 4-10) consist of 31-byte subfields. The values of those fields are important because they tell the payment application and payment processor how to handle the card during payment acceptance.

Table 4-10: Service Code Location on Magnetic Tracks

TRACK	DATA
1	%B4005554444444403^GOMZIN/SLAVA^1512**101**000000012300?
2	;4005554444444403=1512**101**000000012300?

The most common service codes are 101 and 201. The seemingly small one-digit difference is, in fact, very significant for cardholders. The first digit determines whether the card has the EMV chip or not. Thus, the 101 cards are simple magnetic stripe cards which can be accepted virtually anywhere in the United States (thanks to ignoring the European EMV revolution), while 201 cards contain the chip which puts some limitations on the card (the swipe might not be accepted by an EMV-enabled POI device).

Table 4-11 shows additional important instructions to payment applications and processors that are defined by the service codes. Those instructions can include acceptance region (international or domestic), prompt for PIN requirement, and product restrictions (goods and services only, ATM only, or no restrictions).

Table 4-11: Service Code Instructions

INSTRUCTION		SERVICE CODE		
		1ST DIGIT	2ND DIGIT	3RD DIGIT
Technology	The card has a chip	2 or 6		
Acceptance	International	1 or 2		
	Domestic	5 or 6		
Authorization	Normal		0	
	By Issuer		2	
Restrictions	No restrictions	0, 1, or 6		
	Goods and services only			2, 5, or 7
	ATM only			3
PIN requirements	PIN required			0, 3, or 5

Note that most of these service code instructions are usually ignored by local point-of-sale systems and analyzed only by processor or acquirer host.

Card Verification Values

Now it's time to understand what all those three-letter abbreviations using the letters C and V mean. Card Verification Value (CVV) was invented by payment brands in order to fight the massive credit card fraud. There are two types of CVV, which are often confused, and the fact that each payment brand has its own naming convention for virtually the same code adds to the confusion and demonstrates another example of the lack of standardization in the industry.[20]

The first group of codes, which are listed in Table 4-12—let's call them CVV, although each credit company uses different combinations of three letters—is embedded into the discretional data of the magnetic Tracks 1 and 2.

Table 4-12: Card Verification Values Encoded on Magnetic Stripes

PAYMENT BRAND	CODE	NAME	LOCATION	LENGTH
American Express	CSC	Card Security Code	Track 1,2	3
Discover	CVV	Card Verification Value	Track 1,2	3
JCB	CAV	Card Authentication Value	Track 1,2	3
MasterCard	CVC	Card Validation Code	Track 1,2	3
Visa	CVV	Card Verification Value	Track 1,2	3

The second group of codes is usually called CVV2 but, as in the case with CVV, each payment brand has its own names (Table 4-13). Those numbers are printed on the front or back of the plastic payment cards.

Table 4-13: Card Verification Values Printed on Plastic

PAYMENT BRAND	CODE	NAME	LOCATION	LENGTH
American Express	CID	Card Identification Number	Card front	4
Discover	CID	Card Identification Number	Card back	3
JCB	CAV2	Card Authentication Value 2	Card back	3
MasterCard	CVC2	Card Validation Code 2	Card back	3
Visa	CVV2	Card Verification Value 2	Card back	3

CVV Encoded on Magnetic Tracks

CVV (also known as CSC, CAV, and CVC depending on payment brand), which is encoded in a discretional area of magnetic Tracks 1 and 2 as shown in Table 4-14, was introduced before CVV2. It is derived from the track data elements using a special cryptographic function.

Table 4-14: CVV Location on Magnetic Tracks

TRACK	DATA
1	%B4005554444444403^GOMZIN/SLAVA^15121010000000**123**00?
2	;4005554444444403=15121010000000**123**00?

CVV is verified by the acquirer's host during the authorization phase when the POS sends full Track 1 or 2 data, or both. The idea behind this validation is simple—before PCI security standards were introduced and even after, when merchants just started encrypting the data storage, it was easy to steal the PAN numbers because they are usually stored for long periods of time for settlement processing and customer services enquiries. During the early days of credit card fraud, the thieves' job was much easier—they did not have to steal the entire tracks in order to create fake plastic cards. Back then, PAN and expiration date (which is not validated by many authorizers and can be randomly generated to match simple validation criteria) contained enough information for crafting the full Track 2, as follows:

Start sentinels: always ";"

+

PAN: "1234567890123456"

+

Separator: always "="

+

Expiration date: "1512" (just put any year and month in the future)

+

End sentinels: always "?"

=

Track 2: ;1234567890123456=1512?

Nowadays, thanks to the CVV validation feature, the tracks cannot be so easily reconstructed. The thieves need to either obtain the entire track (which is somewhat more difficult but not impossible) or guess the value of CVV which is problematic with 1,000 possible values.

The Track 1 or 2 reconstructed from only PAN can still be used to make counterfeit cards for use in offline transactions because no payment application has the capability of validating CVV offline.

CROSS-REFERENCE   See Chapter 5, "Penetrating Security Free Zones," for more details about forcing offline authorization attack.

CVV2 Printed on Plastic

CVV2 (also known as CAD, CAV2, and CVC2 depending on payment brand) validation is optional and can be provided as an additional service for the merchants.[21] This code is rarely validated in brick-and-mortar stores since the card is physically present and can be validated by an attendant. CVV2 is mostly important for card-not-present transactions (online and phone payments) as it helps to verify that the actual physical card (not just its account number) is in hands of the customer. This is made possible by the fact that CVV2 is not present on the magnetic stripe but only printed on the front or back of the plastic card, as shown in Figure 4-2.

If the card data (Tracks 1 and 2) is stolen from the in-store payment system that is processing the card-present transactions, it normally does not contain CVV2 and, therefore, it can't be used for online shopping (although there are still alternative monetization methods explained later). On the contrary, if the card data (PAN) is stolen from the online payment system, the "dump" may contain CVV2 but it will not contain full magnetic tracks (and CVV1).

Regular Expressions

A special programming technique called *regular expressions* (or *regex*) is employed by malware to find Track 1, Track 2, and PAN components in computer memory or disk files. Regular expressions are a notation for specifying patterns of text as opposed to exact strings of characters.[22] Credit and debit card numbers have known format patterns which are easily translated to instructions written in special regular expression syntax. Those instructions can be interpreted by software in order to filter out the actual tracks and account numbers from huge streams of data loaded from memory or disk files. For example, all MasterCard accounts start with the numbers 51 through 55, and the remaining 14 digits contain any number from 0 through 9, for example, 51000000000000. So the regular expression for a MasterCard PAN would be ^5[1-5][0-9]{14}$.

If you just use simple patterns, however, the search results will also return many false positives—random numbers which look like PAN but in fact contain garbage. The example above with fourteen zeros is not a real MasterCard account number but it fits the right pattern. In order to filter out false positives, various methods of validation are utilized by scanning software. One of them is Mod 10 validation. The last digit of a credit card account number is always checksum which can be compared with the Mod 10 calculated for the remaining numbers (See the "PAN Check Digit" section earlier in this chapter for sample Mod 10 code.) Regular expressions for the PANs of major payment brands are shown in Table 4-15.

Table 4-15: Regular Expressions for the PAN of Major Payment Card Brands

PAYMENT BRAND	REGULAR EXPRESSION
Visa	^4[09]{12}(?:[0-9]{3})?$

PAYMENT BRAND	REGULAR EXPRESSION
MasterCard	^5[1-5][0-9]{14}5
American Express	^3[47][0-9]{13}$
Diners Club	^3(?:0[0-5]|[68][0-9])[0-9]{11}$
Discover	^6(?:01115(0-9)(2))(0-9){12}$
JCB	^(?:2131|1800|35\d{3})\d{11}$

The following C# code samples contain additional false positive filters. They include patterns for all major credit card brands.

Regex searching for PAN only (all card brands):

```
string pan_regex = @"(?<![\d])(?:4[0-9]{12}|4[0-9]{3}\s?[0-9]{4}\s?[0-9]
{4}\s?[0-9]{4}|5[1-5][0-9]{14}|6(?:011|5[0-9][0-9])[0-9]{12}|3[47]
[0-9]{13}|3(?:0[0-5]|[68][0-9])[0-9]{11}|(?:2131|1800|35\d{3})\d{11})
(?![\d])";
```

Search for Tracks 1 and 2 (starts from PAN regex which is followed by additional regex for Track 1 and 2 patterns):

```
string track_pan_regex = @"(?:4[0-9]{12}|4[0-9]{15}|5[1-5][0-9]
{14}|6(?:011|5[0-9][0-9])[0-9]{12}|3[47][0-9]{13}|3(?:0[0-5]|[68][0-9])
[0-9]{11}|(?:2131|1800|35\d{3})\d{11})";
string track_main_regex = @"(?:(?:\=[0-2][0-9][0-1][0-2]|\^.+\^[0-2]
[0-9][0-1][0-2]))";
string full_track_regex = track_pan_regex + track_main_regex;
```

Chapters 5 and 6 contain practical examples of regular expression applications.

Getting the Dumps: Hackers

I am not a hacker. I never wanted to be one. There are so many interesting things I could do without breaking the law and making trouble for innocent people. However, it does not mean I could not become a hacker. In fact, anyone can. If you think about hackers as super gurus with above average IQs and abnormal skills, you are wrong—there are very few like that. Usually, they are ordinary people who simply want to do something unauthorized which would position them above the crowd. And this is good news for us, because it means that we do not have to be super smart in order to defend against them. What we do have to do though, in order to protect ourselves, is understand our vulnerabilities and learn how to mitigate them in the most efficient way.

As for many other cyber targets, there are three major motivations for a hacker to break into a payment system: fun, politics and terrorism, or money. This book is focused on the third reason which is the most dangerous for electronic payments. However, all three still should be taken into account when performing risk assessment and threat modeling.

Security Breach

The activities listed in Table 4-16 can be described by a single word: security breach. The term *Security Breach* (or *Data Breach*) is widely used in the payment industry and security community to name the sequence of events related to the leak and fraudulent use of sensitive cardholder data. There are references to this term found in official documents, such as PCI DSS and PA-DSS security standards.[23, 24] It is not so simple to find detailed information about card data breaches. Companies do not rush to disclose their security breaches, even though in most states they are required to do so by state laws.[25, 26, 27] Even if a data breach is disclosed, they try to minimize the amount of facts that are being published and distract public attention from the event. When a security breach happened in 2008 at one of the nation's biggest payment processors, the public announcement was made on the day of President Obama's Inauguration.[28]

Table 4-16: Phases of Typical Card Data Breach

PHASE	ACTION	DURATION
1. Gathering Information	Learning about retail store environment controls (for example, vulnerability scanning). Learning about target payment application technology and vulnerabilities.	Days to Weeks
2. Preparing Malware	Based on information about payment application, customizing existing malware, or creating a new one.	Days to Weeks
3. Penetrating Store Environment	Breaking physical or/and logical controls of the store. Installing malware.	Hours to Days
4. Retrieving Sensitive Data	Collecting sensitive data from memory, disk storage or communication, and uploading it to the attacker's computer.	Hours to Years
5. Carding	Hackers selling "dumps" to monetization gangs.	Hours to Weeks

PHASE	ACTION	DURATION
6. Monetization	For credit cards:	Hours to Years
	Making online purchases or shopping in retail stores.	
	Selling purchased goods and getting cash.	
	For PIN (Debit) cards:	
	Withdrawing cash from ATM.	
7. Disclosure	Internal discovery (abnormal system behavior) of public disclosure (customers reporting about fraudulent transactions).	Days to Months
	Investigation and mitigation.	

Privacy Rights Clearinghouse maintains a history of every reported security breach since 2005 including data breaches of payment systems.[29]

The most sophisticated types of security breaches do not happen often. In fact, some of them have not happened yet. Why would hackers want to spend more time and resources on a difficult attack scenario if a simpler vulnerability can be exploited and bring the same result? However, as time goes on and more security measures are being implemented to protect against simple intrusions, new attacks do become more sophisticated. Security is a perpetual competition.

There are several steps that would need to be performed in order to make money from stolen credit card data (refer to Table 4-16). First of all, the sensitive records need to be obtained by breaking into the store payment system and exploiting one of the vulnerabilities described in next two chapters. So the very first step is penetrating the store environment, which can be done either remotely from the Internet, or from inside by breaking the physical security of the store or using the help of insiders or social engineering.[30] Once physical and/or logical (network) protection layers are broken, the next step is installing *malware*—specially crafted software that breaks the payment application controls, retrieves and records sensitive data, and finally, uploads it to the "command center" of the attacker.

Largest Point-of-sale Breach

The data breach at The TJX Companies, Inc. (TJX), which is the parent company of T.J. Maxx and Marshalls, was the largest example in the history of merchants' payment card data theft.[31] The initial attacks were performed using a method of *wardriving*—hacking into the stores' networks through the wireless communication that was poorly protected by Wired Equivalent Privacy (WEP) encryption, which can be broken in minutes. Millions of records containing sensitive authentication data were stored by POS systems on the company servers and included full magnetic tracks, CVV2, and even debit PIN numbers.[32] According to one report, in addition to TJX stores, the breach also affected "OfficeMax, Barnes & Noble, Target, Sports Authority, and Boston Market, and probably many other companies that never detected a breach or notified the authorities."[33]

The main figure who organized the TJX and other similar "operations"—Albert Gonzales—was sent to jail for 20 years.

Converting the Bits into Cash: Carders

Once the sensitive data is retrieved, transmitted, and stored outside the targeted store environment, the batches of stolen records, which are called *dumps*, are usually sold online through special forums to other people.[34, 35] This market is called *carding*, and people making deals with stolen records of card data are called, accordingly, *carders*. Misha Glenny, the author of *Dark Market*: *Cyberthieves, Cybercops and You* (Knopf, 2011), defines carding as "the practice of buying or selling stolen or hacked credit-card details" and calls it "the daily bread of cyber-crime."[36] Usually, hackers who steal card data do not deal with monetization issues directly. They make money by selling dumps to individuals or groups who specialize in converting the bits into money. After those "operations" guys buy the dumps from hackers on a carding website, they manufacture fake plastics and finally switch from virtual reality to the real world in order to perform the last step which depends on the type of their dump.

With regular credit cards they make online purchases (which do not even require creating the plastics), or shop at retail stores for fancy goods, and then sell these items online to get cash. With debit cards, if they also have the PIN codes, they withdraw money directly from the ATM. Debit card dumps eliminate the risk of making purchases with fake cards, as well as remove any trouble and expense associated with obtaining the cash by selling the goods. In addition, requirements to the exterior look of the fake credit cards are much higher because they must pass visual inspection by a cashier at the time of purchase. A bogus debit card can be as simple as a piece of white plastic with a magnetic stripe on it in order to be accepted by an unattended ATM terminal. According to *BankInfoSecurity*, in January 2013 "Visa issued an advisory to U.S. payment card issuers" warning about a "recent case involving a limited number of stolen payment cards used to conduct thousands of withdrawals at ATMs in numerous countries over the course of a single weekend."[37]

Even though CVV2 validation has become very common these days, there are still some websites that do not prompt for card verification codes. For example, many non-profit organizations collecting donations on their websites still employ payment applications that do not require CVV2. And even if CVV2 is required, such websites can still be used by carders for testing the validity of their dumps.[38, 39] Here is how it works: First, they find a non-profit organization's website which does not require any further interaction such as shipment details (there is no purchase—it is donation!). Then, they try to donate a very small amount ($1 or even less). If the transaction goes through, the PAN is valid and the dump most definitely can be used to create the fake card and go shopping.

NOTE Unfortunately, many interesting details in every step of this process remain beyond the scope of this book which is focused mostly on the technical side of this phenomenon. More information about the carding world can be found in references 40, 41, and 42 listed at the end of this chapter.

Monetization Strategies: Cashers

After the credit or debit dumps are obtained using one of the methods described previously, it's time to make some money. This is where *cashers* enter the game.

There are two major kinds of monetization strategies which require different technical and psychological skills, as well as different types of card data dumps. Thus, cashers typically stick with one of the two strategies: *online* or *real-world action*.

The online monetization strategy includes any cashing activities that can be performed via the Internet, such as *online shopping* and *games*, and can be completed almost entirely through the computer without even leaving home. In addition to the fact that they don't have to leave their couch, online monetization has another undisputable benefit: it is dependent solely on technology and does not require having any special psychological, social engineering, or communication skills. The dump for online cashing often contains the PAN, expiration date, and CVV2 required for online payment processing.

In contrast, the real-world action monetization strategy requires interaction with the material world—shopping at brick-and-mortar stores or cash withdrawal at ATMs. In some cases additional investments in manufacturing equipment are necessary for creating good-looking fake credit cards. The dump for in-store cashing includes Track 1 or Track 2 or both (having only one readable track is sufficient for payment authorization by most systems).

Producing Counterfeit Cards

As previously described, at least two monetization strategies require having a physical card in-hand: in-store purchase and ATM withdrawal. The process of credit or debit card counterfeiting is much easier than it may seem at first. There are 4 to 5 steps in the process, depending on the desired quality of the resulting product, and only the encoding step is necessary in *all* cases. Each step requires special equipment which may cost from a couple of hundred dollars to a few thousand dollars, depending on the desired quality and final look of the product. Each step is defined as follows:

1. *Encoding* is writing the dump into the magnetic stripe of the blank card template with a special device called a *magnetic stripe encoder*.

2. *Printing* is necessary in order to apply background colors, the payment brand logo, and any other images (such as the cardholder photo) to the card. A special thermal PVC or inkjet printer (Figures 4-5 and 4-6) can produce very decent images that sometimes cannot be easily distinguished from the original. Also, invisible UV marks can be printed at this stage.

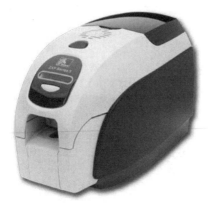

Figure 4-5: Thermal PVC printer

3. *Embossing* is necessary to create the embossed PAN, cardholder name, and expiration date. It is done using an *embosser*, shown in Figure 4-7.

4. *Tipping* is the process of painting the embossed numbers and letters using gold or silver foil using a *tipper* like the one shown in Figure 4-8.

Figure 4-6: Inkjet printer for printing on flat surfaces

Figure 4-7: Embosser

Various types of embossers and tippers can be purchased online.[43, 44]

The printing, embossing, and tipping steps are only needed when a perfect-looking card is needed to be presented to the salesperson in a fancy boutique for quite expensive booty without arousing any suspicion. In such cases, replication of additional security features such as holograms might be needed in order to achieve a top quality card.

For a debit card that is going to be used in an ATM for cash withdrawal, or a credit card that is going to be swiped at the point of sale by an "insider" (an accomplice who works as a cashier), simple white plastic will work just fine: there will be no need for embossing or fancy pictures.

Figure 4-8: Tipper

Encoders

A magnetic stripe reader (MSR) device can be a simple reader or both a reader and a writer (encoder). Readers are utilized in legitimate POS systems as well as in skimming attacks (see Chapter 7). Magnetic stripe encoders are considered in this chapter because they are capable of writing any information into the magnetic stripe of blank plastic card templates. Both card encoders and blank card templates can be purchased online and used for manufacturing fake cards.[45, 46] With a simple encoder such as the one shown in Figure 4-9, which can be purchased anonymously online for less than $200, magnetic tracks stolen from payment systems ("dumps") can be written into blank plastic card templates. After some additional artwork, the resulting product can be used for making fraudulent transactions.

Usually, a brand new device includes drivers for a major OS, a simple managing application with an intuitive graphic user interface, and several blank plastic cards to start using on the spot. A typical encoder can be connected to any computer via a USB or serial port. The track data (Tracks 1 and 2 only—Track 3 is not used in financial transactions) from the dump can simply be copied and pasted into the managing utility interface window, as shown in Figure 4-10.

Figure 4-9: Magnetic Stripe Encoder

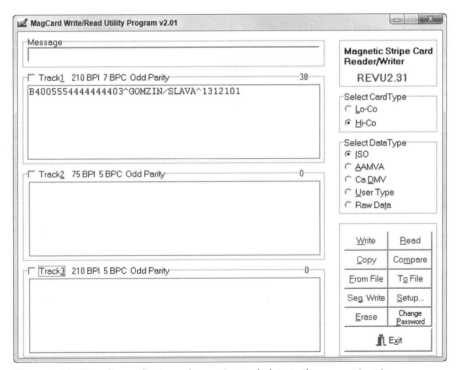

Figure 4-10: Encoding utility is ready to write track data to the magnetic stripe

After the track data is entered into the corresponding text boxes, only a single click on the "Write" button and a quick card-swipe separate us from the complete card (Figure 4-11).

Figure 4-11: Encoding is done

If the dump has debit card tracks with a complementary PIN code, no further steps are required: the card is ready to be used to withdraw cash because the ATM does not validate the exterior of the plastics. Payment cards do not have physical controls (besides the magnetic stripe which is replicated by encoding) that could be verified by ATM.

Printers

There are two types of printing devices capable of creating images on blank PVC cards:

1. *Thermal PVC printers* cost from $1,000 and up[47] (see Figure 4-5). It is capable of producing high quality color images of background and payment brand logos on blank plastic cards.

2. *Inkjet printers capable of printing on flat surfaces* (shown on Figure 4-6) are cheap compared to thermal PVC printers.[48] Such printers, while initially

designed to print images on CD and DVD, can be easily upgraded to print on PVC cards by adding a special PVC card tray for just $25.[49] However, the quality and especially the durability of the image produced by a thermal printer is higher.

Another important function that can be performed by inkjet printers is creating UV marks. In order to do this, the ink cartridge should be reloaded with special UV ink, which is invisible in normal conditions but glows under a black light.

Summary

Magnetic stripe payment cards are insecure by design, primarily due to the following:

- There are multiple physical security features which still do not provide adequate protection from theft.
- Sensitive cardholder information is encoded on a magnetic track in clear text.

Card data breach, which consists of several stages, can remain undisclosed for many months and result in thousands of stolen credit and debit card records.

Counterfeited cards can be relatively easily manufactured using full Track 1 and 2 data from the original cards. The main steps of this process are encoding, printing, embossing, and tipping.

- Only encoding is necessary for ATM cash withdrawal (if PIN is available).
- Selected elements of card track data (PAN and CVV) can be used for online shopping without the need to produce the physical plastic card.

Notes

1. *The Encyclopedia Britannica, A Dictionary of Arts, Science, Literature, and General Information, 11th Edition*, Volume 7 (New York: The Encyclopedia Britannica Company, 1910), p.390.

2. Slava Gomzin, "Free Two-Factor Authentication with Your Smartphone," *PayAppSec* blog (June 2011), http://www.gomzin.com/1/post/2011/06/free-two-factor-authentication-with-your-smartphone1.html

3. American Express cards security features, American Express, https://secure.cmax.americanexpress.com/Internet/International

`/japa/SG_en/Merchant/PROSPECT/WorkingWithUs/AvoidingCardFraud` `/HowToCheckCardFaces/Files/Guide_to_checking_Card_Faces.pdf`

4. *VISA Card Security Features,* Visa Inc. (2012), `http://usa.visa.com` `/download/merchants/card-security-features-mini-vcp-111512.pdf`

5. *Help Prevent Fraud with MasterCard Card Security Features,* MasterCard Worldwide, 2008, `http://www.mastercard.com/us/merchant/pdf` `/MST08004_CardFeatures_r4.pdf`

6. *Discover Card Identification Features,* Discover, `http://www.` `discovernetwork.com/merchants/fraud-protection/prevention.html`

7. Holographic magnetic stripe JCB Cards, JCB Co. Ltd., `http://partner` `.jcbcard.com/acceptance/holographicstripe.html`

8. *How to verify US Dollars, Credit Cards, and Travelers Cheques,* AccuBanker, `http://www.accubanker.com/docs/verify_en.pdf`

9. UV flashlights on Amazon, `http://www.amazon.com/s/ref=nb` `_sb_noss?url=search-alias%3Daps&field-keywords=UV+flashlight`

10. Invisible UV ink on Amazon.com, `http://www.amazon.com/s/ref=nb` `_sb_noss_1?url=search-alias%3Daps&field-keywords=invisible+uv+ink`

11. *International Standard ISO/IEC 7813, Information technology – Identification cards – Financial transaction cards,* ISO/IEC, 2006.

12. David S. Evans and Richard Schmalensee, *Paying with Plastic*: *The Digital Revolution in Buying and Borrowing,* 2nd ed., (Cambridge, MA: The MIT Press, 2005), p.9.

13. *International Standard ISO/IEC 7811-2, Identification cards — Recording technique — Part 2: Magnetic stripe — Low coercivity,* ISO, 2001.

14. *Technical Reference Guide, Open Terminal Requirement Specification - Book 1,* Nets (December 2012), pp. 2-4-7, `http://www.nets.eu/dk-da/Service` `/verifikation-af-betalingsloesninger/Documents/ct-trg-otrs-en.pdf`

15. *Requirements for POS Software Applications and Devices Support for Discover*® *Network Cards,* Discover (April 2012), `http://www.discovernetwork.com` `/value-added-reseller/images/Discover_IIN_Bulletin_Apr_2012.pdf`

16. "Card Identification and Validation,", Range and Rules, Barclaycard (March 2013), `http://www.barclaycard.co.uk/business/documents` `/pdfs/bin_rules.pdf`

17. Visa BIN Lookup Information, `bin-iin.com`, `http://bin-iin.com` `/visa-BIN-range.html`

18. Carolyn Watters, *Dictionary of Information Science and Technology* (New York: Academic Press, 1992), p. 132.

19. *International Standard ISO/IEC 7812-1, Identification cards — Identification of issuers — Part 1: Numbering system*, ISO/IEC, 2006.

20. *PCI Forensic Investigator (PFI) Program Guide*, Version 2.0, PCI SSC (November 2012), `https://www.pcisecuritystandards.org/documents/PFI_Program_Guide.pdf`

21. *Fraud*, CVV/CVC and CVV2/CVC2 Checking, Pulse, A Discover Financial Services Company, `https://www.pulsenetwork.com/fraud/index.html`

22. *Findstr*, Windows XP Professional Product Documentation, Microsoft, `http://www.microsoft.com/resources/documentation/windows/xp/all/proddocs/en-us/findstr.mspx?mfr=true`

23. *PCI PA-DSS Requirements and Security Assessment Procedures Version 2.0*, PCI SSC (October 2010), `https://www.pcisecuritystandards.org/documents/pa-dss_v2.pdf`

24. *PCI DSS Requirements and Security Assessment Procedures Version 2.0*, PCI SSC (October 2010), `https://www.pcisecuritystandards.org/documents/pci_dss_v2.pdf`

25. *California Bill SB-1386*, California State Senate (July 2003), `http://info.sen.ca.gov/pub/01-02/bill/sen/sb_1351-1400/sb_1386_bill_20020926_chaptered.html`

26. *State Security Breach Notification Laws*, The National Conference of State Legislatures, `http://www.ncsl.org/issues-research/telecom/security-breach-notification-laws.aspx`

27. *Security Breach Disclosure Law Matrix by State*, VigilantMinds, Inc. (February 2007), `http://www.contrib.andrew.cmu.edu/~dmarkiew/docs/breach_matrix_200702.pdf`

28. Brian Krebs, "Payment Processor Breach May Be Largest Ever," *The Washington Post* (January 2009), `http://voices.washingtonpost.com/securityfix/2009/01/payment_processor_breach_may_b.html`

29. *Chronology of Data Breaches: Security Breaches 2005 – Present*, Privacy Rights Clearinghouse, `https://www.privacyrights.org/data-breach`

30. *Anatomy of an Attack, From Spear Phishing Attack to Compromise in Ten Steps*, Mandiant, `http://www.mandiant.com/threat-landscape/anatomy-of-an-attack/`

31. "TJX hack the biggest in history," *ComputerWeekly.com* (April 2007), `http://www.computerweekly.com/news/2240080607/TJX-hack-the-biggest-in-history`

32. Gary G. Berg, Michelle S. Freeman, and Kent N. Schneider, "Analyzing the T.J. Maxx Data Security Fiasco: Lessons for Auditors," *The CPA*

Journal (August 2008), `http://www.nysscpa.org/cpajournal/2008/808/essentials/p34.htm`

33. James Verini, "The Great Cyberheist," *The New York Times* (November 2010), `http://www.nytimes.com/2010/11/14/magazine/14Hacker-t.html?pagewanted=all&_r=0`

34. Carding Forum, Forum Jar, `http://www.forumjar.com/forums/Carding`

35. Skimmed Dumps Seller Forum, `http://www.voy.com/195759/36.html`

36. Misha Glenny, *Dark Market: Cyberthives, Cybercops and You* (New York: Alfred A. Knopf, 2011), p. 8.

37. "Visa Issues ATM Cash-Out Warning," *BankInfoSecurity* (January 22, 2013), `http://www.bankinfosecurity.com/visa-warns-banks-atm-fraud-a-5438/op-1`

38. Brian Krebs, "Scammers Play Robin Hood to Test Stolen Credit Cards," *The Washington Post* (July 2007), `http://voices.washingtonpost.com/securityfix/2007/07/odd_charity_donations_could_pr.html`

39. "Bank to refund fees to children's charity," *Irish Examiner* (July 2013), `http://www.irishexaminer.com/archives/2013/0722/ireland/bank-to-refund-fees-to-childrenaposs-charity-237504.html`

40. Misha Glenny, *Dark Market: Cyberthives, Cybercops and You* (New York: Alfred A. Knopf, 2011).

41. Kevin Poulsen, *Kingpin: How One Hacker Took Over the Billion-Dollar Cybercrime Underground* (New York: Crown, 2011).

42. Carding School, `http://browse.feedreader.com/c/Carding_School`

43. PVC Card Embossers on eBay, `http://www.ebay.com/bhp/pvc-card-embosser`

44. Credit Card Tippers on eBay, `http://www.ebay.com/bhp/credit-card-tipper`

45. Credit Card Encoders on eBay, `http://www.ebay.com/bhp/credit-card-encoder`

46. Blank magnetic plastic cards on eBay, `http://www.ebay.com/sch/i.html?_trksid=m570.l1313&_nkw=Blank+Magnetic+Plastic+Card&_sacat=0&_from=R40`

47. Thermal PVC printers on Amazon, `http://www.amazon.com/s/ref=nb_sb_noss?url=search-alias%3Doffice-products&field-keywords=thermal+pvc+printers`

48. Inkjet PVC printers on Amazon, `http://www.amazon.com/s/ref=nb_sb_noss?url=search-alias%3Daps&field-keywords=inkjet+pvc+printers`

49. PVC card trays for inkjet PVC printers on Amazon.com, `http://www.amazon.com/s/ref=nb_sb_noss_1?url=search-alias%3Daps&field-keywords=PVC+ID+Card+Tray`

Penetrating Security Free Zones

If you give to a thief he cannot steal from you, and then he is no longer a thief.
—William Saroyan

PCI security standards put the responsibility for implementing security controls on the payment processing industry—merchants, payment gateways and processors, and software vendors. An interesting trend is emerging, however, where instead of requiring payment system vendors (either hardware or software—in this case, there is no big difference from the merchant's viewpoint) to supply secure systems "out of the box," the standards allow multiple vulnerabilities to be built into software and hardware by design. At the same time, merchants are required to implement security controls that compensate for the lack of security in their payment systems. The merchants hope that security comes from the software and hardware vendors, who are in turn relying on the merchants to secure their own store environments. The results: multiple security breaches. Examples of this scenario include unprotected data in memory, unencrypted local network traffic, and other vulnerabilities, which are discussed in this chapter.

Payment Application Memory

In November 2009, Visa issued its Data Security Alert called "Targeted Hospitality Sector Vulnerabilities" where the biggest payment card brand admitted that "the increasing use of debugging tools that parse data from volatile memory suggests that attackers may have successfully adapted their techniques to obtain payment card data that is not written to POS system disks."[1] In April 2013, Visa issued a new version of the Security Alert with the subtitle "Preventing Memory-Parsing Malware Attacks on Grocery Merchants" which warned about an "increase in network intrusions involving grocery merchants. Once inside a merchant's network, hackers install memory-parsing malware on Windows-based cash register systems or back-of-house (BOH) servers to extract full magnetic-stripe data."[2]

RAM Scraping

Memory Scraping, also known as *RAM (Random Access Memory) Scraping* or *Memory Parsing*, is a technology used for retrieving sensitive payment card data from the memory of the payment application process. Memory scraping is implemented in specially crafted malware which attacks payment applications by stealing cardholder information from the memory.[3, 4] Most payment applications, even if they encrypt the secret fields (Track 1, 2, and PAN) at rest and in transit, still have to have such data in clear text in volatile memory in order to retrieve parameters they need for routing, processing cashier and customer prompts, and many other functions. There is no reliable software technology today that would easily resolve this problem without investing in new systems which introduce new protection methods such as encrypting the data end to end. Therefore, payment software vendors are currently not obligated by any standards to protect the memory of their applications. Instead, the merchants—users of the software—are obligated to protect the memory of their computers running such applications by implementing different types of compensating mechanisms, such as physical and network controls listed in PCI DSS requirements (more details in Chapter 3).

It is relatively easy to connect to a payment application process and scrape its memory, especially, if the malware has managed to become a part of the payment application. Memory scraping malware was reported in additional Visa Data Security Alerts.[5, 6]

WinHex

It's possible to see the memory of the Windows system using special tools. WinHex is one such tool used for security testing and forensics investigations.[7] WinHex has an ability to load, view, and edit the entire image of computer memory or hard disk, as shown in Figure 5-1. The utility also has search capabilities required for this task. QSA uses WinHex during PA-DSS and PCI DSS assessments by running various types of transactions with a predefined card number and then searching the entire disk for this number. However, even if the PAN is found in clear text in memory, the audit is still passed because PCI standards do not require memory protection. Figure 5-2 shows Track 1 found in the memory of a payment application.

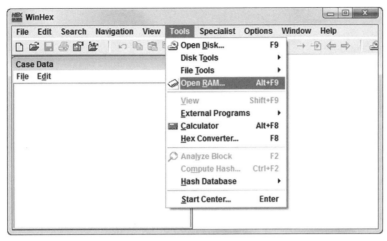

Figure 5-1: WinHex utility

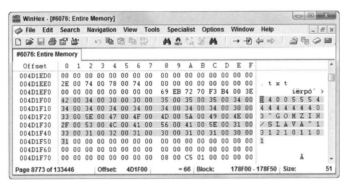

Figure 5-2: WinHex memory search results with Track 1 in clear text

MemoryScraper Utility

This section describes the implementation of a sample .NET C# utility that can attach to any Windows application process and search for payment card PANs and tracks using regular expressions. If you are not a programmer, you can skip the following details and simply test this code on your favorite POS application. Just launch the MemoryScraper.exe along with your payment software, then select the application's process from the combo box and click the Start button (Figure 5-3). As soon as the search is complete, if any cards were found in the memory of the selected application, the numbers of the records will be displayed and the View Log button will be enabled (Figure 5-4). The detailed search results will be available in the log file located in the MemoryScraper home directory (Figure 5-5).

Figure 5-3: MemoryScraper utility

Figure 5-4: MemoryScraper scan results

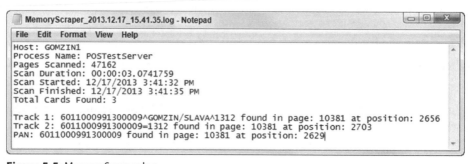

Figure 5-5: MemoryScraper log

This is not the code that would normally be used by actual malware. Hackers mostly write in languages that can be built into binary executables like Assembler,

C, C++, or Delphi (Pascal). Such code has fewer (or no) dependencies on other libraries, so it can be executed in any environment. However, this utility demonstrates some basics of the memory scraping process.

The full source code and compiled executable of MemoryScraper can be downloaded from Wiley's website at www.wiley.com/go/hackingpos.

Loading Data from Memory

Windows OS provides the ability to connect to any application process and load data from its memory. There are three *Windows API* functions that should be imported and called in order to do this (ProcessMemoryLoader class). The names and the order of those methods are self-explanatory:

```
DllImport("kernel32.dll")]
public static extern IntPtr OpenProcess(
    UInt32 dwDesiredAccess,Int32 bInheritHandle, UInt32 dwProcessId);

DllImport("kernel32.dll")]
public static extern Int32 ReadProcessMemory(
    IntPtr hProcess, IntPtr lpBaseAddress, [In, Out] byte[] buffer,
    UInt32 size, out IntPtr lpNumberOfBytesRead);

DllImport("kernel32.dll")]
public static extern Int32 CloseHandle(IntPtr hObject);
```

The process memory cannot be read all at once, so multiple ReadProcessMemory function calls are required in order to load the data chunk by chunk. The default memory page size is 4 KB (4,048 bytes) so we will use it as the value of the chunk size parameter for each iteration (MemoryScanner class):

```
const int MEM_PAGE_SIZE = 4096;
```

Another parameter required for the ReadProcessMemory API call is *lpBaseAddress*. Obviously, we want to start from the beginning of the process memory (address 0) and move forward until the end by incrementing the base address by *MEM_PAGE_SIZE*:

```
while (memAddress + MEM_PAGE_SIZE <= processMemSize)
{
    buffer = loader.LoadMemory(
        (IntPtr)memAddress,(uint)bufferSize, out readCount);
    if (readCount > 0)
    {
        // regex search code
    }
    memAddress += MEM_PAGE_SIZE;
}
```

The maximum address (`processMemSize`) can be calculated using one of the process's parameters:

```
long processMemSize = process.PeakVirtualMemorySize64;
```

Looking for Card Data

In order to filter out the PAN and track data of the payment cards from the byte stream of the payment application memory, the MemoryScraper uses regular expressions (regex) which were briefly described in Chapter 4. Since regex should be applied to a string data type, the chunk of memory that is being scanned for sensitive data should first be converted from binary format to string. There are different types of *data encoding* that can be used by payment applications for PAN and to track data in-memory storage. Various development environments may represent the same string in different formats, but most probably are either ASCII or *Unicode*. For example, .NET will use the Unicode string by default, while a Delphi or C++ coded application would probably store the PAN and tracks as an array of ASCII characters. The difference between ASCII and Unicode strings is simple: an ASCII string stores each character as a single byte (8 bits), while a Unicode string reserves 2 bytes (16 bits) for each character. However, they both use the same ASCII codes for digits and basic symbols which are used by regular expressions to match the PAN and track patterns (as shown in Table 5-1).

Table 5-1: ASCII and Unicode Codes for Digits and Track Data Field Separators

CHARACTER	ASCII CODE (DECIMAL)	ASCII CODE (HEXADECIMAL)	UNICODE (DECIMAL)	UNICODE (HEXADECIMAL)
0	48	30	0 48	00 30
1	49	31	0 49	00 31
2	50	32	0 50	00 32
3	51	33	0 51	00 33
4	52	34	0 52	00 34
5	53	35	0 53	00 35
6	54	36	0 54	00 36
7	55	37	0 55	00 37
8	56	38	0 56	00 38
9	57	39	0 57	00 39
=	61	3D	0 61	00 3D
^	94	5E	0 94	00 5E

The only difference is that Unicode characters contain an extra zero byte. Table 5-2 shows an example of PAN as it is stored in memory in ASCII and Unicode formats. The actual data in memory is usually displayed in hexadecimal format. In source code, the hexadecimal number usually has a "0x" prefix so it can be distinguished from decimal numbers. For example, the "0" character has ASCII code 48 (decimal) or 0x30 (hexadecimal).

Table 5-2: ASCII and Unicode Encoding of Sample PAN

ENCODING	STRING REPRESENTATION	ACTUAL DATA IN MEMORY (HEXADECIMAL FORMAT)	LENGTH (BYTES)
ASCII	4005554444444403	34 30 30 35 35 35 34 34 34 34 34 34 34 34 30 33	16
Unicode	4 0 0 5 5 5 4 4 4 4 4 4 4 4 0 3	00 34 00 30 00 30 00 35 00 35 00 35 00 34 00 34 00 34 00 34 00 34 00 34 00 34 00 34 00 30 00 33	32

Since it is probably unknown in advance whether the application uses ASCII or Unicode strings (or may be even both!), the MemoryScraper will transform the memory buffer (and scan it using regex) twice (`MemoryScanner` class):

```
string ASCIItext = Encoding.ASCII.GetString(buffer);
string Unicodetext = Encoding.Unicode.GetString(buffer);
searchLine.Search(
    ASCIItext, pageNumber.ToString(), string.Empty, ref res);
searchLine.Search(
    Unicodetext, pageNumber.ToString(), string.Empty, ref res);
```

The results and statistics of the search are accumulated in the `res` list and logged in the text file once the scraping is done:

```
ScanInfo scanInfo = new ScanInfo();
scanInfo.searchResults = res;
Logger.GetLogger(LogType.MemoryScraper).AddToLog(scanInfo);
```

How Regex Search Works

Regular expressions use patterns, or a set of consistent parameters, of the object that's being searched. In our case, the objects are PAN, Track 1, and Track 2. Those parameters are translated into special instructions (see Table 5-3) which create the final expression.

Table 5-3: Regex Instructions Used in PAN and Tracks Search Expressions

INSTRUCTION	DESCRIPTION	USAGE
\s?	\s matches any white-space character. ? matches the previous element zero or one time.	4[0-9]{3}\s?[0-9]{4}\s?[0-9]{4}\s?[0-9]{4} finds account numbers grouped by 4 digits, for example: 4005 5544 4444 4403
[x-y]	[x-y] matches any digit in the range between x and y.	Example 1: 5[1-5][0-9]{14} finds all cards with ISO prefixes 51, 52, 53, 54, and 55 Example 2: [0-2][0-9][0-1][0-2] finds expiration data in yymm format, for example: 1402
{n}	{n} matches the previous element exactly n times.	5[1-5][0-9]{14} finds the body of the PAN after the prefix, for example: 54**99830000000601**
x	Matches the exact digit x.	5[1-5][0-9]{14} finds any PAN with prefix 5, for example: 5499830000000601
+	Matches the previous element one or more times.	\^.+\^ finds cardholder name field of Track 1 which has variable length and is located between two field separators '^', for example: 4005554444444403^**GOMZIN/SLAVA**^1512

Regular Expression Language - Quick Reference[8]

PAN has a known length, contains only digits, and starts with known prefixes. Those properties are translated into the set of regex instructions:

```
(?:4[0-9]{12}|4[0-9]{3}\s?[0-9]{4}\s?[0-9]{4}\s?[0-9]{4}|5[1-5][0-9]
{14}|6(?:011|5[0-9][0-9])[0-9]{12}|3[47][0-9]{13}|3(?:0[0-5]|[68][0-9])
[0-9]{11}|(?:2131|1800|35\d{3})\d{11})
```

In addition to the PAN recognition patterns, Tracks 1 and 2 also have a fixed structure with a predetermined sequence of components: PAN plus 4-digit expiration date in *yymm* format, separated by the field separator characters = for Track 2 and ^ for Track 1:

```
(?:(?:\=[0-2][0-9][0-1][0-2]|\^.+\^[0-2][0-9][0-1][0-2]))
```

Fighting False Positives

One of the issues with using regular expressions for PAN lookup is the high probability of catching *false positives*—random sequences of numbers which look exactly like normal PAN. There are several methods that can be used in order to avoid such bad results.

Let's take a look at the regex that is used to search for standalone PAN. It is started and concluded with `(?<!)` and `(?!)` expressions. For example, the regex `4[0-9]{12}` will find the 13-digit Visa PAN which always starts with 4 and is followed by 12 digits. In order to search for all card types at once, several regex can be combined into one:

```
string pan_pattern =
    @"(?<![\d])(?:4[0-9]{12}|4[0-9]{3}\s?[0-9]{4}\s?[0-9]{4}\s?[0-9]
{4}|5[1-5][0-9]{14}|6(?:011|5[0-9][0-9])[0-9]{12}|3[47][0-9]
{13}|3(?:0[0-5]|[68][0-9])[0-9]{11}|(?:2131|1800|35\d{3})\d{11})
(?![\d])";
```

`(?<! subexpression)` is a zero-width negative look-behind assertion, `(?! subexpression)` is a zero-width negative look-ahead assertion, and `[\d]` matches any decimal digit. Thus, `(?<![\d])` and `(?![\d])` expressions are added in order to make sure the PAN is not a part of a random stream of numbers, by checking that there are no digits before and after the PAN.

The `test_pattern` is used by `test_rgx` regex as another method of false positive prevention:

```
string test_pattern =
    @"(?:0{7}|1{7}|2{7}|3{7}|4{7}|5{7}|6{7}|7{7}|8{7}|9{7})";
```

The PAN of test cards, which are generated by payment brands and processors and used by payment software vendors for testing their systems, often have the same digit repeated several times, usually 7 or more times (see Table 5-4).

Table 5-4: Examples of False Positive Test Cards

TEST CARD PAN	CARD TYPE
4005554444444403	Visa
4485530000000127	Visa
5499830000000601	MasterCard
5567300000000016	MasterCard
371111111111114	American Express

The `test_rgx` regex will filter out any test card numbers containing 7 or more repeated digits:

```
test_rgx = new Regex(test_pattern, RegexOptions.IgnoreCase);
MatchCollection test_matches = test_rgx.Matches(result.PAN);
if (test_matches.Count > 0)
    break;
```

Validating the Mod 10 check-digit is also one of the basic protection measures for catching multiple false positives (the Mod 10 [Luhn] verification procedure and code were discussed in Chapter 4):

```
if (!PassesLuhnTest(result.PAN))
    break;
```

Note that all these measures against false positives are not necessary for the PAN part of the regex looking for Track 1 and Track 2. That's because Tracks 1 and 2 have very distinguishable marks—field separators and expiration date format, also discussed in detail in Chapter 4.

Windows Page File

Windows page file (*pagefile.sys*, sometimes also called the *swap file*) is normally located in the root directory (C:\) and contains the OS memory image. When Windows is running out of physical memory, it starts using virtual memory by saving currently unused memory pages (for example, the ones belonging to applications that have been inactive for a long time) to the disk. The less physical memory is available in the system, the more frequently the memory pages are stored to or loaded from the hard drive. Since this process is managed by the operating system, it is transparent to the applications. Payment applications are no exception, so when they perform any operation with sensitive cardholder information in memory, such data is most definitely being swapped as well. The content of the page file is not encrypted by default and can be scanned by malware in order to extract the cardholder data.[9]

Sniffing

Wiretapping on data in transit is probably the second most dangerous security threat to payment applications, after memory scraping. Modern POS systems, both hardware and software, have modular architecture, meaning they consist of different, often physically separated modules, such as POS machine and

Store Server, POS app and Payment Application, Payment Application and POI device, Payment Application and Payment Gateway, and others. Thus, those modules have to communicate with each other using different technologies such as Ethernet (LAN, TCP sockets), Serial (COM), or in-memory (Windows COM, DLL API). Since payment software vendors are not obligated by PA-DSS to encrypt such connectivity[10] and merchants are not required by PCI DSS to encrypt their local networks[11], wiretapping, especially of store LAN, remains one of the biggest vulnerabilities of payment applications.

CROSS-REFERENCE   Refer to Chapter 2 for more detailed information on payment application architecture.

Traffic on Local Networks

There are different ways to "tap into the wire."[12] One of various sniffing attack scenarios would be a hidden network tap device plugged into the store network. The tap device will catch the payment application traffic and mirror it to the remote control center.[13] This little computer which costs less than $1,000 can be masked as an air freshener or power strip, and equipped with 4 G/GSM cellular, Wireless (802.11b/g/n), high-gain Bluetooth, and USB-Ethernet adapters.[14]

Let's focus on understanding how dangerous this type of vulnerability can be when it happens at the brick-and-mortar merchant location. Both PCI DSS and PA-DSS require network traffic encryption only when communication is implemented on public networks, such as the Internet. Communication between modules of a payment system, which are often located at different machines, is done through the store LAN. This type of attack is especially dangerous for Hybrid POS/Store Server architecture because they send sensitive cardholder payment data from each POS to the Store Server for further processing. However, POS EPS or Store EPS systems can also be affected because of the links they maintain to payment processors.

Network Sniffers

Special software called a *network sniffer*, or a *packet analyzer*, is used to intercept the network traffic. If payload is not encrypted, the sensitive data can be easily filtered out using the methods similar to what's been described previously for memory scraping. *Wireshark* is an example of a network sniffer application.[15] Figure 5-6 shows the TCP/IP packets between POS client and server (upper window) and Track 1 data in clear text inside the TCP packet payload.

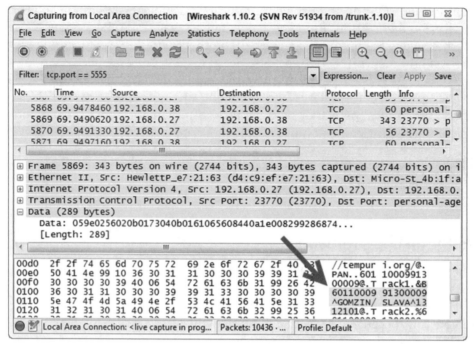

Figure 5-6: Wireshark network sniffer displays Track 1 inside TCP/IP packet

References to network sniffing malware can be found in Visa Data Security Alerts.[16, 17] Of course, malware does not use such tools directly, but it may contain the sniffing code written using similar principles.

NetScraper Utility

NetScraper is an example .NET C# application which demonstrates the ability to extract and store the payment card sensitive data from the network communication traffic while installed on a POS machine. As with the previously described MemoryScraper utility, if you are not interested in the details of this implementation, you can just test the executable which can be downloaded from the Wiley website, and skip to the next section.

After the NetScraper application is launched, it checks for local active network interfaces and prompts to select the *IP address* which will be scanned. The first IP address in the list will be preselected automatically (Figure 5-7).

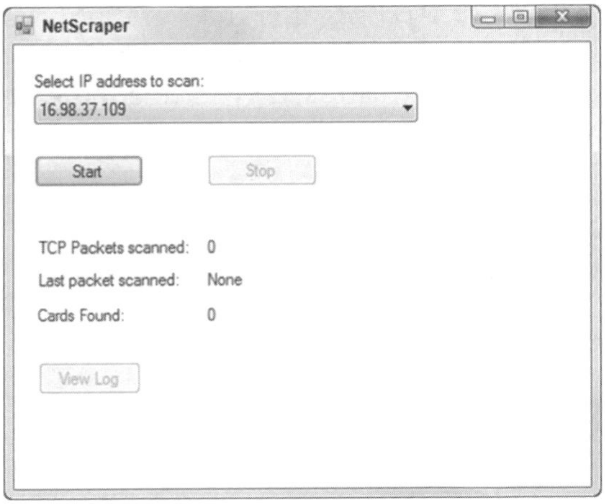

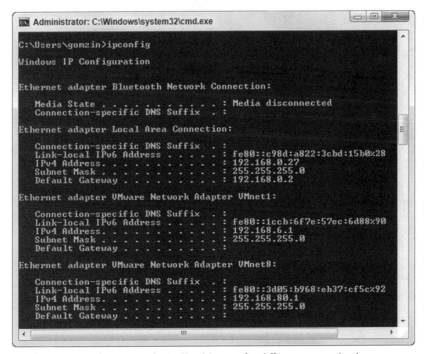

Figure 5-7: NetScraper Utility

Since there may be more than one network adapter installed in the system (Ethernet, Wireless card, VMware, for example), the correct address can be determined using the Windows *ipconfig* utility. Figure 5-8 shows an example of ipconfig output which shows the local LAN IP address 192.168.0.27.

Figure 5-8: Ipconfig output shows IP addresses for different network adapters.

The NetScraper begins scanning the TCP/IP *packets* after the Start button is pressed (Figure 5-9) and continues until the Stop button is pressed. Then it creates the log file with search results which can be accessed by hitting the *View Log* button (Figure 5-10).

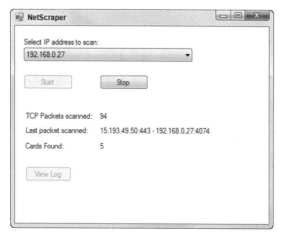

Figure 5-9: NetScraper scanning the traffic on a local network at 192.168.0.27

```
NetScraper_2013.12.18_12.45.00.log - Notepad
File  Edit  Format  View  Help
Host: TEST1
IP Address: 192.168.0.27
Packets Scanned: 110
Scan Duration: 00:07:04.7524710
Scan Started: 12/18/2013 12:37:55 PM
Scan Finished: 12/18/2013 12:45:00 PM
Total Cards Found: 5

Track 1: 6011000991300009^GOMZIN/SLAVA^1312 found in packet: 192.168.0.27:13818 -
192.168.0.38:5555 at position: 222
Track 2: 6011000991300009=1312 found in packet: 192.168.0.27:13818 - 192.168.0.38:5555 at
position: 269
PAN: 6011000991300009 found in packet: 192.168.0.27:13818 - 192.168.0.38:5555 at position: 195
PAN: 6011000991300009 found in packet: 192.168.0.27:13818 - 192.168.0.38:5555 at position: 222
PAN: 6011000991300009 found in packet: 192.168.0.27:13818 - 192.168.0.38:5555 at position: 269
```

Figure 5-10: NetScraper log with the results of a network scan

Scanning the Net

The code of NetScraper is pretty simple. First it creates a socket that listens for the IP address selected by the user:

```
socket = new Socket(
    AddressFamily.InterNetwork, SocketType.Raw, ProtocolType.IP);
socket.Bind(new IPEndPoint(IPAddress.Parse(listeningAddress), 0));
```

The socket is set to capture any IP-level packet data:

```
socket.SetSocketOption(
    SocketOptionLevel.IP, SocketOptionName.HeaderIncluded, true);
```

This way, several protocols that are based on IP can be captured—UDP and TCP, for example.

The socket will raise an event (captured by OnDataReceived procedure) each time the IP packets are sent back and forth through the specified address:

```
socket.BeginReceive(
    dataBuffer, 0, dataBuffer.Length, SocketFlags.None,
    new AsyncCallback(OnDataReceived), null);
```

Once the data is received, the IP packet is first analyzed to check the protocol ID of the data it carries:

```
IPHeader ipHeader = new IPHeader(dataBuffer, dataLength);
if (ipHeader.ProtocolID == BaseHeader.PROTOCOL_TCP)
    TCPHeader tcpHeader = new TCPHeader(
        ipHeader.Payload, ipHeader.PayloadLength);
```

NetScraper is interested only in TCP packets because TCP/IP is used mostly in application communication, but other protocols can also be captured if needed (UDP, for example).

Once the TCP packet payload is retrieved, NetScraper scans it for the tracks and PAN traces exactly the same way as MemoryScraper does it with the data extracted from the application memory:

```
string ASCIItext = Encoding.ASCII.GetString(ipHeader.Payload);
string Unicodetext = Encoding.Unicode.GetString(ipHeader.Payload);
string route =
    ipHeader.SourceAddress + ":" + tcpHeader.SourcePort +
    " - " + ipHeader.DestinationAddress + ":" +
    tcpHeader.DestinationPort;
searchLine.Search(ASCIItext, route, "", ref res);
searchLine.Search(Unicodetext, route, "", ref res);
```

In fact, both NetScraper and MemoryScraper use the same search logic, which is encapsulated in the PANandTracksSearch class located in HackingPOS .Scrapers.Common.dll.

More Communication Vulnerability Points

Although LAN communication is probably the most convenient way to wiretap sensitive data, there are other possible methods related to communication.

Communication Between POS and POI Devices

POS devices are usually connected to the hosting (POS) machine via a serial (COM) port, USB, or LAN. Even though COM ports look archaic these days, they are still widely used in retail. POI devices connected via serial ports can even be accessed remotely through the network.[18]

Communication Between POS and PA

This sort of communication can be done in two different ways—remotely or locally—depending on system architecture and deployment. If POS and PA physically reside on the same machine, they communicate locally using Windows COM, DLL API, or even TCP sockets. In any case, the data transfer goes through the local machine memory and can be tapped using memory scraping. When POS and PA are physically separated (for example, several POS talking to a single PA located at the store server), they most definitely communicate using LAN, so the traffic can be wiretapped using network sniffing.

Exploiting Other Vulnerabilities

Besides the "standard" exploitations which are focused primarily on stealing sensitive data through the software, there are exotic deviations of attack vectors in two different areas. First, there are attacks against the hardware rather than software. Secondly, there are attacks when confidentiality of sensitive cardholder data is not targeted, but instead the same financial results are achieved through compromising the integrity or availability of the payment application.

Tampering With the Application

There are several payment application attack vectors that can be grouped by one feature: they exploit the vulnerabilities of the application code. The difference between "mainstream" attacks (such as memory scraping and network sniffing) and attacks on application code is that in order to perform the latter the attackers have to have significant knowledge about the application. The former are more generic methods which can be applied to virtually any payment application. The following sections provide brief scenarios of some attacks on applications.

Abusing Exposed PA API

Sensitive data can be exposed through the payment application API, which is supposed to be exposed to POS only. However, since PA API is usually not protected by access controls such as client application authentication, malware applications can pretend to be POS and call special API methods that return unmasked PAN or Tracks 1 and 2 in clear text.

Tampering Configuration

The application configuration (`.config` file in .NET applications, or `.cfg` files in legacy applications) can be modified to change the workflow of the application. For example, the server address can be changed in order to route all the communication traffic to a bogus server which scans the packets for sensitive data before rerouting them to the legitimate server.

Tampering Software Updates

All software providers periodically issue new versions of their applications with new features as well as patches which fix bugs or security issues. There are different update systems, either commercial or proprietary, that can be tampered with in order to insert the malware that pretends to be a legitimate update patch.

Disassembling the Application Code

The payment application code is compiled and built into binary files which are installed on the POS systems. Those files can be *disassembled*, or *reverse engineered*, to get the original source code, analyze the application logic, and as a result modify it or retrieve some hard-coded sensitive information such as cryptographic key components. Modern languages like C# and Java are mostly vulnerable to this type of attack because they use *intermediate code* that can be easily reversed to the source code which looks almost like the original one.

Spoofing Client Credentials

POS systems with client/server architecture, where the client is located at the POS machine and the server is running in the data center, store server, or cloud, are vulnerable to spoofing attacks. Even if the system has some sort of authentication mechanism between the client and the server, there is really no safe place at the client to store the credentials. If an attacker has access to the client POS machine, the client credentials can be stolen and used to access the server from a different location by the bogus client software which pretends to be a legitimate client.

Tampering With the Hardware

Hacking POS software is very reliable, but it's not the only way to steal cardholder data. Hardware is an essential part of any payment solution, and it can be attacked as well.[19]

Injecting Malicious Code into POI Devices

The malicious code can be injected into POI devices to modify the device behavior, install plug-ins that retrieve sensitive data, and translate it to the command center. Examples of unauthorized malicious code injection were presented at the Black Hat 2012 security conference.[20]

Skimming POI devices

In general, *skimming* is modification of the original payment terminal by installing bogus hardware parts that duplicate the original MSR and keypad functions. They capture cardholder data and send it to the attacker.[21] The skimming threat is big enough to be treated as a separate topic by PCI.[22] In fact, this is probably one of the most promising attack methods as the industry moves toward hardware point-to-point encryption, and the software hacking becomes a more complex task. Information about pinpad device skimming attacks is available in Visa Security Alerts.[23]

Targeting New Technologies

As new payment processing and data protection technologies evolve, new hacking methods emerge as well. There is not enough information available yet about specific attack vectors for two reasons: those technologies are not yet widely implemented, and it is still too easy to steal cardholder data using traditional software hacking methods such as memory scraping and network sniffing. Therefore, we can only speculate on potential methods of hacking future POS systems.

Hardware P2PE

The idea of Hardware P2PE is to prevent the stealing of sensitive data through software. In response to Hardware P2PE, hackers will probably develop alternative attack vectors—such as hacking the hardware and social engineering—to break the P2PE. For example, the same hardware skimming used today to attack payment terminals could still be applied to future P2PE solutions. The encryption key components can be obtained by either social engineering methods (for instance, from key custodians) or by intercepting the communication between the solution provider and key injection facility.

Mobile Payments

Mobile Payments (payments made using smartphones) are vulnerable because this is relatively new area which is not yet regulated by security standards.

In addition, most smartphones are not protected by antivirus and other security software. Smartphones are consumer-grade devices, so their maintenance cannot be controlled by corporate security policies, and malware can be installed and remain unrevealed for a long time.[24]

EMV

Even though EMV is old technology, it is still new for some countries such as the United States which is still using magnetic stripes. However, even in countries where EMV is already implemented, there are ways to bypass the chip. According to PCI EMV guidelines, "Most EMV cards contain a magnetic stripe, for either backwards compatibility in non-EMV environments, or to support technical fallback if the EMV-enabled chip is unreadable (technical fallback describes an exception process wherein the magnetic stripe, rather than the chip data on an EMV card, is read by an EMV-capable device). In such situations the security mechanisms provided by EMV are effectively bypassed, and the transaction security reverts to that of a magnetic stripe."[25]

Attacks on Integrity and Availability

Although this book is mainly focused on vulnerabilities related to software rather than the payment processing system itself, I think it is important to demonstrate that the payment application is not the only target, and even if it was fully protected from attack via software vulnerabilities (which is virtually impossible), the entire payment system is still imperfect and can be attacked from other directions.

Fake Voice Authorization

This type of attack on system integrity exploits the vulnerability of standard *Force Post* (also known as *Voice Authorization*) feature. Force Post means that a payment transaction can be authorized ("forced") by the merchant even if it was rejected by the payment processor. Normally this type of authorization is obtained via the phone (which is why it is called "Voice Authorization"). When a credit card is rejected after it is swiped at the POS, the cashier may decide to call the telephone number usually located on the back of the card and ask for voice authorization. The bank operator checks the cardholder account and may decide to approve the transaction. In this case, a special authorization code is given to the cashier (usually 6 digits or letters), who manually enters it into the POS. There is a security flaw in this system: usually the voice authorization code is not validated online, thus any combination of digits or letters can be entered.[26, 27]

Forcing Offline Authorization

When a payment processing host or network goes down, most POS systems switch to offline authorization (also called Store and Forward) mode. Payment transactions are authorized locally by the payment application, with no real validation of the cardholder information. Thus, any card swiped at the POS that passes the basic validations (PAN check digit and expiration date) would be accepted for payment. This fact can be used by attackers if they manage to force the network connectivity to go down. For example, if a remote store uses satellite antenna to communicate with the payment network, the attackers cover the antenna receiver with tin foil which disturbs the reception and puts the payment application into Store and Forward mode.[28, 29]

Summary

There are two major payment application attack vectors: POS memory scraping and local network sniffing. PCI security standards lack explicit requirements that would protect these areas. The malware installed on a POS machine can use regular expressions to scan the payment application memory or communication traffic between remote payment application modules. MemoryScraper and NetScraper are sample utilities that demonstrate how to write the code needed to find and collect sensitive card data in memory and on networks. In addition to these two "mainstream" attack vectors, there are many alternative ways to attack POS systems by exploiting vulnerabilities in application code, hardware, or the integrity of payment systems.

Notes

1. *Targeted Hospitality Sector Vulnerabilities*, Visa Data Security Alert (November 2009), `http://usa.visa.com/download/merchants/targeted-hospitality-sector-vulnerabilities-110609.pdf`

2. *Preventing Memory-Parsing Malware Attacks on Grocery Merchants*, Visa Data Security Alert (April 2013), `http://usa.visa.com/download/merchants/alert-prevent-grocer-malware-attacks-04112013.pdf`

3. McAfee Labs, *VSkimmer Botnet Targets Credit Card Payment Terminals*, `https://blogs.mcafee.com/mcafee-labs/vskimmer-botnet-targets-credit-card-payment-terminals/comment-page-1#comment-453678`

4. *Point-of-Sale and memory scrappers* (December 2012), `http://www.xylibox.com/2012/12/point-of-sale-and-memory-scrappers.html`

5. *Dexter Malware Targeting Point-of-Sale (POS) Systems*, Visa Data Security Alert (December 2012), `http://usa.visa.com/download/merchants/alert-dexter-122012.pdf`

6. *Retail Merchants Targeted by Memory-Parsing Malware – UPDATE*, Visa Data Security Alert (August 2013), `http://usa.visa.com/download/merchants/Bulletin__Memory_Parser_Update_082013.pdf`

7. X-Ways Software Technology AG, *WinHex: Computer Forensics & Data Recovery Software, Hex Editor & Disk Editor*, `http://winhex.com/winhex/index-m.html`

8. Microsoft, *Regular Expression Language - Quick Reference*, `http://msdn.microsoft.com/en-us/library/az24scfc.aspx`

9. Swap file may contain sensitive data, Stackexchange, `http://security.stackexchange.com/questions/29350/swap-file-may-contain-sensitive-data`

10. *PCI PA-DSS Requirements and Security Assessment Procedures Version 2.0* (October 2010), Req. 11.1, p. 43, `https://www.pcisecuritystandards.org/documents/pa-dss_v2.pdf`

11. *PCI DSS Requirements and Security Assessment Procedures Version 2.0* (October 2010), Req. 4.1, p. 35, `https://www.pcisecuritystandards.org/documents/pci_dss_v2.pdf`

12. Chris Sanders, *Practical Packet Analysis, Using Wireshark to Solve Real-World Network Problems, 2nd Edition* (San Francisco: No Starch Press, 2011), pp. 17–33,

13. Robert McMillan, "The Little White Box That Can Hack Your Network," *Wired*, (March 2012), `http://www.wired.com/wiredenterprise/2012/03/pwnie/`

14. *Pwn Plug Elite, Pwnie Express*, `http://pwnieexpress.com/products/pwnplug-elite`

15. Wireshark download, `http://www.wireshark.org/download.html`

16. *Malicious Software and Internet Protocol Addresses*, Visa Data Security Alert (April 2009), `http://usa.visa.com/download/merchants/20090401_malware_ip.pdf`

17. *Top Vulnerability - Packet Sniffing*, Visa Data Security Alert (February 2009), `http://usa.visa.com/download/merchants/20090202_packet_sniffing.pdf`

18. H.D. Moore, "Serial Offenders: Widespread Flaws in Serial Port Servers," *Security Street Rapid7* (April 2013), `https://community.rapid7.com/community/metasploit/blog/2013/04/23/serial-offenders-widespread-flaws-in-serial-port-servers`

19. *5 Ways Thieves Steal Credit Card Data*, Bankrate.com, `http://www.bankrate` `.com/finance/credit-cards/5-ways-thieves-steal-credit-` `card-data-1.aspx`

20. Henry Schwarz, *PinPadPwn*, `http://henryschwarz.blogspot.com/2012/07` `/black-hat-usa-2012-versus-atm-and-eft.html`

21. *Don't Get Sucker Pumped*, Krebs on Security (July 2013), `http://` `krebsonsecurity.com/2013/07/dont-get-sucker-pumped/`

22. *Skimming Prevention: Overview of Best Practices for Merchants*, PCI SSC (2009), `https://www.pcisecuritystandards.org/documents/skimming_preven-` `tion_overview_one_sheet.pdf`

23. *Help Protect Cardholder Data from Attacks on PIN Entry Devices*, Visa Security Alert (November 2012), `http://usa.visa.com/download/merchants` `/alert-compromised-PED-reminder.pdf`

24. "Report: Fraud Threat to Mobile Payments to Grow in 2013," *Mobile Payments Today* (December 2012), `http://www.mobilepaymentstoday.com` `/article/205561/Report-fraud-threat-to-mobile-payments-to-` `grow-in-2013`

25. *PCI DSS Applicability in an EMV Environment – A Guidance Document*, PCI Security Standards Council (October 2010), p. 7, `https://www.` `pcisecuritystandards.org/documents/pci_dss_emv.pdf`

26. "New Credit Card Scam Making the Rounds," *The Dealertrack Sales, F&I, and Compliance Blog*, `http://www.dealertracksfi.com/content` `/new-credit-card-scam-making-the-rounds`

27. "What if you get a Card Declined or Pick Up Card message?," *John Mayleben Blog, Michigan Retailers Association* (April 2013), `http://www.retail-` `ers.com/john-mayleben-blog/what_if_you_get_a_card_declined_or_` `pick_up_card_message#.Unrzv_nbOPZ`

28. "'Tin Foil' Fraud Resurfaces at Gas Stations," *ISO & Agent Weekly* (August 29, 2013), p. 5, `http://www.isoandagent.com/media/pdfs/29Aug2013ISOAgent` `.pdf?ET=isoandagent:e17675:`

29. "Station's Satellite Blocked to Steal Gas," *Northwest Times* (October 22, 2012), `http://www.nwitimes.com/news/local/laporte/michigan-city` `/station-s-satellite-blocked-to-steal-gas/article_50980df5-d933-` `5e4c-9721-c287557458e9.html`

Breaking into PCI-protected Areas

And when memory failed and written records were falsified-when that happened, the claim of the Party to have improved the conditions of human life had got to be accepted, because there did not exist, and never again could exist, any standard against which it could be tested.

—George Orwell

Most payment application vendors today sell PA-DSS validated software, and many merchants are PCI DSS compliant. It would be reasonable to assume that vulnerability areas which are protected already by PCI rules are in practice less vulnerable than others. However, even though this is true to a certain extent, it is not the case for all of them and there are security holes in PCI-protected areas.

PCI Areas of Interest

For mostly historical reasons, PCI security standards take care of very specific places where sensitive card data can be intercepted. If you take a look at the detailed review of PCI DSS and PA-DSS requirements provided in Chapter 3, you will be able to easily distinguish those two key zones: *data at rest* and *data in transit*. It is important to note that data-at-rest protection is supported by PCI almost in full, while data in transit protection is very limited and mostly ineffective inside the store or data center. These findings are summarized in Table 6-1.

Table 6-1: Payment Application Protection Provided by PCI

VULNERABILITY AREA	SUB-AREA	MANDATORY PROTECTION	PCI DSS REQUIREMENT
Data in memory		-	
Data at rest	Temporary storage (S&F, TOR, active transaction databases)	●	Requirement 3: Protect stored cardholder data
	Long-term storage (batch, settlement, archive records)	●	Requirement 3: Protect stored cardholder data
	Log files	●	Requirement 3: Protect stored cardholder data
Data in transit	Local communication	-	
	Communication between POI device and POS	-	
	Communication to processors	○	Requirement 4: Encrypt transmission of cardholder data across open, public networks
Application code and configuration	Application code	-	
	Application configuration	-	

● – full protection is required by PCI DSS

○ – only limited protection is required by PCI DSS

- – no particular protection measures required by PCI DSS

Data at Rest: The Mantra of PCI

Data at rest is a security term for information stored on hard drives. To a certain extent, it is the opposite of data in transit, which is information that travels between various devices and computers. And it is also mostly what PCI is after. PCI rules are focused mainly on defense against attacks on data at rest because historically it was one of the two easiest ways to steal cardholder information (another one is "data in transit" which is discussed in the next section).

Before the PCI era, sensitive data was stored on hard disks and backup drives unencrypted, and it was only protected by merchants' network and physical security controls, which were often weak or in many cases missing completely. Since PCI was introduced, payment software vendors started protecting stored information by using cryptography which significantly reduced the possibility of exploiting these kinds of vulnerabilities. However, the level of protection provided by cryptography depends on specific implementation which includes different factors such as encryption algorithm, key length, and key management scheme. Using weak algorithms and poor key management for database and log protection is common practice, even in PA-DSS validated software.

The situation with application configuration is even grimmer: PCI does not require payment software vendors or users to encrypt application configuration, and it is usually stored in clear text and open to uncontrolled modifications. At first glance, this does not seem to be too dangerous since configuration information itself does not contain sensitive cardholder data. However, in the following paragraphs, you will see how the payment application can also be compromised through misconfiguration.

Temporary Storage

Some payment application vendors claim that they do not store sensitive data on POS machines, and as a result their systems are not vulnerable to attacks on data at rest. Such statements can be untrue, even though it is possible that they do not lie, and here is why. Product managers typically think about storage as long-term records of information, such as archive databases, while developers know that there are many occasions when data is stored temporarily. "There is nothing in this world constant, but inconstancy."[1]

The best examples of such temporary storage are S&F (Store and Forward) and TOR (Timeout Reversals) records which can be implemented as either local database tables or simply flat data files. Without entering into discussion about the importance and functional necessity of these two containers (for more details about S&F and TOR, see Chapter 2), just note that they exist in almost any POS payment system. Most important is the fact that despite the famous PCI prohibition of sensitive authentication data storage.

Sensitive authentication data must not be stored after authorization (even if encrypted).[2]

In practice these files still include full Tracks 1 and 2, which makes them very desirable targets for hacking. There is a simple explanation to such a severe "violation" of PCI rules: S&F and TOR records are normally generated when the authorization host is offline, which means no authorization is received, and thus storage of sensitive authentication data is allowed.

> *By prohibiting storage of sensitive authentication data after authorization, the assumption is that the transaction has completed the authorization process and the customer has received the final transaction approval.*[3]

An important characteristic of S&F and TOR implementation is the necessity to perform both encryption and decryption operations at the same machine because those records are encrypted when temporarily stored to hard disk, but must also be decrypted immediately after they are restored so they can be further processed. Therefore, only a symmetric encryption scheme can be utilized. The inability to use hashing or public key cryptography means that the cryptosystem is vulnerable because the decryption key (the same as the encryption key in symmetric algorithms) is always available in the system, even if it is hidden and encrypted, and will be found sooner or later by an attacker.

Additional common security issues with such temporary storage are weak encryption algorithms and poor cryptographic key management, such as lack of key rotation, hard-coded key components, or insecure key storage (these vulnerabilities are discussed in more detail later in this chapter). Poorly designed key management can easily compromise even the strongest encryption algorithm.

That said, the temporary character of S&F and TOR data often leads to them being overlooked during security assessments, and their exploitability level not being adequately protected.

Application Logs

Payment application log files may contain much more interesting information for hackers than you can even imagine. Unlike primary application functions which are supervised by product management, log files and their content are usually controlled by developers who often do not care about security. Developers want to know as much as they can about their application runtime in order to troubleshoot it remotely, and log files containing as much detail as possible are their only way to gather such information. Thus developers may decide (without telling anyone) to write everything to the log files, including card tracks and account numbers. Yes, at best they may encrypt the sensitive data. However, the encryption keys can either be hard-coded or badly managed. If the same key is used for encrypting all the data for a long period of time, the history of the log files may contain enough information for *cryptanalysis*: "the art and science of breaking ciphertext."[4]

Another threat associated with logging is tokens generated using the hash function of the PAN. At first glance, tokens are supposed to be safe by definition and are recommended to replace the actual card account numbers. However, when generated using hashing, they can be relatively easy to crack (more details about vulnerabilities of PAN hash functions are discussed in the next section).

Locating Temporary Storage and Log Files

Both temporary storage and logs are usually present in one of the following forms:

- Databases
- Flat data files
- Text files

Many POS and payment applications store temporary data using commercial *database management systems* such as Microsoft SQL Server, Oracle, Interbase, or MySQL. The fact that one of those systems is installed at the POS machine or store server means that the POS and/or payment application most likely uses this particular database for data storage.

The databases are typically password protected. However, payment applications often use default, well known administrative accounts with default passwords (as shown in Table 6-2) or passwords stored in clear text (either hard-coded or in configuration files).[5, 6]

Table 6-2: Examples of Default Database Accounts and Passwords

DATABASE	LOGIN	PASSWORD
Interbase	SYSDBA	masterkey
Microsoft SQL Server	sa	
Oracle	system/manager	sys/change_on_install
MySQL	root	

The following fragment of a PA configuration file containing the SQL server database connection string is an example of the database password stored in clear text:

```
Server=localhost;Database=Payments;User Id=sa;Password=1d50fAnkesOTSUMW;
```

At first glance, the value of *Password* may look like it is encrypted, but this is just a password in clear text.

Flat data files can be used by custom in-house implementations of database management systems. The data in such files can be stored in binary format when information is encoded using all possible byte values (0–255) rather than just the ASCII codes (32–126) typically used in text files. Flat data files often have .dat file extensions.

POS and payment applications normally use *text file* format for logs so they could be easily read by developers and technical support personnel. They typically have `.log` or `.txt` file extensions.

Hashed PAN

The standard use of hash functions is producing a short digest of a message or file. The hash function is also called *one-way encryption* because it is mathematically impossible to reconstruct the original message from its digest, or more precisely, we "know of no easy way to reverse them."[7] This property of hashing is utilized by payment systems for "encryption" of credit card account numbers without the need to secure the encryption keys (simply because there is no key in most hash implementations). Table 6-3 shows different types of hash functions utilized for PAN encryption. The SHA-256 algorithm is considered safe today, while MD5 is obsolete.

Table 6-3: Examples of PAN Hash Functions

HASH FUNCTION	SIZE	EXAMPLE
PAN in clear text	16	4005554444444403
MD5	32	73bd8d04cc59610c368e4af76e62b3f1
SHA-1	40	f9b5eededb928241974368cbd97c055141813970
SHA-256	64	f85d4630aabe6d0d037ccb0ec0d95429aef6927b1e45a26da62cb-d0bc344f6b4

Brute Forcing and Rainbow Tables

The problem with hashing of credit card numbers is the fact that those numbers are "predictable" in that they consist of digits only and have a fixed length (15–19 digits, but usually 16) predetermined by card brand, with well-known 6-digit prefixes, and the last digit reserved for the Mod 10 checksum which can be validated. More than that, the first six and last four digits are often exposed in clear text, which is allowed by PCI and other standards, so in reality it's only six digits (16 - 6 - 4) that need to be guessed (Table 6-4). These factors provide an ability to conduct a relatively simple *brute-force attack* on credit card numbers.[8]

Table 6-4: Examples of PAN Masking According to PCI Rules

CARD TYPE	MASKED PAN	NUMBER OF DIGITS TO GUESS
Visa	400555******4403	6
MasterCard	557552******7645	6
Amex	379640*****1007	5

A brute-force attack in the case of PAN means going through all possible combinations (10^{16}) of account number digits (or only 10^6 in case the first six and last four digits are known), performing a hash function, and comparing the results with the "encrypted" (hashed) number obtained from the payment application log files or database. *Rainbow tables* can be used to simplify the process.

Rainbow tables are pre-compiled hash results that can be compared dynamically with the hashed PAN without the need to go through all the combinations and conduct hash functions for each permutation. It is possible to reduce the size of a rainbow table (and thus the lookup time) by excluding prefixes that are not used by major payment card brands (such as 0, 7, 8, and 9) and account numbers with invalid Mod 10 check digits. Table 6-5 shows a fragment of a rainbow table calculated for SHA-1 functions of major credit card account numbers. Note that the combinations with invalid Mod 10 are omitted.

Table 6-5: Example of PAN Rainbow Table Fragment

PAN	SHA-1
. . .	. . .
4005554444444395	e690e41f949423016e9346df2b4e7d6eb205c3b6
4005554444444403	f9b5eededb928241974368cbd97c055141813970
4005554444444411	96e8bddce2202451c828d57be33c94ae747f3594
. . .	. . .

Insecure Storage of Encryption Keys

Strong requirements for data-at-rest protection are the most powerful side of the PCI standards, and they are implemented by many software vendors and merchants, mostly through use of symmetric encryption algorithms. More details about symmetric and asymmetric encryption can be found in Chapter 7, but for now just note that there is an important characteristic of symmetric encryption algorithms: the same cryptographic key can be used for both encryption and decryption. With respect to payment applications, this means that if the POS was able to encrypt the data (for example, before dumping it into the temporary storage or log file), there is almost always the possibility of decrypting the data on the same machine, even if the application is not programmed to do so. This is because the encryption key (which is also decryption key!) is present somewhere at that computer.

There are fewer options to hide the keys, which can be stored either in hardware or software. A hardware option is out of scope because it is too expensive (at least in most merchants' opinions) to use cryptographic hardware modules on each POS machine. The software options for key storage usually are:

- Hard drive (data file)
- Registry (on Windows-based machines, of course)
- Hard-coded (in the application binary file)
- Any combination of these options

Given the fact that many software vendors today use strong encryption algorithms, finding the cryptographic keys and using them to decrypt the sensitive data is the easiest and most likely scenario for attack on data at rest compared to others, such as cryptanalysis.

But why don't developers use asymmetric algorithms where the encryption and decryption keys are different and encryption keys cannot be used to decrypt the data? Simply because the payment application usually also needs access to the stored information, like in case of temporary S&F or TOR records, which means it must be able to decrypt the data after reading it from storage.

DEK and KEK

In simple cryptographic implementations, the data is encrypted using an encryption key which is stored in clear text in a file, a Registry, or hard-coded in the application code. In more sophisticated applications, the data is encrypted by *Data Encryption Key* (DEK) which is protected by *Key Encryption Key* (KEK). In this case, the DEK is still stored in one of the "secret" places listed above but it is encrypted using KEK (Figure 6-1). The problem with this approach, which is obviously more secure than encryption with just a single key, is that the KEK still needs to be hidden somewhere, and the choices are really the same as for the DEK: hard-coded, file, or Registry (usually, KEK is hard-coded because it is rarely changed). So the attacker's task—finding the key and decrypting the ciphertext—in general remains the same, it simply requires a bit more time and effort to find the KEK first, then find the encrypted DEK, decrypt it using the KEK, and finally decrypt the ciphertext using decrypted DEK.

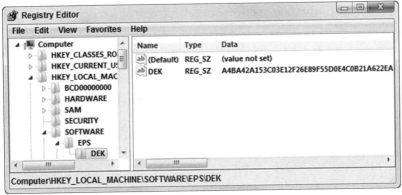

Figure 6-1: Example of encrypted AES 256 DEK "hidden" in Windows Registry

Key Rotation

Key rotation is a security mechanism that was invented to resolve at least two issues:

1. Prevent cryptanalysis. When an attacker has access to a large amount of *ciphertext* (the output of data encryption) which was created using the same encryption key, it is possible in some cases to guess what the key is. When an encryption key is changed (rotated) often, such a task becomes very difficult or even impossible to perform.

2. Minimize the amount of data that can be leaked when a single encryption key is obtained by an attacker. If the keys are rotated often, an attacker must find a way to retrieve the keys on a constant basis in order to steal any significant number of credit card records.

The problem with key rotation is that it is not a simple task to implement, especially to implement it correctly. PCI standards do not contain explicit technological requirements or recommendations for software vendors regarding implementation of automatic key rotation features. The only requirement for key rotation is providing some minimal basic functionality, therefore, many application vendors just provide the merchants with manual instructions on how to change the keys.[9]

Naturally, such merchants never do key rotation because it is infeasible to perform those manual procedures on hundreds or thousands of their POS machines without significant interruption to the business.

In any case, key rotation is a great deterrent control; however, it does not provide ultimate data protection because the symmetric encryption key, even if it is rotated often, still must be present somewhere in the machine and can be retrieved by an attacker.

Default Keys

The problem with using default encryption keys is somewhat related to the issue with key rotation. Many merchants receive payment software from a payment application vendor and install it "as is" using out-of-the-box features and configurations. If the application vendor does not bother to design the automatic key generation and rotation mechanism, it is possible that all their customers' POS machines use the same default encryption keys.

Getting to the Keys

In order to find the keys, an attacker first needs to know where and how they are stored. This information can be obtained either with help of *insiders* or by *reverse engineering*.

Insiders are people who work or used to work for the payment software vendor, integrator, or merchant. They are familiar with the application design and have access to the code and/or documentation. Those current or former employees can abuse their authority and knowledge in order to meet their financial goals, or just for some kind of revenge. Using their knowledge of the system, they may craft malware to retrieve the keys themselves or sell this information to hackers.

Reverse engineering, or *disassembling*, is a process of "decoding the code." Most programming languages used to write the payment application code are either compilers or interpreters. In any case, they create some kind of binary file as the last step of the code-building process. If a compiler creates the machine executable code (examples are C, C++, or Delphi), it is more difficult to disassemble such code to its original representation, which is called *source code*. With modern languages that create *intermediate code* (such as Java or C#), it is much easier to understand the original source unless the binary code is *obfuscated*. In any case, whatever time it takes, reversing the code in order to locate the keys is a feasible task.

CROSS-REFERENCE   See Chapter 9 for more details on code obfuscation.

And finally, we should not forget about the fact that the application has to decrypt the DEK before it can use it for data encryption or decryption. Most payment applications use software encryption which means that all the cryptographic operations are performed in the application memory, so unencrypted DEK must be present in memory and can be captured by the malicious *memory scanning* software installed on a POS machine.

Once the application logic is studied, it is only a matter of time and the programmer's skills to create malware that would be able to retrieve the keys, decrypt the cardholder data stored by payment application, collect it, and send it to the attacker via the Internet, wireless, or even a Bluetooth connection.

DiskScraper Utility

Although encrypting PAN and track data storage is one of the strongest and most famous PCI requirements, it is possible that some records are still sitting out there because somebody forgot to delete them or simply because there is a bug in the POS software. There are several tools—both commercial and open source—available to scan the hard drives for sensitive data. If you run such a tool, you may be surprised that account numbers or even track data that should have been deleted from the PCI DSS compliant machines running PA-DSS validated applications are still there. *DiskScraper* is a sample .NET utility that scans the files which may contain sensitive data (such as .log, .txt, and .dat), and finds the PAN, Track 1, and Track 2 of the payment cards (Figure 6-2). It uses the same search technology—regular expressions—that is also implemented by the MemoryScraper and NetScraper tools that are described in the previous chapter. Run the executable (NetScraper.exe, which along with the source code, is available for download from www.wiley.com/go/hackingpos) on the computer with your favorite POS software. The results of the search will be displayed in the log file (Figure 6-3). And once again, if you are not a programmer and not interested in the code details, skip to the next sections.

Figure 6-2: DiskScraper utility

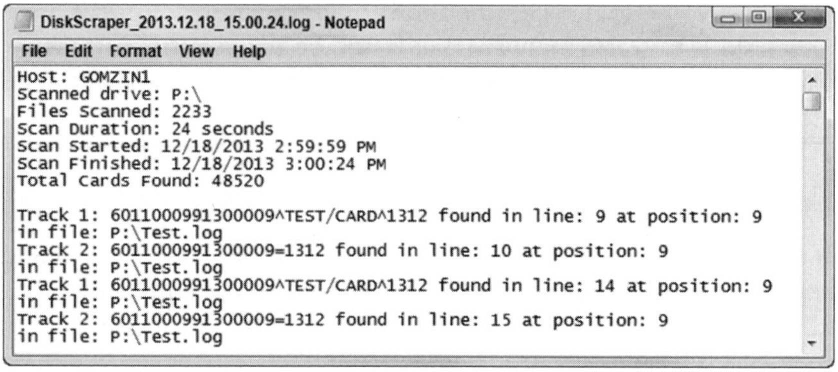

```
DiskScraper_2013.12.18_15.00.24.log - Notepad
File   Edit   Format   View   Help
Host: GOMZIN1
Scanned drive: P:\
Files Scanned: 2233
Scan Duration: 24 seconds
Scan Started: 12/18/2013 2:59:59 PM
Scan Finished: 12/18/2013 3:00:24 PM
Total Cards Found: 48520

Track 1: 6011000991300009^TEST/CARD^1312 found in line: 9 at position: 9
in file: P:\Test.log
Track 2: 6011000991300009=1312 found in line: 10 at position: 9
in file: P:\Test.log
Track 1: 6011000991300009^TEST/CARD^1312 found in line: 14 at position: 9
in file: P:\Test.log
Track 2: 6011000991300009=1312 found in line: 15 at position: 9
in file: P:\Test.log
```

Figure 6-3: DiskScraper search results

Recursive search

When DiskScraper is set up to search all the files on either a single drive or all
the drives, it is using *recursion* which is a simple and elegant method of scanning a tree (a folder tree in our case).

The *recursive function* starts from the root folder and calls itself until it reaches
the "bottom" of the folder tree branch:

```
bool RecursiveScan(DirectoryInfo Directory, bool CountOnly)
{
    …
    IEnumerable<DirectoryInfo> dirs = Directory.EnumerateDirectories();
    foreach (DirectoryInfo dir in dirs)
    {
        if (!RecursiveScan(dir, CountOnly))
            return false;
    }
    …
    return true;
}
```

Then, it scans all the files in that folder and "automatically" moves to the
next branch:

```
IEnumerable<FileInfo> files = Directory.EnumerateFiles();
foreach (FileInfo file in files)
    if (!ProcessFile(file, CountOnly))
        return false;
```

Eventually, it passes all the folder branches and scans all the files.

Text vs. Binary Files

There are two major types of files with different structures: text and binary. Text files consist of lines of ASCII or Unicode characters. The text lines are separated by carriage return (0x0D) and new line (0x0A) ASCII characters. The binary files are arrays of bytes which may have any value. Depending on the file types, there are different ways to open the file and iterate through its content.

The text files can be read using .NET `StreamReader` (`TextFileSearch` class),

```
StreamReader sr = new StreamReader(fName);
```

and then simply scanned line by line:

```
while (sr.Peek() >= 0)
{
  input = sr.ReadLine();
  LineNumber++;
  searchLine.Search(input, LineNumber.ToString(), fName, ref res);
}
```

The binary files should be opened by .NET `FileStream` and `BinaryReader` (`BinaryFileSearch` class):

```
using (FileStream fs = new FileStream(
    fName, FileMode.Open, FileAccess.Read, FileShare.ReadWrite))
{
    using (BinaryReader br = new BinaryReader(fs, new ASCIIEncoding()))
    {
    ...
    }
}
```

They should be read in chunks since they can be too large to load as a single block. The chunk size is set to 4,096 (4 KB) by default but it can be any size depending on desirable performance:

```
chunk = br.ReadBytes(CHUNK_SIZE);
while (chunk.Length > 0)
{
    string ASCIItext = Encoding.ASCII.GetString(chunk);
    string Unicodetext = Encoding.Unicode.GetString(chunk);
    searchLine.Search(ASCIItext, position.ToString(), fName, ref res);
    searchLine.Search(Unicodetext, position.ToString(), fName, ref res);
    chunk = br.ReadBytes(CHUNK_SIZE);
    position += CHUNK_SIZE;
}
```

DiskScraper uses the same code (located in `HackingPOS.Scrapers.Common`) as MemoryScraper and NetScraper for finding the card account numbers and tracks.

Data in Transit: What is Covered by PCI?

In the requirements related to communication protection, PCI standards distinguish between different types of networks: "open, public" and any other network.

"Encrypt transmission of cardholder data across open, public networks."[10]

The problem with such a distinction is that non-"open, public" networks, which include in-store LAN, corporate WAN, and frame relay between merchant and processor, play significant roles in the functionality of payment applications. Moreover, payment applications mostly use those types of networks for sensitive data transmission (Table 6-6).

Table 6-6: Network Protection Requirements

NETWORK TYPE	ENCRYPTION REQUIRED BY PCI?	TYPICALLY USED FOR SENSITIVE DATA TRANSMISSION
Internet	Yes	Between POS and payment gateway/processor
Wireless	Yes	Between POS and store; Server between POS and payment gateway/processor
LAN	No	Between POS and store server; Between POS and payment gateway/processor; Between modules of payment application
WAN	No	Between POS and payment gateway/processor; Between store server and corporate headquarters

With that said, even a simple analysis of PCI DSS requirements makes most "PCI compliant" payment applications vulnerable for basic network-sniffing attacks, which are described in Chapter 5. However, even PCI-protected "open, public" networks are still vulnerable to more sophisticated attacks.

SSL Vulnerabilities

Secure Socket Layer (SSL) is a very popular and established protocol used for protecting data in transit, and payment applications are no exception. However, SSL is not unbreakable and it may have flaws, especially when it is not properly configured.[11]

CROSS-REFERENCE   More details about SSL implementation can be found in Chapter 8.

Outdated Versions of SSL/TLS

SSL went through several modifications since it was first invented by Netscape in 1995.[12] The last version of SSL was 3.0 and since then it has been continued under the name TLS (*Transport Layer Security*) protocol. If a payment application does not use the latest and greatest version of TLS (1.2 at the time of this publication), it is most probably vulnerable to attacks because each version of SSL and TLS included security patches.[13]

Weak Cipher Suits

One of the features of SSL is the ability to negotiate the type and level of encryption between client and server. On the one hand this feature is beneficial because it allows different types of clients and servers to communicate with each other. On the other hand, this feature may allow an attacker to *downgrade* the level of encryption and tamper with a communication that is supposed to be secure.[14]

Man-in-the-Middle

Man-in-the-Middle (MITM) is one of the most famous type of attacks. It allows an attacker to seamlessly tap on-network traffic between unsuspecting clients and servers and steal sensitive payment card data. The client configuration can be manipulated so it establishes communication with the bogus server through a different host address and a server certificate that is valid for that address. If the client does not validate the host URL and the issuer of the *server certificate*, then it assumes it is talking to the legitimate server.

Another possible scenario of a MITM attack is inserting a bogus *proxy* (an intermediary that transmits requests and responses between clients and servers) which intercepts the network traffic between the legitimate client and the server using a fake server certificate as shown on Figure 6-4. The bogus proxy establishes communication with the legitimate server and pretends to be a legitimate client. This can be made possible by several conditions, including:

1. An attacker manages to access the public or proprietary *Certificate Authority* (CA), which issued an original server certificate, and issue a fake certificate on behalf of the legitimate issuer.[15] Some merchants and processors may use "homemade" certificates issued on-premises by a proprietary CA that lacks proper security controls.

2. An attacker "plants" its server certificate into the client's certificate repository as a legitimate certificate. The client assumes that the server certificate is valid and enables communication with the bogus proxy.[16]

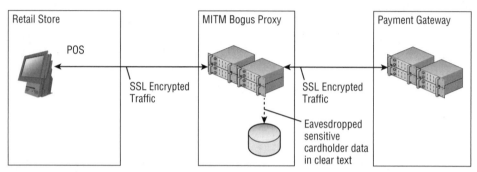

Figure 6-4: Man-in-the-Middle Attack

Summary

PCI Security Standards protect only limited, relatively small areas of payment applications and are mostly focused on data at rest, which includes temporary storage of S&F and TOR data on hard drives, log files, and more. Even though all the sensitive data stored on hard drives must be encrypted according to PCI requirements, payment applications use software encryption with weak key management implementations which are often vulnerable to simple attacks. Encryption keys are "hidden" inside the application code (hard-coded), Windows Registry, or data files, and can be easily located and used to decrypt the sensitive cardholder information.

PCI also protects very limited amounts of sensitive data in transit, which is transmitted only through "open, public networks" such as wireless LAN and Internet. PCI compliant payment applications are not required to encrypt data traffic on store LAN, corporate WAN, or frame relay links to payment processors. Even though the traffic is encrypted on wireless networks and the

Internet, vulnerabilities of security protocols such as SSL can be exploited in order to tap on-network communications and steal sensitive cardholder information.

Notes

1. Jonathan Swift, "A Critical Essay upon the Faculties of the Mind," *The Works of the Rev. Jonathan Swift, D.D. Dean of St. Patrick's, Dublin with Notes, Historical and Critical, Vol. 2*, Arranged by Thomas Sheridan, A.M., (London, 1808), p. 460.

2. PCI DSS Requirements and Security Assessment Procedures Version 2.0, PCI SSC, (October 2010), Req. 3.2, 3.2.1, p. 29, `https://www.pcisecuritystandards.org/documents/pci_dss_v2.pdf`

3. PCI PA-DSS Requirements and Security Assessment Procedures Version 2.0, PCI SSC, (October 2010), Req. 1.1, 1.1.1, pp. 17–18, `https://www.pcisecuritystandards.org/documents/pa-dss_v2.pdf`

4. Bruce Schneier, *Applied Cryptography, Second Edition: Protocols, Algorithms, and Source Code in C*, (Hoboken, NJ: Wiley, 1996), p. 13.

5. Default Passwords, CIRT.net, `http://www.cirt.net/passwords`

6. Default Password Database, Virus.org, `http://www.virus.org/default_passwds`

7. Bruce Schneier, *Applied Cryptography, Second Edition: Protocols, Algorithms, and Source Code in C*, (Hoboken, NJ: Wiley 1996), p. 35.

8. "Hashing Credit Card Numbers: Unsafe Application Practices" (2007), `http://www.integrigy.com/files/Integrigy_Hashing_Credit_Card_Numbers_Unsafe_Practices.pdf`

9. "PCI PA-DSS Requirements and Security Assessment Procedures Version 2.0, PCI SSC" (October 2010). Req. 2.3, pp. 24–26, `https://www.pcisecuritystandards.org/documents/pa-dss_v2.pdf`

10. "PCI DSS Requirements and Security Assessment Procedures Version 2.0, PCI SSC" (October 2010), Req. 4, p.35, `https://www.pcisecuritystandards.org/documents/pci_dss_v2.pdf`

11. David Wagner and Bruce Schneier, "Analysis of the SSL 3.0 protocol," `https://www.schneier.com/paper-ssl.pdf`

12. "The SSL Protocol, Netscape" (1996), `http://web.archive.org/web/19970614020952/http://home.netscape.com/newsref/std/SSL.html`

13. TLS/SSL hardening and compatibility Report 2011, *G-Sec*, `http://www.g-sec.lu/sslharden/SSL_comp_report2011.pdf`

14. WeakCipherSuites: Testing for weak cipher suites, *Sslyze*, (March 2012), `https://code.google.com/p/sslyze/wiki/WeakCipherSuites`

15. "Comodo Fraud Incident, Comodo" (March 2011), `http://www.comodo.com/Comodo-Fraud-Incident-2011-03-23.html`

16. Steven J. Vaughan-Nichols, "How the NSA, and your boss, can intercept and break SSL," *ZDNet*, (June 2003), `http://www.zdnet.com/how-the-nsa-and-your-boss-can-intercept-and-break-ssl-7000016573/`

Part

III

Defense

A general is a man who takes chances. Mostly he takes fifty-fifty chances; if he happens to win three times in succession he is considered a great general.

—Enrico Fermi

In This Part

Cryptography in Payment Applications

All problems are finally scientific problems.
—George Bernard Shaw

Wherever there is information that needs to be protected, there lurks a need for cryptography. Not just a pure cryptography but rather its proper application. In the case of POS applications, there is the presence of sensitive cardholder data that must be hidden from prying eyes during the entire payment-processing cycle. There are remarkable books already written about cryptography.[1] The goal of this chapter is not another explanation of underlying math or algorithm implementations, but cryptography applied to the payment application security through specific methods and implementations. In order to understand what protection mechanisms are available, whether they are appropriate in particular situations, and how to implement them correctly, we still need a bit of theory.

The Tip of the Iceberg

Modern payment applications already use cryptography in many cases; however, they are not always used in the most secure way. Many developers are already familiar with the principle of using well known encryption algorithm implementations rather than trying to create new, unproven, "in-house" code.

The problem is that cryptography is not limited to just an algorithm implementation library, which is only the tip of the iceberg. There is the whole issue of key management, which surrounds any type of encryption and requires appropriate attention when designing the payment application. Adding symmetric keys or public-private-key certificates into the code and forgetting about them isn't the best approach. You must answer several questions, such as: How do you protect those keys? How do you rotate them? How do you generate and deploy a new key (and destroy the old one) if the existing key has been compromised or expired?

While assessing the level of payment application protection, auditors or curious users often ask: "What type of encryption does it use?" Here is an example of a common answer to such a question: "AES"—or perhaps "AES 256" to provide more confidence. Both answers definitely carry some information about the encryption being used, but they still leave many questions, such as: What is the implementation of the algorithm? What is the key management scheme? How is the key generated and protected? How is the key rotated and destroyed? Who has access to the keys or key components? Do you trust those people, applications, and organizations? Obviously there are a lot of questions that must be answered in order to understand the complete real picture.

Symmetric, Asymmetric, or One-way?

The name of the algorithm is usually the first (and in many cases, the only) characteristic of the entire encryption system that is being advertised by the payment application developers. Although the name does not tell much about the details of implementation and key management, at least it identifies the basic behavior of the system along with some potential weaknesses.

There are three major groups of cryptographic functions: *symmetric*, *asymmetric*, and *one-way* encryption (see Table 7-1). Each group is based on different math concepts and is intended for use in different tasks. Another important difference that should be taken into account when selecting the encryption type is the relationship between encryption and decryption keys. In a nutshell, the symmetric key is the same for both encryption and decryption, asymmetric algorithms use different encryption and decryption keys, and a one-way cryptographic hash function has no keys at all (although there are some exceptions). Such diversity in key management mainly dictates the areas of practical application.

Table 7-1: Summary of Differences between Symmetric, Asymmetric, and One-way Encryption

	SYMMETRIC	ASYMMETRIC	ONE-WAY HASH
Keys	The same key for both encryption and decryption	Two different keys: one for encryption and another one decryption	No keys
Decryption	The ciphertext can be decrypted using the same key that was used for encryption	A different key is required in order to decrypt the ciphertext	It is impossible to reverse (decrypt) the one-way hashed data
Performance	High	Low	High
Data Encryption Use Case	❖ Temporary data storage (S&F) ❖ Settlement records ❖ Long-term transaction records ❖ Communication -payload encryption ❖ Software P2PE	❖ Software P2PE	❖ Password encryption ❖ Tokenization
Used as Part of the Cryptosystem	❖ Hardware P2PE ❖ SSL	❖ Digital data signing ❖ Code signing ❖ Client authentication ❖ SSL	❖ Digital data signing ❖ Code signing ❖ SSL
Examples of Algorithms	AES, TDES	RSA	SHA
Acceptable Key/ Digest Length (bits)	AES: 128 TDES: 112 (double-length key)	RSA: 1024	SHA: 160
Recommended Key/Digest Length (bits)	AES: 256 TDES: 168 (triple-length key)	RSA: 2048	SHA: 256

As shown in Table 7-1, symmetric encryption is the most useful type of cryptographic algorithm for data encryption in payment applications. However, all types of encryption are usually involved to some degree in POS software.

Does Size Matter?

As mentioned in the beginning of this chapter, the standard answer to the question about encryption is the name of the encryption algorithm, like "AES." If you are lucky, you can get more information in the form of a 3–4 digit suffix, like "AES-256." Those numbers are the length of the key, in bits. For some algorithms there are "fixed" key lengths linked to their names. For example, Triple DES usually means the key length of 112 bits. "Usually" because there are different flavors of Triple DES: *2TDEA* and *3TDEA*. 2TDEA stands for "Triple DES with double-length key" which means that the key size is 112 bits (the original DES key length is 56 so double-length is 2 × 56 = 112). 3TDEA stands for "Triple DES with triple-length key" which means that the key size is 3 × 56 = 168 bit. The general rule for all the encryption algorithms is "the bigger the better." This is because the simplest way to attack the encryption is a brute-force attack, which goes through all possible combinations of the bits in the key until the right key is found. With data processing capabilities of modern computers, it is possible to brute-force several dozen bits. For example, DES with a 56-bit key (2^{56} possible combinations) can be cracked in less than a day.[2] However, adding more bits to the key will exponentially increase the time required for cracking (see Figure 7-1). That's why 2TDEA with a 112-bit key (2^{112}) is still secure (but not for a very long time as according to Moor's law, computing power doubles every two years[3]).

Asymmetric algorithms have different scales of security related to the key size compared to symmetric encryption. For example, a 1,024-bit RSA key is equivalent to an 80-bit symmetric key.[4]

One-way hash functions, in most cases, do not have the key, so their strength is determined by the length of the digest they produce. For example, SHA-256, which is considered best practice today, would produce a 256-bit result.

Key Entropy

In simple words without math, *entropy* means the predictability of the key value. When generating new keys or key components, it is important to use functions that produce random results. Most cryptographic libraries provide random generators that take some natural events, such as user input and system clock, as initial entropy. For example, .NET `System.Security.Cryptography` contains the

`RandomNumberGenerator` class, which can be used to generate random numbers for key components, keys, or initialization vectors (the next section, "Symmetric Encryption," contains more details on this).

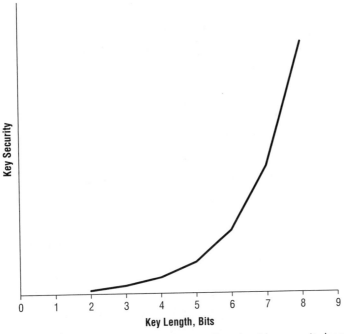

Figure 7-1: Exponential increase of encryption algorithm security by adding extra key bits

Key Stretching

The *key stretching* technique allows you to increase the size and entropy—and as a result—the security of the encryption key that can be derived from regular user input such as password or passphrase.[5] The problem with user-defined passwords or passphrases is that they can be guessed relatively easily using a dictionary and/or brute-force attack. In order to solve this problem, the key stretching algorithms perform multiple passes of transformations (such as hash functions) with the input data, which eventually creates an encryption key with suitable size and level of security. The `Rfc2898DeriveBytes` class in .NET `System.Security.Cryptography` is one example of implementing key stretching according to the rules defined in the *PKCS #5* standard.[6] `Rfc2898DeriveBytes` is used for key generation in the `EncryptionDemo` application, which is described in the following sections.

Symmetric Encryption

It was named "symmetric" because it uses the same key for encryption and decryption (Figure 7-2).

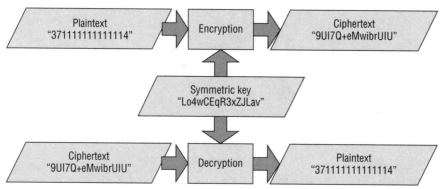

Figure 7-2: Symmetric encryption

This feature is good and bad at the same time. On the one hand, it simplifies the key management—two sides (for example, POS application and payment gateway server) share the same key, so one side can encrypt the message and another side can decrypt it, both using the same key. On the other hand, if one side is compromised, the attacker has the key, which can be used to decrypt the data stored on both sides. Therefore, there are specific cases where it is safe to use symmetric encryption:

1. Both encryption and decryption sides are located on the same machine. In this case, it does not make sense to use asymmetric encryption (the next section explains the details of this) because the decryption key will be accessible anyway if the application is compromised. That's one of the reasons why most payment applications use symmetric algorithms for temporary local data storage.

2. The key is stored in hardware and cannot be retrieved even if the hosting computer is compromised. This is the case for P2PE (see Chapter 8 for more information about P2PE).

3. The keys are often changed ("rotated"). If a new data encryption key is generated for each communication session (like in SSL) or each transaction (like in DUKPT), then even if a single key is compromised it does not compromise the previous or further sessions/transactions, and does not provide the ability to access a large amount of data.

Another important benefit of symmetric encryption is high performance. Symmetric algorithms use simpler math compared to asymmetric ones, therefore, their implementation code requires less CPU cycles and works much faster.

Strong Algorithms

There are many symmetric encryption algorithms that are commonly used both as standalone implementation for data protection, and as an integral part of cryptographic solutions such as digital signatures or SSL. AES (Advanced Encryption Standard) and TDES (Triple Data Encryption Standard) are widely used in payment applications. Triple-DES, along with the DUKPT key management scheme, have a long and well proven track record of being a part of debit PIN encryption technology, while AES is recommended by the NSA (National Security Agency) for encryption of classified information.[7]

EncryptionDemo

The `EncryptionDemo` application (shown in Figure 7-3) demonstrates all three types of encryption—symmetric, asymmetric, and one-way, which are implemented in separate assembly— `HackingPOS.Cryptography.Encryption.dll`—and can be reused by other applications. These binary files can be downloaded from the Wiley website at `www.wiley.com/go/hackingpos` and tested without the need to compile the source code (which is also available for download).

Figure 7-3: EncryptionDemo application: Symmetric encryption

Implementing Symmetric Encryption

Many years ago programmers had to write cryptographic code whenever they needed to encrypt data in their applications. Implementing encryption in modern development environments is a relatively trivial task because there are cryptographic libraries supporting most common algorithms and basic key management functions. However, encryption implementation suitable for payment application is not coming "out of the box" and there are some manipulations with the code that are still required in order to get the robust solution.

Generating the Key

In an `EncryptionDemo` application, the symmetric key is not stored anywhere but is reconstructed dynamically in memory each time it is needed for encryption or decryption. Three key components are used as an input of *deterministic generator* (`Rfc2898DeriveBytes` class):

1. First, the `generateKey` method creates the value of the `Rfc2898DeriveBytes` *salt* parameter from *KeyComponent1*:

   ```
   Random random = new Random(keyComponent1.GetHashCode());
   byte[] salt = new byte[16];
   random.NextBytes(salt);
   ```

2. Then, it creates the value of the `Rfc2898DeriveBytes` *password* parameter from *KeyComponent2* and hard-coded *KeyComponent3*:

   ```
   SHA256 sha256 = SHA256.Create();
   byte[] password = sha256.ComputeHash(
       Encoding.ASCII.GetBytes(keyComponent2 + keyComponent3));
   ```

3. Finally, the instance of the `Rfc2898DeriveBytes` class "generates" the key:

   ```
   Rfc2898DeriveBytes keyGenerator = new Rfc2898DeriveBytes(
       password, salt, ITERATIONS);
   return keyGenerator.GetBytes(KEY_SIZE);
   ```

These three key components can be used to spread out information about the key among different media; for example, component 1 can be hard-coded in the application, component 2 can be written to a file on the hard drive, and component 3 can be stored in the Registry. The attacker will have to have access permissions to all three areas—the application code, the file system, and the Registry—in order to re-create the key.

Another method often used in encryption systems is that the application prompts the user to enter the password and use it as one of the key components. This approach has limited application because the user can forget the password, needs to enter the password for each session, or simply may be unavailable in the case of an unattended standalone service application.

Blocks, Padding, and Initialization Vectors

The *block ciphers* are used when the length of the *plaintext* (the data in clear text to be encrypted) is greater than the key size. The plaintext is then divided into blocks and a cryptographic operation is performed on each block until the entire data stream is encrypted (or decrypted). There are several blocking modes that are different in the way the previous block is connected to the next one. The *CBC* (Cipher Block Chaining) mode connects the block with the previous one by performing the XOR (exclusive OR) operation between the current plaintext block and the previous ciphertext block:

```
provider.Mode = CipherMode.CBC;
```

The *padding* is required when the size of the plaintext is different from the block size (for example, when encrypting the last block of the data stream). *PKCS #7* padding strings consist of a sequence of bytes, each of which is equal to the total number of padding bytes added:[8]

```
provider.Padding = PaddingMode.PKCS7;
```

Initialization Vector (IV) is required for block ciphers in order to provide an input for the first block of plaintext. The IV should be randomly generated:

```
byte[] IV_seed = new byte[IV_SEED_SIZE];
RandomNumberGenerator IVGenerator = RandomNumberGenerator.Create();
IVGenerator.GetNonZeroBytes(IV_seed);
```

The IV seed is added to the output ciphertext stream:

```
result = new byte[IV_SEED_SIZE + ciphertext.Length];
Buffer.BlockCopy(IV_seed, 0, result, 0, IV_SEED_SIZE);
Buffer.BlockCopy(
    ciphertext, 0, result, IV_SEED_SIZE, ciphertext.Length);
```

It can now be read by the decryption function in order to initialize the first block during decryption operation:

```
byte[] IV_seed = new byte[IV_SEED_SIZE];
Buffer.BlockCopy(Ciphertext, 0, IV_seed, 0, IV_SEED_SIZE);
```

Encryption and Decryption

Several streaming classes are involved in the encryption process:

```
using (ICryptoTransform encryptor = provider.CreateEncryptor(
    provider.Key, provider.IV))
```

```
using (MemoryStream memStream = new MemoryStream())
    using (CryptoStream encryptStream = new CryptoStream(
        memStream, encryptor, CryptoStreamMode.Write))
    {
        using (StreamWriter streamWriter = new StreamWriter(
            encryptStream))
            streamWriter.Write(Plaintext);
        byte[] ciphertext = memStream.ToArray();
    }
```

Since this is a symmetric cipher, the code of decryption is similar to one for encryption, they just work in opposite directions:

```
using (ICryptoTransform decryptor = provider.CreateDecryptor(
    provider.Key, provider.IV))
    using (MemoryStream memStream = new MemoryStream(
        actual_ciphertext, 0, actual_ciphertext_length))
        using (CryptoStream decryptStream = new CryptoStream(
            memStream, decryptor, CryptoStreamMode.Read))
            using (StreamReader streamReader = new StreamReader(
                decryptStream))
                result = streamReader.ReadToEnd();
```

Asymmetric Encryption

Asymmetric encryption, which is also called *public-key encryption,* is named so because it uses different keys for encryption and decryption (Figure 7-4).

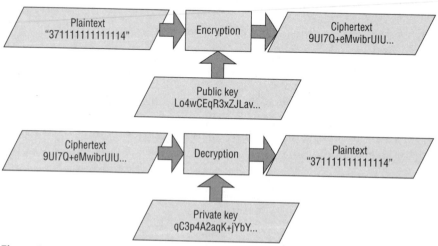

Figure 7-4: Asymmetric (public-key) encryption

The same key cannot be used for both encryption and decryption operations. Asymmetric encryption is one of the greatest inventions in cryptography because for the first time it allows you to encrypt information without fear of disclosure even if the encryption side (encryption key) is compromised. Furthermore, the encryption key can be exposed to everyone (that's why it is called *public key*) so anyone can send the encrypted data to the sender who owns the decryption key (*private key*). These features of asymmetric encryption are used in *Public Key Infrastructure* (PKI) which is, along with SSL protocol, essential for Internet security. In *digital signature* implementations, the asymmetric algorithm works in the opposite direction—the sender encrypts the data using her private key (the digest of the message), while the recipients validate the signature using the public key of the sender.

Implementing Public-key Encryption

In some relatively rare cases, instead of implicit usage—such as client and server certificates, SSL, or digital signatures—payment application developers may need to implement the public-key encryption directly; for example, as a data encryption mechanism for P2PE solution. The `EncryptionDemo` application has a tab for asymmetric encryption which demonstrates the work with the RSA algorithm and asymmetric keys stored as *certificates* (Figure 7-5).

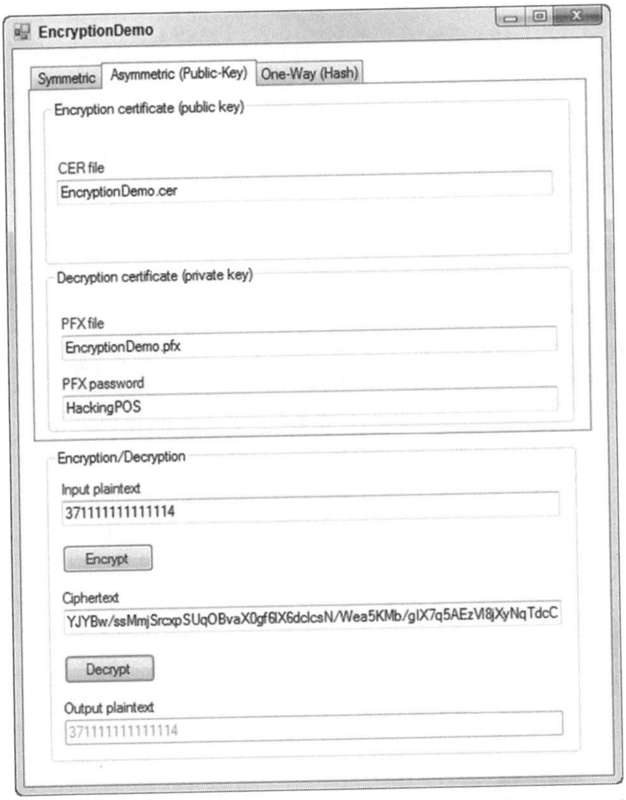

Figure 7-5: EncryptionDemo: Asymmetric (Public-key) encryption

Generating the Keys

Usually, the payment application does not generate the asymmetric keys, but rather receives them in the form of *key container*, or *digital certificate*. An *X.509 certificate* is one of the industry standards for a digital certificate format.[9] Certificates may contain only public keys, or both public and private keys, depending on the function defined for a particular certificate and application. For example, if a POS application implements P2PE encryption, it will have a certificate with a public key only, while the private key will be located only on the P2PE server side.

Self-signed Certificate

`MakeCert.exe` is a certificate creation tool included in the Microsoft .NET Framework SDK (versions 1.1 and later) and in the Microsoft Windows SDK.[10] `MakeCert` can be used to generate a basic self-signed certificate (`.cer` file) which is sufficient for a basic demo application. The private key is created in a separate `.pvk` file:

```
makecert.exe EncryptionDemoCert.cer
-r -a sha256 -len 2048 -n "CN= EncryptionDemo"
-b 01/01/2013 -e 01/01/2023 -sv EncryptionDemo.pvk -sky exchange
```

Table 7-2 contains the list of `MakeCert` parameters and values which were used to generate the self-signed certificate and private key for the `EncryptionDemo` application. `MakeCert` also prompts for the password in order to generate and protect the secret private key, which it stores in the `.pvk` file. As a result of this command execution, `EncryptionDemo.cer` and `EncryptionDemo.pvk` files are created.

Table 7-2: MakeCert Parameters for Generating the Self-signed Certificate and Private Key

PARAMETER	VALUE	DESCRIPTION
N/A	EncryptionDemo.cer	Location and name of the certificate (public-key) file that is being generated
-r	N/A	Create a self-signed certificate
-a	sha256	Use SHA-256 as signature hash algorithm
-len	2048	Create 2,048-bit RSA key (the default length is 1,024 bits)
-n	"CN= EncryptionDemo"	Certificate name

Continues

Table 7-2 (*continued*)

PARAMETER	VALUE	DESCRIPTION
-b	01/01/2013	Validity starting date
-e	01/01/2023	Validity expiration date
-sv	EncryptionDemo.pvk	Location and name of the private-key file that is being generated
-sky	exchange	Set key type for encryption/decryption

PFX Certificate File

After certificate and private-key files are created, the `Pvk2Pfx.exe` tool[11] is used to combine the public and the private keys in a single universal key container—the *PFX (Personal Information Exchange) certificate file*—which can be provided as input for both encryption and decryption procedures:

```
pvk2pfx -pvk EncryptionDemo.pvk -spc EncryptionDemo.cer
-pfx EncryptionDemo.pfx -pi HackingPOS
```

As a result of this command, an `EncryptionDemo.pfx` file is created. Table 7-3 contains the list of `Pvk2pfx` parameters and values that were used to create the single-file certificate in PFX format.

Table 7-3: Pvk2pfx Parameters for Creating Single-file Certificate in PFX Format

PARAMETER	VALUE	DESCRIPTION
-pvk	EncryptionDemo. pvk	Location and name of the input private-key file
-spc	EncryptionDemo.cer	Location and name of the input certificate (public-key) file
-pfx	EncryptionDemo.pfx	Location and name of the output PFX certificate file
-pi	HackingPOS	Password for private key (prompted during previous MakeCert session)

The `Pvk2pfx` tool is part of the Windows SDK and is located in the `bin\x86` folder (Win32) or `bin\x64` folder (Win64).

In order to just run the `EncryptionDemo` application and test asymmetric encryption, it is not necessary to generate a new certificate because the `EncryptionDemo` application comes with pre-generated test certificate files (`EncryptionDemo.cer` and `EncryptionDemo.pfx`), which can be downloaded along with all the binary files from the Wiley website.

When the client and server are remote, `MakeCert` and `Pvk2pfx` tools can be used to create various certificates for client and server authentication.[12] More sophisticated scenarios of SSL encryption, client authentication, and digital signing are described in Chapters 8 and 9.

Encryption

After the keys are generated and packed into the certificate files using appropriate formats, the encryption and decryption code itself (`AsymmetricEncryption` class) is not too complicated. As discussed before, the main advantage of asymmetric encryption is having different keys for encryption and decryption. In order to encrypt, only the public key component is required. The `X509Certificate2` class is used to load and parse the public key from the `EncryptionDemo.cer` certificate file:

```
X509Certificate2 certificate = new X509Certificate2(CERName);
```

The instance of the `RSACryptoServiceProvider` class encrypts the plaintext when it is initialized with the public key loaded from the certificate:

```
using (RSACryptoServiceProvider RSA = (RSACryptoServiceProvider)
    certificate.PublicKey.Key)
{
    encryptedData = RSA.Encrypt(PlainText, false);
    return encryptedData;
}
```

Decryption

In order to decrypt the ciphertext that was encrypted with the public key, the instance of the `X509Certificate2` class loads and parses the PFX certificate file. The second argument that should be provided when constructing the instance of `X509Certificate2` class is the password for the private key, which was prompted when generating the PVK file by the `MakeCert` command:

```
X509Certificate2 certificate = new X509Certificate2(PFXName, Password);
```

The instance of `RSACryptoServiceProvider` class decrypts the ciphertext when it is initialized with the private key:

```
using (RSACryptoServiceProvider RSA = (RSACryptoServiceProvider)
    certificate.PrivateKey)
{
    plaintext = RSA.Decrypt(Ciphertext, false);
    return plaintext;
}
```

One-way Encryption

One-way encryption, which is also called *hash function*, according to its name works in only one way: it can encrypt the message without providing the ability to decrypt it (Figure 7-6).

Figure 7-6: One-way encryption (hash function)

Hash function guarantees that it creates a unique result (*digest*) for each unique data input. (In practice, however, there is a very small probability of *collision*, which is when two different data inputs produce the same hash.) One of the important features of hash function is the fact that no key is required for encryption. This feature has both advantages and disadvantages. On the one hand, it is very convenient to implement encryption that does not require any key management. On the other hand, hash function, when used without any additional security measures, can be easily broken by using brute-force attacks or rainbow tables (see Chapter 6 for more details). Thus, hash functions are secure only if they are implemented with extra protection mechanisms such as *salt*.

There are two major areas of direct hash function applicability in payment systems: Tokenization and password encryption. In addition, hashing is an essential component of digital signatures and public key infrastructure.

Implementing One-way Encryption

The EncryptionDemo application has another tab for one-way encryption, which shows how to work with the SHA-256 hash algorithm (Figure 7-7).

Hashing implementation can be extremely simple and done by a couple of lines of code when using a cryptographic library (.NET `System.Security .Cryptography`):

```
SHA256 sha256 = SHA256.Create();
byte[] hash_result = sha256.ComputeHash(pan_bytes);
```

However, as discussed in Chapter 6, using just a straightforward hash function can be dangerous due to exposure to rainbow table and brute-forcing attacks. Thus, salt should be added in order to prevent, or at least to reduce the possibility of such attacks. The `EncryptionDemo` has an example of salt constructed from three parts:

1. **Constant component**—hard-coded in the application

2. **User-defined component**—can vary per customer and can be stored in an application configuration file

3. **Variable component:**

   ■ For tokens—can be taken from the user input that is not included in the data being hashed; for example, expiration date and CVV (which is present on both Track 1 and Track 2 and not supposed to be stored after the transaction is done)

   ■ For passwords—a unique value randomly generated for each function call

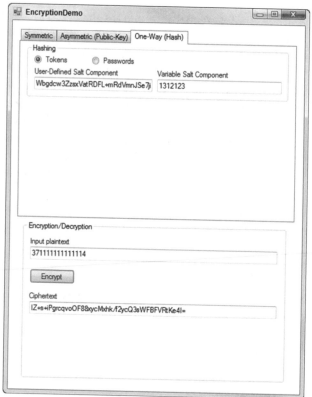

Figure 7-7: EncryptionDemo: One-way Encryption (Hash)

Salting Tokens

Hash functions are often used to create a *token*—a unique ID that represents the payment card throughout the merchant's payment and enterprise systems, without exposure of actual sensitive cardholder information. Such a token is usually created by applying one of the hash algorithms to the PAN value, because PAN is present in both Track 1 and Track 2 and can always uniquely identify the card.

The `Random` class is used in order to stretch the `VariableSaltComponent`, which can be too small to be a good input for the `saltGenerator`, via its hash code:

```
Random random = new Random(VariableSaltComponent.GetHashCode());
byte[] variable_salt_bytes = new byte[SALT_SIZE];
random.NextBytes(variable_salt_bytes);
```

The `hash` method dynamically constructs the salt from three components: `CONSTANT_SALT_COMPONENT`, `user_defined_salt_component`, and `VariableSaltComponent`, which are mixed together using the `Rfc2898DeriveBytes` class:

```
Rfc2898DeriveBytes saltGenerator = new Rfc2898DeriveBytes(
    Encoding.ASCII.GetBytes(
    CONSTANT_SALT_COMPONENT + user_defined_salt_component),
    variable_salt_component,    ITERATIONS);
salt_bytes = saltGenerator.GetBytes(SALT_SIZE);
```

Once the salt is constructed from the three components, it is combined with the input plaintext in a single buffer to form the input for the final hash function (Figure 7-8):

```
byte[] plaintext_bytes = new byte[SALT_SIZE + pan_bytes.Length];
Buffer.BlockCopy(salt_bytes, 0, plaintext_bytes, 0, SALT_SIZE);
Buffer.BlockCopy(
    pan_bytes, 0, plaintext_bytes, SALT_SIZE, pan_bytes.Length);
SHA256 sha256 = SHA256.Create();
return sha256.ComputeHash(hash_input);
```

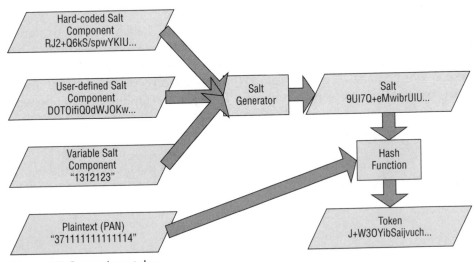

Figure 7-8: Generating a token

Salting Passwords

In some hash applications, such as password encryption and validation, it is necessary to add a randomly generated salt component in order to get a different ciphertext (encrypted password) for the same input (password in clear text) for each new hash function call. It is done this way in order to prevent the possibility of password disclosure, even if an attacker has access to the password file. The `encryptPassword` method uses the same hash logic as the previously described `CreateToken`, the only difference is that instead of a variable component stretched by the `Random` class, it generates the random salt component using `RandomNumberGenerator`:

```
dynamic_password_salt_component = new byte[16];
RandomNumberGenerator generator = RandomNumberGenerator.Create();
generator.GetNonZeroBytes(dynamic_password_salt_component);
```

Without a random salt component, two identical passwords will produce the same hash output, so the attacker may enter the same password as a legitimate user and determine the user's password value by looking at the password file. The random salt component also must be added to the result of hashing in order to validate the password by hashing the user input and comparing the result with the original password hash stored in the password file (as shown in Figure 7-9):

```
byte[] encrypted_password =
    new byte[SALT_COMPONENT_SIZE + hash_result.Length];
Buffer.BlockCopy(
    random_password_salt_component, 0,
    encrypted_password, 0, SALT_COMPONENT_SIZE);
Buffer.BlockCopy(
    hash_result, 0, encrypted_password,
    SALT_COMPONENT_SIZE, hash_result.Length);
```

The constant and user-defined salt components can be hard-coded or stored separately from the code; the idea behind this is to make it impossible to retrieve the entire salt value from the password record. Thus, if an attacker has access to the password database but no access to the application code and configuration, she won't be able to re-create the salt value from just one random salt component.

Validating Passwords

Password validation is based on the assumption that the encrypted password record is linked to a particular user account and, therefore, there is no need to perform the search using the hashed data. Thus, the encrypted password can be randomly salted and the random salt component can be added to the output along with the ciphertext. The `ValidatePassword` method retrieves the random salt component from the original record:

```
byte[] original_random_salt_component = new byte[SALT_COMPONENT_SIZE];
Buffer.BlockCopy(
    original_password_hash, 0,
    original_random_salt_component, 0, SALT_COMPONENT_SIZE);
```

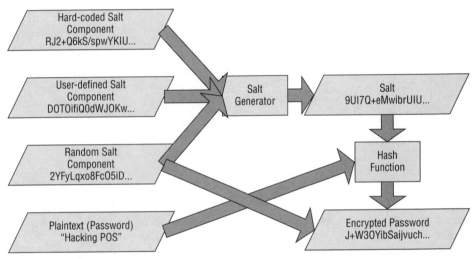

Figure 7-9: Password encryption

Then it creates the hash for the password being validated (exactly the same way it was created for the original password):

```
string encrypted_password_to_validate = encryptPassword(
    PasswordToValidate, original_random_salt_component);
```

The last step is just comparing the two encrypted passwords:

```
return encrypted_password_to_validate.Equals(OriginalPasswordHash);
```

If the two strings are identical, the validation is passed which means the user has entered the correct password (Figure 7-10).

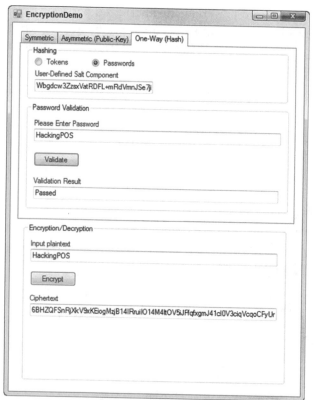

Figure 7-10: EncryptionDemo: Password validation

Digital Signatures

Digital Signature is one of most remarkable applications of cryptography. It provides the ability to authenticate the author of digital documents, messages, and data records as well as software code, which is an important feature when working with payment applications and financial transactions. Public-key and one-way cryptography are used in order to create the signature which consists of the message digest encrypted with the private key of the signer. Thus, in order to validate the digital signature, the recipients of the message or document use the public key to decrypt the digest and compare it with their own hashing result.

Attached vs. Detached Signatures

There are two types of digital signatures: attached and detached. The former is part of the data that is being signed—for example, the *Authenticode* signature embedded into the binary file. The latter is created as a separate entity—for example, as the `.p7s` file containing the e-mail digital signature according to *S/MIME* (Secure/Multipurpose Internet Mail Extensions) standard.

A detached signature can be used for signing any file type because it does not modify the content of the file that's being signed. An attached signature can be used only with specific file types and custom message formats.

The format defined in the *PKCS #7* standard, which is based on the more common X.509 certificate standard, can be used when implementing the detached signature container.[13] The `.p7s` file type can be used to store the content of a detached digital signature.[14] Table 7-4 shows various use cases for attached and detached signatures.

Table 7-4: Examples of Well-known Attached and Detached Signature Implementations

OBJECT TO SIGN	ATTACHED SIGNATURES	DETACHED SIGNATURES
Code files	Authenticode[15]	
	.NET Strong-name Signing[16]	
Data files	XML Signature[17]	
Messages		E-mail Signing: S/MIME[18]

Code and Configuration Signing

This is one of most important digital signature use cases for payment applications. *Code signing* provides protection from application code tampering, while signed configuration allows mitigating the threat of unauthorized configuration changes. The details of code and configuration signing implementation are described in Chapter 9.

Data File and Message Signing

Speaking of signing the data, especially sensitive cardholder data, it is important to understand that a digital signature does not protect confidentiality. Therefore, in addition to signing, other security measures (encryption) are required to avoid information disclosure. However, a digital signature can be used to protect information that is not sensitive to disclosure threat from modification by unauthorized personnel or malware. For example, POS transaction files (the information about complete customer transactions circulating between the POS, store server, and corporate headquarters) would be a good candidate for digital signing.

Cryptographic Hardware

Any cryptographic functions can be implemented in software. In practice, however, many cryptographic functions are delegated to dedicated hardware modules and appliances. There are two functions of cryptographic hardware that are very important for payment applications:

1. Performing CPU-intensive cryptographic operations (encryption, decryption, key management) and, therefore, removing the load from the hosting computers running POS front-end or back-end applications.

2. Creating a barrier between unsafe computers and networks exposed to hackers and the secure zone located inside the hardware which is isolated from hazardous environments by physical and logical controls.

TRSM and HSM are examples of cryptographic hardware mostly used in payment application solutions:

- *TRSM (Tamper-Resistant Security Module)* is a hardware module that is installed in payment terminals in order to store and generate the encryption keys, and perform encryption. TRSM is designed to recognize a physical intrusion and destroy the keys if someone attempts to retrieve them.

- *HSM (Hardware Security Module)* is a cryptographic hardware appliance or extension card used mostly in back-end systems for secure key management and decryption. HSM provides the ability to manage the keys according to the requirements of X9.24-1, TR-39, and PCI HW-P2PE standards (with multiple key components and custodians). Special HSM are also used as key injection machines for injecting the PIN and P2PE keys into payment terminals and standalone secure card readers.

Cryptographic Standards

PCI is not the only player in payment card security regulations, even though it is probably the most famous one these days. There are other standards that came from adjacent and more generic areas, such as financial and banking industries, application security, and cryptography. Several years ago, FIPS 140-2 and TR-39 had been known mostly to security experts dealing with ATM machines and PIN transactions. As the payment industry invests more and more into its security, professional-level cryptography comes to retail card payment processing as well. Today, payment applications call the encryption libraries, which had been known only to professional cryptographers just several years ago. Hardware point-to-point encryption solutions utilize highly-secure cryptographic hardware for encryption of sensitive data at the merchant store and decryption at the payment processor's data centers.

NIST and FIPS

The *National Institute of Standards and Technology* (NIST) plays a leading role in development of cryptographic standards as well as validation and certification of cryptographic implementations. NIST has developed a series of *Federal Information Processing Standards* (FIPS) defining requirements for cryptographic algorithms and systems.

One of the famous NIST products is *FIPS 197*, which is well known to a wide audience as *AES* (Advanced Encryption Standard).[19] Another one is *FIPS 180-4*, also known as *SHA* (Secure Hash Algorithm).[20] They are both widely used in application security (payment applications are not an exception) for data protection.

FIPS are mandatory for government organizations but are also widely used by the commercial sector as de facto information security standards. There are different types of FIPS: cryptographic algorithms (such as FIPS 197 for AES) and validation programs (such as FIPS 140-2 for cryptographic modules validation).

Retired Algorithms: DES vs. Triple DES

DES used to be a standard encryption algorithm defined in *FIPS 46-3*. Its implementation was an encryption algorithm used along with the DUKPT key management for debit PIN protection. DES was cracked for the first time in 1997 and was eventually replaced by AES.

> *FIPS 46-3, Data Encryption Standard (DES), was withdrawn May 19, 2005 because the cryptographic algorithm no longer provided the security that is needed to protect Federal government information. DES is no longer an approved algorithm.*[21]

However, the financial industry could not break from DES completely and still uses its reaffirmed version *Triple DES* (TDEA), which is basically a DES applied three times to each data block and is allowed until 2030.[22, 23] Triple DES is more secure than DES because it uses a triple-length 168-bit key (3 × 56-bit DES keys). In practice, however, double-length (two-key) 112-bit keys (where K1 and K3 key components are the same) are still often used. After December 31, 2015, two-key Triple DES will not be used for encryption.[24]

Table 7-5 shows NIST-approved encryption algorithms, both current and deprecated. Note that allowance of the algorithms depends on their key (or digest in case of hash) length. As a general rule of thumb, the more bits in the key or digest, the stronger the algorithm. However, AES with a 128-bit key is more secure than Triple DES with a 168-bit key.

Table 7-5: NIST-approved Encryption Algorithms

ALGORITHM	STANDARD	KEY/DIGEST LENGTH, BITS	USE
DES	FIPS 46-3	56	Disallowed
Single-length Triple-DES	N/A	56	Disallowed
Double-length Triple-DES (2TDEA)	NIST SP 800-67	112	Disallowed after 2015
Triple-length Triple-DES (3TDEA)	NIST SP 800-67	168	Disallowed after 2030
AES 128	FIPS 197	128	Acceptable
AES 192	FIPS 197	192	Acceptable
AES 256	FIPS 197	256	Acceptable
SHA-1 (non-digital signatures applications)	FIPS 180-4	160	Acceptable
SHA-1 in digital signatures	FIPS 180-4	160	Disallowed after 2013
SHA-224	FIPS 180-4	224	Acceptable
SHA-256	FIPS 180-4	256	Acceptable
SHA-384	FIPS 180-4	384	Acceptable
SHA-512	FIPS 180-4	512	Acceptable

FIPS 140-2

FIPS 140-2 is a validation program for cryptographic modules. There are four levels of security defined in FIPS 140-2. The program is open for both software and hardware implementations; however, software modules cannot achieve higher levels (3 and 4) due to strict physical security requirements. HSM appliances are usually validated to Level 2 or 3. The PCI HW-P2PE standard requires that HSM used for decryption and key management be approved to Level 3 or higher. The validation results are published online.[25]

ANSI

There are two *ANSI* (American National Standards Institute) standards that are related to P2PE: *X9.24-1* and *TR-39*.

X9.24-1: DUKPT

X9.24-1 defines *DUKPT*, which is a common technology for symmetric key management in debit PIN encryption and P2PE solutions.

TR-39: Key Injection

TR-39 (also known as *TG-3*) is a security standard that regulates the key injection facilities, which are an important part of debit PIN and P2PE solutions.[26] TR-39 is maintained by the ANSI X9F6 Working Group and is required by debit processing networks (such as STAR, NYCE, PULSE, etc.) in order to be allowed to perform the key injections. The TR-39 certification is conducted by certified TG-2 auditors (CTGA) and expires every 2 years.

PKCS

Public-Key Cryptography Standards (PKCS) were created by RSA Security, Inc. The most famous is *PKCS #1*, which defines the RSA algorithm. *PKCS #7* is important for digital-signing implementations.[27] *PKCS #12* defines the container format commonly used to store multiple private-key and public-key certificates (.P12 or .PFX files).

Summary

Cryptography is an essential part of modern POS and payment applications. There are three main groups of cryptographic algorithms: symmetric, asymmetric (public-key), and one-way hash. Symmetric algorithms use the same key for encryption and decryption. Asymmetric algorithms have two keys, public and private, and the same key cannot be used for both encryption and decryption. One-way hash functions create a digital digest of the input plaintext and in most cases do not require keys. Both public-key and hash algorithms are used in digital signing and digital certificates. There are several cryptographic standards that provide implementation requirements for encryption algorithms and cryptographic hardware.

Notes

1. Bruce Schneier, *Applied Cryptography: Protocols, Algorithms, and Source Code in C, Second Edition*, (Wiley, 1996).

2. SciEngines, "Break DES in less than a single day," http://www.sciengines.com/company/news-a-events/74-des-in-1-day.html?eab1dd0ce8f296f6302f76f8761818c0=0b59c5b91984fe01986ef3bbc6de9871

3. Intel, Moore's Law Timeline, http://download.intel.com/pressroom/kits/events/moores_law_40th/MLTimeline.pdf

4. *EMC2*, "What Key Size Should Be Used?" http://www.emc.com/emc-plus/rsa-labs/standards-initiatives/key-size.htm

5. John Kelsey, Bruce Schneier, Chris Hall, David Wagner, "Secure Applications of Low-Entropy Keys" (2000), https://www.schneier.com/paper-low-entropy.pdf

6. IETF, "PKCS #5: Password-Based Cryptography Specification Version 2.0," http://tools.ietf.org/html/rfc2898

7. NSA, "Suite B Cryptography / Cryptographic Interoperability," http://www.nsa.gov/ia/programs/suiteb_cryptography/index.shtml

8. MSDN, "PaddingMode Enumeration," http://msdn.microsoft.com/en-us/library/system.security.cryptography.paddingmode(v=vs.110).aspx

9. IETF, "Internet X.509 Public Key Infrastructure: Certification Path Building," http://tools.ietf.org/html/rfc4158

10. MSDN, "MakeCert. Exe (Certificate Creation Tool)," http://msdn.microsoft.com/en-us/library/bfsktky3.aspx

11. MSDN, "Pvk2Pfx," http://msdn.microsoft.com/en-us/library/windows/hardware/ff550672(v=vs.85).aspx

12. Slava Gomzin, "Securing .NET Web Services with SSL: How to Protect 'Data in Transit' between Client and Remote Server," http://www.gomzin.com/securing-net-web-services-with-ssl.html

13. IETF, "Public-Key Infrastructure (X.509)," http://datatracker.ietf.org/wg/pkix/charter/

14. IETF, "RFC 5751 - Secure/Multipurpose Internet Mail Extensions (S/MIME) Version 3.2 Message Specification," http://tools.ietf.org/pdf/rfc5751.pdf

15. Microsoft TechNet, "Authenticode," `http://technet.microsoft.com/en-us/library/cc750035.aspx`

16. MSDN, "Strong-Name Signing for Managed Applications," `http://msdn.microsoft.com/en-us/library/h4fa028b(v=vs.90).aspx`

17. W3C, *XML Signature Syntax and Processing* (*Second Edition*), `http://www.w3.org/TR/xmldsig-core/`

18. Microsoft TechNet, "Understanding S/MIME," `http://technet.microsoft.com/en-us/library/aa995740(v=exchg.65).aspx`

19. NIST, "Advanced Encryption Standard (AES)," FIPS Publication 197, (June 2008), `http://csrc.nist.gov/publications/fips/fips197/fips-197.pdf`

20. FIPS, "Secure Hash Standard (SHS)," FIPS Publication 180-4, (March 2012), `http://csrc.nist.gov/publications/fips/fips180-4/fips-180-4.pdf`

21. NIST, "Retired Validation Testing, Data Encryption Standard (DES)," `http://csrc.nist.gov/groups/STM/cavp/`

22. NIST, "Recommendation for the Triple Data Encryption Algorithm (TDEA) Block Cipher," Special Publication 800-67, (Revised January 2012), `http://csrc.nist.gov/publications/nistpubs/800-67-Rev1/SP-800-67-Rev1.pdf`

23. NIST, "Recommendation for Key Management – Part 1: General (Revision 3)," Special Publication 800-57, (July 2012), `http://csrc.nist.gov/publications/nistpubs/800-57/sp800-57_part1_rev3_general.pdf`

24. NIST, "Transitions: Recommendation for Transitioning the Use of Cryptographic Algorithms and Key Lengths," Special Publication 800-131A, (January 2011), `http://csrc.nist.gov/publications/nistpubs/800-131A/sp800-131A.pdf`

25. NIST, "FIPS 140-1 and FIPS 140-2 Vendor List," `http://csrc.nist.gov/groups/STM/cmvp/documents/140-1/1401vend.htm`

26. ANSI, "TG-3 Retail Financial Services Compliance Guideline - Part 1: PIN Security and Key Management," `http://webstore.ansi.org/RecordDetail.aspx?sku=ANSI%2fX9+TR-39-2009`

27. "PKCS #7: Cryptographic Message Syntax Standard, An RSA Laboratories Technical Note," `http://www.emc.com/emc-plus/rsa-labs/standards-initiatives/pkcs-7-cryptographic-message-syntax-standar.htm`

CHAPTER

8

Protecting Cardholder Data

*It is easier to produce ten volumes of philosophical writing
than to put one principle into practice.*

—Leo Tolstoy

PCI standards require only disk storage encryption, and in some cases communication encryption. Since the core technology around payment card processing
has fundamental security flaws, the payment application should encrypt the
sensitive cardholder data wherever possible: in memory, at rest, and in transit.
In addition, it's a good idea to implement the *defense in depth* principle — put in
extra layers of protection wherever possible. For example, when sending data via
a network, a payment application can encrypt the sensitive data elements using
symmetric algorithms, and also encrypt the entire communication session by a
transport security mechanism such as SSL, HTTPS, or IPSec. In theory, physical
and logical security controls can form another layer of protection. However,
they are not effective in the hazardous working environment of POS which is
directly exposed to the public.

Data in Memory

The answer to questions about memory protection is simple: the sensitive cardholder data can't be completely safe if it is not encrypted before it is placed in
memory. There are no existing reliable security mechanisms that would prevent
memory scraping. If an attacker gains access to the POS hosting computer, the
chances that the data will be leaked are very high because most of the operations

(including encryption, decryption, and cryptographic key management) with sensitive data are performed in memory.[1]

Minimizing Data Exposure

There are some preventive measures that can be implemented to minimize data exposure or, more precisely, to reduce the duration of data in clear text in memory, so that less sensitive and sophisticated memory scrapers do not have enough time to catch the tracks. In order to do that, the payment application needs to store the sensitive data in memory encrypted most of the time, and decrypt it only for a short period of time when it is needed for processing in clear text.

Secure Strings

The .NET *SecureString* class can be used as a secure storage container that automatically encrypts its content.[2] Note that SecureString still provides very limited protection. Until many classes natively support SecureString, it must still be converted to regular string in order to perform any work on its content.

Cleaning Up

It is important that the data in clear text is cleaned up after it is used. For example, the *memory buffers* (byte arrays) containing sensitive data should not be left for garbage collection (which may happen after an indefinite time), but zeroed using special methods before the reference to the buffer is lost. Therefore, using buffers is preferable to strings, especially in managed runtime environments such as .NET Framework or Java Virtual Machine where a programmer has no direct control of strings.

Encrypting Data End to End

There is no doubt that the only reliable way to protect data in memory is not to have it in memory in clear text. End-to-end, or point-to-point, encryption (P2PE) technologies provide the ability to encrypt the data before it even reaches the memory of the hosting machine (inside the payment terminal or standalone MSR device), and decrypt it only after it has left the POS (in the payment gateway's data center). Even software P2PE, where data is encrypted in the application running on the POI device, while still vulnerable provides a much higher level of confidentiality than not having P2PE at all and exposing data to the POS RAM. Moreover, P2PE doesn't just protect memory, but also ensures that sensitive data is unreachable in transit and at rest.

Data in Transit

Sensitive data that is being transmitted over the network can be protected in two ways:

1. Payload encryption: selected sensitive fields are encrypted using symmetric or asymmetric methods.

2. Transport encryption: the entire communication is encrypted using secure protocols such as SSL, HTTPS, or IPSec.

CROSS-REFERENCE   See Chapter 7, "Cryptography in Payment Applications" for more information on symmetric and asymmetric encryption methods.

Both methods can be combined in order to provide layered protection that makes a hacker's job more difficult: if one layer is broken, there is still another layer to work on.

Implementing SSL

Netscape developed The Secure Sockets Layer Protocol (SSL) in 1994 as a response to the growing concern over security on the Internet.[3] SSL is a secure protocol that prevents eavesdropping, tampering, or message forgery over the network. The use of SSL for confidentiality as well as for authentication has been phenomenally successful.[4] Recent versions of SSL are called *Transport Layer Security* (TLS), but the two abbreviations are still interchangeable in many cases. There are many books describing interesting low-level details of SSL.[5]

Server Certificate

SSL is one example of a payment application using encryption algorithms indirectly, as part of a larger encryption system. An SSL client (which can be an Internet browser or POS application) uses a *server certificate* to authenticate the server and make sure it communicates with a legitimate entity. The server certificate, which is downloaded by the client during the *SSL handshake process*[6], contains the public part of the asymmetric key pair, while the private key is stored at the server (see Figure 8-1). SSL uses public-key encryption algorithms for *key exchange*. Once the key exchange process is done, the data transmitted between client and server is encrypted using symmetric algorithms, because they have better performance than asymmetric algorithms.

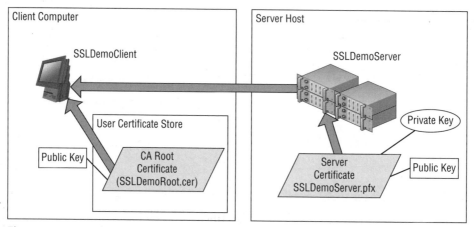

Figure 8-1: Server certificate validation

In order to establish an SSL connection, the server application needs to provide the SSL server certificate with a public key to the client during the handshake. The server certificate has two roles:

1. Server authentication: the client ensures that the server it is communicating with is a legitimate application.

2. Communication encryption: the certificate's public key is used in the initial SSL handshake in order to exchange symmetric keys for data encryption.

SSLDemo Application

SSLDemo demonstrates a secure communication between the Windows Communication Foundation (WCF) client (`SSLDemoClient.exe` shown in Figure 8-2) and the WCF self-hosted server (`SSLDemoServer.exe` shown in Figure 8-3) applications.

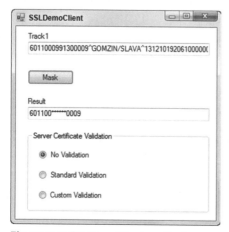

Figure 8-2: SSLDemoClient application

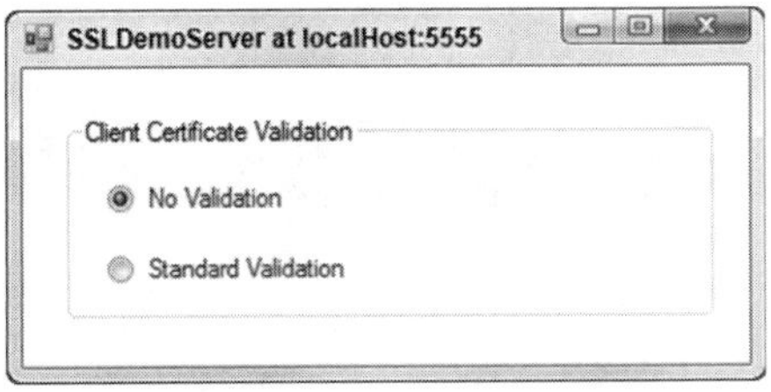

Figure 8-3: SSLDemoServer is waiting for client calls at port 5555

Certificate Authority

Using a self-signed certificate (similar to the one used in the asymmetric encryption demo in Chapter 7) as the server SSL certificate is possible, but not enough to ensure the complete security of the communication. With a self-signed certificate, the client has no ability to verify the authenticity of the server, so confidentiality of the data being encrypted can be compromised by using a fake certificate in a *man-in-the-middle* (MITM) attack. Therefore, there should be a way to validate the authenticity of the server certificate. Such a way is provided by a *certificate authority* (CA) which issues and signs server certificates to ensure their authenticity. In order to be able to validate the server certificate, the client has to have access to the certificate authority's *root certificate* which contains the CA's public key. The CA root certificate's public key is used to verify the digital signature of the server certificate created by the CA using its root private key. There are different ways to obtain a server certificate signed by the CA:

- Public CA such as VeriSign[7]
- Proprietary CA service such as Microsoft Certificate Services[8]
- Proprietary CA created manually using free tools such as MakeCert or OpenSSL[9]

The third option is the best candidate for testing and experiments with SSL and digital certificates.

Creating Certificate Authority

Creating a proprietary CA for testing purposes is much easier than you might imagine. You only need to generate a couple of files: a self-signed root certificate with a CA public key and private key, both located in a dedicated folder (for more convenience and security). The MakeCert tool[10] can be used to generate a root certificate and private key for a local CA with the parameters described in Table 8-1:

```
makecert -r -a sha256 -len 2048
-n "CN=SSLDemoRoot,O=HackingPOS,S=Texas,C=US"
-cy authority -sv SSLDemoRoot.pvk
-b 01/01/2013 -e 01/01/2023 SSLDemoRoot.cer
```

Table 8-1: MakeCert Parameters for Generating the Self-signed Root Certificate and Private Key for Certificate Authority

PARAMETER	VALUE	DESCRIPTION
N/A	SSLDemo.cer	Location and name of the CA root certificate file (with public key) that is being generated
-r	N/A	Create a self-signed certificate (root certificate is self-signed)
-a	sha256	Use SHA-256 as signature hash algorithm
-len	2048	Create 2,048-bit RSA key (the default length is 1,024-bit)
-n	"CN= SSLDemoRoot"	CA name
-b	01/01/2013	CA validity starting date
-e	01/01/2023	CA validity expiration date
-sv	SSLDemoRoot.pvk	Location and name of the CA root private-key file that is being generated
-cy	authority	Create CA root certificate

MakeCert will prompt for a private key password three times. Just enter the same password each time and commit it to memory because it will be used later to issue server certificates.

Installing CA Root Certificate

When SSL implementation, such as .NET crypto library, verifies the server certificate, it needs a public key from a CA in order to verify the certificate's digital signature. Without access to the public key packed in the CA root certificate, the client validation logic won't be able to trace the certificate up the chain to its root, and it will throw the exception shown in Figure 8-4.

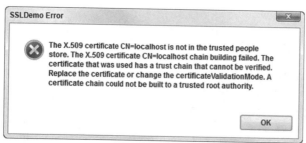

Figure 8-4: Exception is thrown by SSLDemoClient when CA root certificate is not found

In order to tell the system that the certificate belongs to a trusted root CA, install it by clicking the SSLDemoRoot.cer file, and then on the Install Certificate... button in the Certificate dialog (Figure 8-5).

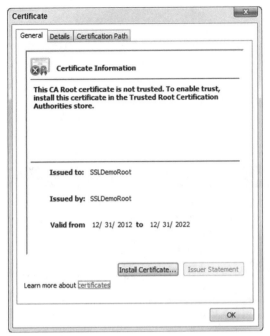

Figure 8-5: Root certificate installation dialog

Then, click the Next button. In the Certificate Import Wizard dialog, select "Place all certificates in the following store" and press the Browse… button (Figure 8-6). In the Select Certificate Store dialog, select Trusted Root Certification Authorities and then click OK, Next, and, Finish.

Figure 8-6: Certificate Import Wizard and Select Certificate Store dialogs

Issuing SSL Server Certificate

A server certificate can be issued using the same MakeCert tool with the parameters described in Table 8.2.

```
makecert -a sha256 -len 2048 -n "CN=localhost"
-ic SSLDemoRoot.cer -iv SSLDemoRoot.pvk -sv SSLDemoServer.pvk
-sky exchange SSLDemoServer.cer
```

Table 8-2: MakeCert Parameters for Issuing the SSL Server Certificate

PARAMETER	VALUE	DESCRIPTION
N/A	SSLDemoServer.cer	The name and location of the server certificate file (with public key) that is being generated
-a	sha256	Use SHA-256 as signature hash algorithm
-len	2048	Create 2,048-bit RSA key (the default length is 1,024-bit)
-n	"CN= localhost"	Host name; The sample certificate is issued for local IP address (127.0.0.1); In a production environment, the network host (domain) name should be used instead
-b	01/01/2013	Server certificate validity starting date
-e	01/01/2023	Server certificate validity expiration date
-sv	SSLDemoServer.pvk	Location and name of the server certificate's private-key file that is being generated
-ic	SSLDemoRoot.cer	The name of the issuing CA root certificate file (with public key)
-iv	SSLDemoRoot.pvk	The name of the issuing CA root private key file
-sky	exchange	Set key type for key exchange

.NET will be confused if only the .cer file (which does not contain the private key) is provided as an input for the X509Certificate2 class constructor. Therefore, the additional command Pvk2pfx with the parameters described in Table 8-3 are required in order to compile the public and private keys into a single PFX file:

```
pvk2pfx -pvk SSLDemoServer.pvk -spc SSLDemoServer.cer
-pfx SSLDemoServer.pfx -pi 1
```

Table 8-3: Pvk2pfx Parameters for Creating Single-file SSL Server Certificates in PFX Format

PARAMETER	VALUE	DESCRIPTION
-pvk	SSLDemoServer. pvk	Location and name of the input SSL server certificate's private-key file
-spc	SSLDemoServer.cer	Location and name of the input SSL server certificate's public-key file
-pfx	SSLDemoServer.pfx	Location and name of the output PFX SSL server certificate file
-pi	1	Password for private key (prompted during the MakeCert command)

SSLDemoServer Code

In order to enable SSL encryption, two changes should be made in the server application:

1. The following parameters should be added in the server configuration initialization code:

```
binding.Security.Mode = SecurityMode.Transport;
binding.Security.Transport.ProtectionLevel =
    System.Net.Security.ProtectionLevel.EncryptAndSign;
binding.Security.Transport.ClientCredentialType =
    TcpClientCredentialType.None;
```

2. The following code, which loads the server SSL certificate and its corresponding private key from the PFX file, should be added in the `ServiceHost` initialization section before `host.Open()`:

```
var certificate = new X509Certificate2("SSLDemoServer.pfx", "1");
host.Credentials.ServiceCertificate.Certificate = certificate;
```

SSLDemoClient Code

In order to enable SSL, the same change is required in the client application configuration code:

```
binding.Security.Mode = SecurityMode.Transport;
binding.Security.Transport.ProtectionLevel =
    System.Net.Security.ProtectionLevel.EncryptAndSign;
binding.Security.Transport.ClientCredentialType =
    TcpClientCredentialType.None;
```

Certificate Revocation List

In theory, no additional changes are required in the client application besides the previous binding configuration. However, there is one line of code needed in a test application to avoid failure to check the *Certificate Revocation List* (CRL):

```
channelFactory.Credentials.ServiceCertificate.Authentication.
    RevocationMode = X509RevocationMode.NoCheck;
```

CRL is a tool used by the CA to revoke certificates — for example, in case the CA was compromised and fraudulent certificates were issued.[11] In our root CA we did not generate the CRL in order to simplify the testing process. In real life, however, the CRL is another important validation point, so that line of code should be commented out (or the value of the RevocationMode parameter set to X509RevocationMode.Online) before switching to production certificates.

Custom Server Certificate Validation

Standard certificate validations might not be enough if more scrupulous verification is desired. In this case, custom validation can be performed. Validating extra parameters of the server certificate, such as thumbprint, may prevent more refined MITM attacks. In order to perform a custom validation, the CertificateValidationMode property should be set to X509CertificateValidationMode.Custom, and custom validation procedure should be defined:

```
channelFactory.Credentials.ServiceCertificate.Authentication.
    CertificateValidationMode = X509CertificateValidationMode.Custom;
channelFactory.Credentials.ServiceCertificate.Authentication.
    CustomCertificateValidator = new CustomServerCertificateValidator();
```

The custom validation code that checks the thumbprint of the server certificate is simple:

```
if (certificate.Thumbprint !=
    "904CE1DE2A2858E6938081CEB7063F08C8F61D9F")
{
    throw new ApplicationException("certificate is invalid");
}
```

Note that checking the thumbprint is a practical solution only if the server certificate is issued for a long period of time. If server certificates are intended to be rotated quite often, the value of the thumbprint should be either configurable, or the client software version should be easily upgradable to a version containing a new thumbprint value. In both cases, the thumbprint value — either hard-coded or stored in configuration file — should be protected from tampering by a digital signature.

CROSS-REFERENCE   See Chapter 9 "Securing Application Code" for information about implementation of code and configuration signing.

Client Authentication

In the SSL scheme reviewed in previous sections, we used a server certificate for server authentication, which provides the client with the ability to ensure that it talks to a legitimate entity (as was shown in Figure 8-1). A similar technique can be used in the opposite direction — in order to authenticate clients so the server application ensures it talks to legitimate clients (see Figure 8-7). This feature is necessary, for example, to prevent a situation where a bogus POS terminal conducts fraudulent transactions with the remote payment gateway.

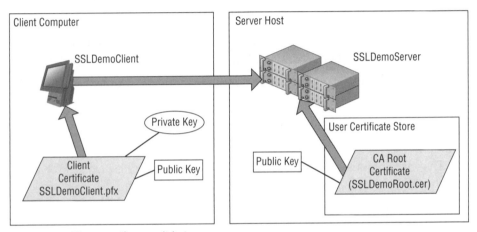

Figure 8-7: Client certificate validation

Creating a Client Certificate

A client certificate can be generated using the same MakeCert and Pvk2pfx tools with the parameters similar to the server certificate:

```
makecert -a sha256 -len 2048 -n "CN=SSLDemoClient"
-b 01/01/2013 -e 01/01/2023 -ic SSLDemoRoot.cer
-iv SSLDemoRoot.pvk -sky exchange
-sv SSLDemoClient.pvk SSLDemoClient.cer

pvk2pfx -pvk SSLDemoClient.pvk -spc SSLDemoClient.cer
-pfx SSLDemoClient.pfx -pi 1
```

In practice, when there are hundreds or thousands of clients spread over the network, the process of creating client certificates should be automated — for example, by using the *autoenrollment* functionality provided by a proprietary CA.[12]

Configuring the Client for Client Authentication

Two changes should be made in order to configure the client for authentication with a certificate:

1. The value of the `ClientCredentialType` property should be set to Certificate:

```
binding.Security.Transport.ClientCredentialType =
    TcpClientCredentialType.Certificate;
```

2. The client certificate should be loaded from the PFX file:

```
var certificate = new X509Certificate2("SSLDemoClient.pfx", "1");
channelFactory.Credentials.ClientCertificate.Certificate = certificate;
```

Configuring the Server for Client Authentication

Two changes should also be made to the server code in order to set up the client authentication with a client certificate:

1. The value of the `ClientCredentialType` property should be also set to Certificate:

```
binding.Security.Transport.ClientCredentialType =
    TcpClientCredentialType.Certificate;
```

2. The validation mode should be set to ChainTrust, and TrustedStoreLocation should be pointed to CurrentUser store:

```
host.Credentials.ClientCertificate.Authentication.
    CertificateValidationMode =
    X509CertificateValidationMode.ChainTrust;
host.Credentials.ClientCertificate.Authentication.
    TrustedStoreLocation = StoreLocation.CurrentUser;
```

Note that in order to validate the chain of trust of the client certificates, the CA root certificate (SSLDemoRoot.cer) should be installed in the user certificate store the same way it was done for the client. The CRL check should also be disabled while working with test certificates:

```
host.Credentials.ClientCertificate.Authentication.RevocationMode =
    X509RevocationMode.NoCheck;
```

Using Encrypted Tunnels

Encrypted tunnels are an alternative to secure communication protocols such as SSL and HTTPS. The advantage of encrypted tunnels — provided by Virtual Private Network (VPN) protocols or tunneling protocols such *IPSec* — is that they do not require any changes in application code and configuration on either the client side or server side. This feature can be useful when working with legacy software, which was created without security in mind and does not support encryption out of the box. The disadvantage of tunneling protocols is that they require special setup or even software installed on client systems, which is often beyond the control of the payment application provider.

IPSec

IPSec (Internet Protocol security) is the best alternative to SSL when working with multiple clients because usually it does not require any additional software to be installed on the client or server system, and doesn't require any changes in the client or server application that is being protected. Windows OS comes with IPSec out of the box and can be configured using network configuration and certificates issued by a proprietary CA.[13]

Data at Rest

The best approach to the data at rest protection problem is avoiding the storage of sensitive data at all, which is easy to say but difficult to do. In practice, there are many cases when a payment application must temporarily store the data — such as S&F, TOR, settlement batch records, and more. The second best approach is using point-to-point encryption. If P2PE is also impossible for some reason, then regular (usually symmetric) encryption can be used.

CROSS-REFERENCE   See Chapter 7 for more information on symmetric encryption.

Secure Key Management

Any software implementation of encryption is vulnerable, by definition, because there is no physical barrier between the cryptographic module and the attacker. There are, however, a few useful tricks that can make a hacker's life a little bit more complicated.

Multiple Key Components

Constructing the encryption key in runtime from multiple *key components*, rather than having a whole key available in memory all the time, provides some level of protection. This is because it makes it more difficult to retrieve the key and decrypt the sensitive data (see Figure 8-8). Chapter 7 has an example of the code that constructs the symmetric key from three key components.

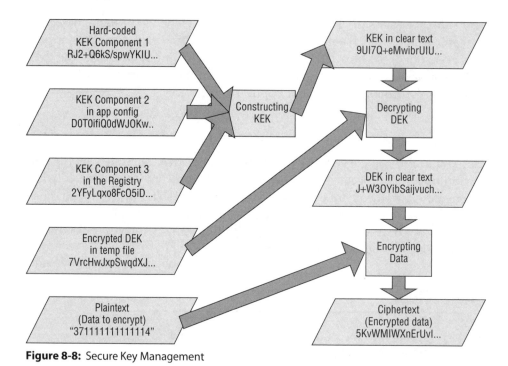

Figure 8-8: Secure Key Management

Spreading the Key Components Between Different Media

The key components can be stored in different places, such as an application code, a configuration file, and the Registry. So in order to reconstruct the key, the hacker needs to get simultaneous access to all those places (also shown in Figure 8-8).

KEK and DEK

Another best practice illustrated in Figure 8-8 is implementing two (or even more) encryption keys: *key encryption key* (KEK) and *data encryption key* (DEK). The KEK is constructed in runtime from multiple components, as previously described. Its only purpose is to protect the DEK which encrypts the sensitive data itself. The idea behind the KEK is to complicate the task of key retrieval by adding more steps. Another benefit of having KEK is that it allows the DEK to be dynamically generated for each data encryption session (for example, for each POS transaction similar to DUKPT, which is described in next section).

Key Rotation

Key rotation is a process of changing (generating a new key and discarding the old one) the encryption/decryption key without disrupting the encryption/decryption functionality. Frequent key rotation helps to avoid full information disclosure if the single key is compromised. Even if attackers managed to retrieve the value of the single DEK, they cannot use it to pump out the sensitive data for the rest of their lives if proper key rotation is in place.

Point-to-point Encryption

Point-to-point encryption, which allows simultaneous protection of data in memory, in transit, and at rest, is very strong and a popular trend. This technology is already implemented or in the process of development by many payment software vendors, payment gateways, and merchants.

What Point-to-point Really Means

The idea of P2PE in general is simple: the sensitive data is encrypted at one end of the communication and decrypted at the other end. However, when P2PE technology is applied to the brick-and-mortar merchant environment, there are several important conditions that should be taken into account:

- The data should be encrypted as close as possible to the entry point. In a case of hardware P2PE, the magnetic tracks are encrypted inside the *tamper-resistant security module* (TRSM) of the MSR device.
- The encryption end can be located in a hazardous environment, such as a retail store. The decryption end must therefore be located in a highly secure (both logically and physically) environment such as a *hardware security module* (HSM) installed in the data center.
- Cryptographic keys should be managed using special secure procedures and equipment that will prevent them from disclosure.

Levels of P2PE

P2PE solutions come in different flavors that are dictated by underlying technology (see Table 8-4). First of all, all P2PE solutions can be divided into two main groups: *Hardware P2PE (HW-P2PE)* and *Software P2PE (SW-P2PE)*. The difference is that the former uses hardware for cryptographic operations, while the latter performs encryption (and sometimes decryption) in software. HW-P2PE is much more secure because cryptographic hardware (such as TRSM and HSM) is much more protected (both logically and physically) from intrusions than is software. However, SW-P2PE is also a viable option — at least, it is better than not having P2PE at all.

Table 8-4: Different Types of P2PE Technologies

P2PE TYPE	ENCRYPTION END	DECRYPTION END	PCI STANDARD
Hardware P2PE (HW-P2PE, Hardware/ Hardware P2PE)	Encryption and key management is done in hardware (TRSM)	Decryption and key management is done in hardware (HSM)	PCI Hardware/ Hardware P2PE[14] (initially released in September 2011)
Hardware/Hybrid P2PE	Encryption and key management is done in hardware (TRSM)	Decryption and key management is done in software	PCI Hardware/Hybrid P2PE[15] (released in December 2012)
Software P2PE (SW-P2PE, Software/ Software P2PE)	Encryption and key management is done in software	Decryption is done in software; Key management is done in hardware (HSM)	N/A (expected in 2014)

There are also mixed P2PE solutions which have elements of both hardware and software implementations. PCI distinguishes them by the technology used at the client side (encryption) and at the server side (decryption) — for example, Software/Hardware. The designation before the slash indicates the encryption technology, while the name after the slash indicates the decryption implementation. So in the Software/Hardware example, the encryption is done in software but decryption and key management at the server side is implemented using HSM.

Another type of P2PE is *Hybrid P2PE* where both software and hardware are used at the same time. Hybrid means that the encryption or decryption operations are performed in software, but the keys are managed in hardware. For example, Hardware/Hybrid P2PE means that the encryption (and key management) at the POS side is implemented inside TRSM, while decryption at the data center level is done in software with the key management performed by HSM.

Hardware P2PE

The high-level architecture of typical Hardware/Hardware P2PE solutions is illustrated in Figure 8-9.

The magnetic tracks are encrypted in the MSR's TRSM as soon as the payment card is swiped. No sensitive authentication data in clear text is ever available in the memory, storage, or network transmission at the POS or store environment. The tracks are decrypted in the HSM located in the payment gateway's data center, so the server application could process the transaction and route it for authorization to the appropriate payment processor.

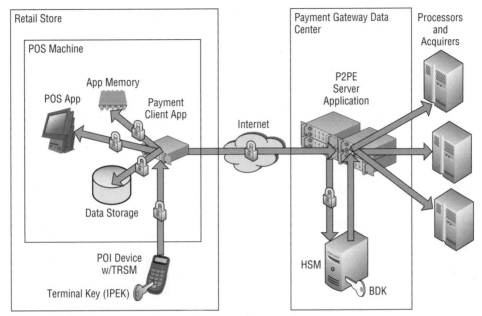

Figure 8-9: Typical Hardware/Hardware P2PE solution architecture

PCI Hardware/Hardware P2PE certification requirements are very extensive and include the following mandatory prerequisites:

- PCI PTS SRED certified encryption devices
- FIPS 140-2 Level 3 certified decryption devices
- PCI HW-P2PE certified key injection environment
- PCI DSS certified decryption environment
- TR-39 compatible key management procedures

DUKPT Key Management

Derived Unique Key Per Transaction (DUKPT) is a symmetric key management scheme which dynamically generates new encryption keys for each new encryption session (transaction). In conjunction with the Triple DES encryption algorithm, DUKPT is used in debit PIN encryption, and is defined in ANSI standard X9.24-1. DUKPT was invented in the 1980s and has been used for debit PIN encryption since the 1990s. Nowadays, this successful technology is being widely adopted by P2PE solution providers.

"The specified key management technique provides a unique key per transaction with no information about any previous key retained in the PIN Entry Device. It also provides for a derived key system in which the Acquirer's security module can determine any key used at any time in any PIN Entry Device based on information included in the transaction."[16]

The advantage of DUKPT is that it defines the hierarchy of keys so that disclosure of a single key does not compromise other keys. This means that disclosure of a single session key does not compromise other transactions, and disclosure of a single terminal's key does not compromise other devices. Another remarkable feature of DUKPT is that only one master key is needed in order to decrypt the data coming from multiple terminals.

BDK

The *base derivation key* (BDK) is the master key — the highest key in the DUKPT hierarchy (Table 8-5), which must be highly secure. If BDK is disclosed, the entire key hierarchy (which can be an entire retail chain or a large payment network segment) will be compromised. The protection of BDK is done by using the *split knowledge* principle: the key is constructed from several key components inside the HSM and never exposed in clear text outside the hardware. The key components (usually three or more) are stored on smart cards or on paper in tamper-evident envelopes and owned by different people known as *key custodians*. All key custodians must be present in order to re-create the entire BDK — for example, to set up a new HSM device. When the BDK needs to be shared with a third-party organization (for example, a key injection facility), the key components are sent in separate tamper-evident envelopes by each key custodian using different shipment carriers on different dates.

Table 8-5: DUKPT Keys

KEY	ENCRYPTION DEVICE	DECRYPTION ENVIRONMENT	KEY INJECTION FACILITY
BDK	N/A	Stored in Decryption HSM.	Stored in Key Injection Machine.
Initial Key (IPEK)	Injected during key injection. Then, discarded after first series of Future Keys is generated during key injection.	Reconstructed by encrypting the Initial KSN with BDK. Then used to derive the session key.	Generated at the time of key injection by encrypting the Initial KSN with BDK.
Future (Session) Key	Used for data encryption and generation of new Future Keys. New key is used for each new encryption session. Discarded after encryption session. There are 21 Future Keys of 34 hexadecimal digits each.	Derived from Initial Key and Transaction Counter using special algorithm.	N/A

Initial Key and KSN

According to the DUKPT scheme, each *PIN encryption device* (PED) or *secure card reader* (SCR) is injected with a unique *initial key* (Table 8-5). The initial key, which is also called the *initial PIN encryption key* (IPEK) in PIN encryption implementations, is derived from the BDK during the *key injection* process at a special *key injection facility* (KIF). Each new PED or SCR is assigned with the *initial key serial number* (Initial KSN) which is also injected into the terminal along with the initial key. The initial KSN consists of a *BDK ID* and a *TRSM ID* (Table 8-6). The BDK ID allows the decryption part to select an appropriate BDK to decrypt the data. The TRSM ID is the unique device identifier within the scope of the given BDK. The *key injection machine*, which is an HSM that is specialized for key injection, creates the initial key by encrypting the initial KSN with BDK and injects it into the memory located in TRSM along with the initial KSN. The initial key is not stored in the terminal but used for generation of the series of *future keys* at the time of injection. The DUKPT-enabled encryption device also has an *encryption counter* which is initiated to 0 during the key injection process.

Table 8-6: DUKPT Data Elements

DATA ELEMENT	CONTENT	DESCRIPTION
BDK ID	Key Identifier	Identifies the BDK associated with the encryption device. Injected to the encryption device as part of the Initial KSN during key injection.
TRSM ID	Device Identifier	Identifies the encryption device in a scope of given BDK. Injected to the encryption device as part of the Initial KSN during key injection.
Encryption Counter	Transaction Counter	Set to 0 during key injection. Incremented after each encryption session.
Initial KSN	BDK ID + TRSM ID	When encrypted by BDK during key injection produces the Initial Key (IPEK).
KSN	Initial KSN + Encryption Counter	Used by decryption end to re-create the session key.
Encrypted PIN Block	KSN + ciphertext	Sent from encryption device to decryption end.

Future (Session) Key

The future key has two functions:

1. It is used as a one-time *session key* for data encryption.
2. It is used for nonreversible generation of the next future key by encrypting the value of the encryption counter which is incremented after each encryption session.

The future (session) key is discarded as soon as it is used for encryption and generation of the next future keys. Thus, no information about previous keys is ever stored in the TRSM. The size of the encryption counter (21 bits) allows 1 million transactions to be performed without the need for another initial key injection.

Decryption

For each transaction, the PED or SCR send to the decryption part the specially formatted data block, which is called *encrypted PIN block* in PIN encryption implementations. The encrypted PIN block consists of KSN (20 bytes) and ciphertext. The KSN consists of the initial KSN (BDK ID plus TRSM ID) and the encryption counter value. The software or the HSM at the decryption back end uses the KSN elements to select the appropriate BDK and re-create the appropriate session key using special a algorithm defined in the standard.[17]

EMV

EMV (also known as *Chip & Pin*) stands for *Europay, MasterCard and Visa* and is a global standard for *Integrated Circuit Cards* (ICC) also known as "Chip and PIN." EMV cards can be accepted at POS terminals and ATM machines that are equipped with special *Integrated Circuit Card Reader* (ICCR) device. The EMV cards are regulated by the EMV Integrated Circuit Card Specifications[18] which are managed by EMVCo LLC.[19], a global company owned by American Express, JCB, MasterCard, and Visa. The EMVCo standard consists of a set of four "Books" which are based on a series of ISO/IEC 7816 standards (from 7816-1 to 7816-16) for contact cards. For example, the ISO/IEC 7816-4 standard defines the "Organization, security and commands for interchange."[20] According to EMVCo, their specifications "contain a selection of options taken from the ISO 7816 standards that are relevant for the financial sector."[21]

The EMV Integrated Circuit Card Specifications for Payment Systems are:

- Book 1 — Application Independent ICC to Terminal Interface Requirements
- Book 2 — Security and Key Management
- Book 3 — Application Specification
- Book 4 — Cardholder, Attendant, and Acquirer Interface Requirements

EMV is still uncommon in the United States and many other countries, and we are still years away from its global implementation. This technology is mostly focused on cardholder authentication and fraud protection. The PCI DSS standard requires the same rules be applied to merchants using EMV because sensitive cardholder information can still be obtained through the payment application. Many Chip and PIN card issuers still retain the magnetic stripe so their cards will be accepted in U.S. stores not equipped by EMV readers. Such "dual" cards allow the hackers to manipulate the service codes or kill the chip in order to force the payment system to switch into fallback processing of ordinary magnetic swipes, which disables new security features.

Mobile and Contactless Payments

NFC-based payment solutions use existing contactless payment terminals to enter the card data into the POS. They store the card data in the mobile device, which can be compromised. In addition, the contactless MSD (Magnetic Stripe Data) readers aren't more secure than regular MSR. Once the data is transmitted via NFC from the card chip (or mobile device NFC transmitter) to the payment terminal, it is handled internally by POS and the payment application in exactly the same way as the data read by regular MSR.

Non-NFC solutions can resolve these issues listed. Such solutions use the POS to link a mobile device to the payment transaction. All the sensitive data is exchanged between the POS and mobile payment server so no sensitive data is ever present at the store level. The traditional format of the credit cards can be preserved so no technological revolution (such as EMV) is even necessary at the card level — the card data is stored securely in the data centers which have all the necessary prerequisites to be adequately protected. I proposed such a solution back in 2009.[22] It uses a barcode with a one-time randomly generated token displayed on the mobile device screen to link the cell phone and POS in order to start the payment session. Once the transaction is finalized, the logical link between the POS and mobile phone is destroyed and cannot be reused. The connection between the POS and the customer is kept at the data center level.

Summary

PCI DSS and PA-DSS require only data at rest and some limited data in transit encryption. In order to provide complete protection to sensitive cardholder information, the data should be encrypted everywhere: in memory, in transit, and at rest. SSL is a reliable solution for data in-transit protection. Point-to-point encryption is the best choice when shopping for a comprehensive solution. There are different flavors of P2PE: hardware, software, hybrid, and their combinations. Hardware/Hardware P2PE is the most secure and complicated option from both implementation and certification viewpoints. EMV and mobile payment technologies provide additional protection to sensitive cardholder data.

Notes

1. *NetworkWorld*, "Memory scraping malware goes after encrypted private information," `http://www.networkworld.com/news/2011/022211-pervasive-memory-malware.html`

2. MSDN, "SecureString Class," `http://msdn.microsoft.com/en-us/library/system.security.securestring(v=vs.110).aspx`

3. IBM, "History of SSL," `http://publib.boulder.ibm.com/infocenter/iseries/v5r3/index.jsp?topic=/rzain/rzainhistory.htm`

4. Mark O'Neil, *Web Services Security*, (New York: McGraw-Hill/Osborne, 2003), pp. 37, 43.

5. Joshua Davies, *Implementing SSL / TLS Using Cryptography and PKI*, (Hoboken, NJ: Wiley, 2011)

6. SSLShopper, "SSL Details," `http://www.sslshopper.com/ssl-details.html`

7. Symantec/Verisign, "SSL Certificates," `http://www.symantec.com/verisign/ssl-certificates`

8. Microsoft, "Setting Up a Certification Authority," `http://technet.microsoft.com/en-us/library/cc770827.aspx`

9. OpenSSL, `http://www.openssl.org/`

10. MSDN, "MakeCert.exe (Certificate Creation Tool)," `http://msdn.microsoft.com/en-us/library/bfsktky3.aspx`

11. Mike Wood, "Fraudulent certificates issued by Comodo, is it time to rethink who we trust?" (March 24, 2011), `http://nakedsecurity.sophos.com/2011/03/24/fraudulent-certificates-issued-by-comodo-is-it-time-to-rethink-who-we-trust/`

12. TechNet, "Auto-Enrollment—Avoid the challenges of making end users manage their certificates" (TechNet, 2010), `http://blogs.technet.com/b/meamcs/archive/2010/12/01/auto-enrollment-avoid-the-challenges-of-making-end-users-manage-their-certificates.aspx`

13. Slava Gomzin, "Securing Communication of Legacy Applications with IPSec: Step-by-Step Guide to Protecting "Data in Transit" without Changes in Your Existing Software," `http://www.gomzin.com/securing-communication-of-legacy-applications-with-ipsec.html`

14. "Payment Card Industry (PCI) Point-to-Point Encryption Solution Requirements and Testing Procedures: Encryption, Decryption, and Key Management within Secure Cryptographic Devices (Hardware/Hardware),

Version 1.1.1" (July 2013), `https://www.pcisecuritystandards.org/documents/P2PE_v1-1.pdf`

15. "Payment Card Industry (PCI) Point-to-Point Encryption Solution Requirements and Testing Procedures: Encryption and Key Management within Secure Cryptographic Devices, and Decryption of Account Data in Software (Hardware/Hybrid)" *Version 1.1.1*, (July 2013), `https://www.pcisecuritystandards.org/documents/P2PE_Hybrid_v1.1.1.pdf`

16. ANSI, "Retail Financial Services Symmetric Key Management Part 1: Using Symmetric Techniques, Accredited Standards Committee X9, Inc" (October 13, 2009), `http://webstore.ansi.org/RecordDetail.aspx?sku=ANSI+X9.24-1%3A2009`

17. Ibid.

18. EMVCo, LLC., "EMV Integrated Circuit Card Specifications for Payment Systems Version 4.3" (November 2011), `http://www.emvco.com/specifications.aspx?id=223`

19. EMVCo, LLC., `http://www.emvco.com/`

20. ISO/IEC, "INTERNATIONAL STANDARD ISO/IEC 7816-4, Identification cards—Integrated circuit cards—Part 4: Organization, security and commands for interchange," (2005).

21. EMVCo, LLC., "General FAQ," `http://www.emvco.com/faq.aspx?id=37#1`

22. Slava Gomzin, "Mobile Checkout: Secure Mobile Payments Solution Proposal" (April 2009), `http://www.gomzin.com/mobile-checkout.html`

CHAPTER 9

Securing Application Code

Any sufficiently advanced technology is undistinguishable from magic.

—Arthur C. Clarke

While designing secure POS and payment applications, developers first think about sensitive data protection. However, they often forget about the fact that the data protection mechanisms by themselves should be protected as well. Insecure application code and configuration open the back doors for hackers.

Code Signing

Code signing is the mechanism that protects software applications from tampering during all stages of the application life cycle, including initial deployment, runtime, and updates. Digital signatures are calculated by the software vendor for each binary file in the application package as the final part of the build and release process. The signature can then be verified by end users to ensure that the code was not modified since it was built by the vendor. In addition, code signing allows recognition of counterfeited binaries that pretend to be legitimate parts of the application, since such files wouldn't have a digital signature at all or their signature would be fake.

Code signing has been used with software distributed through the Internet for a long time. However, the importance of digital signing is often underestimated for "regular" desktop and server software, such as POS and payment applications. Many security breaches could be prevented if merchants had the ability to verify the authenticity of all the code files that are present on their POS and store server machines.

Authenticode

Microsoft *Authenticode* technology allows for the signing of binary files using attached digital signatures.[1] The signature is contained inside the signed file which simplifies all operations involving both the file and its signature. SignTool[2] provides the ability to sign the application files as well as verify digital signatures. Unlike *strong name signing*[3], which is only intended for signing .NET assemblies, Authenticode can be used for protection of any executable and Dynamic Link Library (.dll) files.

Code Signing Certificates

For a real production environment, it is recommended to purchase the *code signing certificate* from one of *public certification authorities*.[4, 5] The point is that root certificates of well-known CA are pre-installed in most operating systems and browsers, so the code singing certificate issued by public CA will be trusted at virtually any client machine "out of the box," without a need to pre-install proprietary root CA certificates on target systems.

For development and testing purposes, the *MakeCert* tool, already discussed in Chapters 7 and 8, can be used to issue the code signing certificate, which looks the same (at least from the viewpoint of the application being tested) as the one issued by the public CA. In order to sign the code signing certificate, you can also reuse the test root CA that was created to issue SSL certificates:

```
makecert -a sha256 -len 4096 -n "CN=CodeSignDemo"
-b 01/01/2013 -e 01/01/2023 -ic SSLDemoRoot.cer -iv SSLDemoRoot.pvk
-sky signature -sv CodeSignDemo.pvk CodeSignDemo.cer

pvk2pfx -pvk CodeSignDemo.pvk -spc CodeSignDemo.cer
-pfx CodeSignDemo.pfx -pi 1
```

CROSS-REFERENCE See the "Creating Certificate Authority" section of Chapter 8 for more details on the test root CA.

Don't forget to install the root CA certificate to the Trusted Root Certification Authorities store by clicking the SSLDemoRoot.cer file as described in Chapter 8 (the trusted root CA certificate should be available during both signing and validation operations). However, there is an alternative path that can be taken for generating both root CA and code signing private keys and certificates: using an open source cryptographic toolkit and SDK called *OpenSSL*.[6]

Creating the Root CA Using OpenSSL

First, download and install OpenSSL.[7] During the installation, use the default target folder `c:\OpenSSL-Win32` and check the option to install OpenSSL binaries into the `[OpenSSL]\bin` directory. After the installation, use the Windows command prompt (`Start->Run...->cmd`) to set the OpenSSL configuration path:

```
set OPENSSL_CONF=c:\OpenSSL-Win32\bin\openssl.cfg
```

Now generate the root CA private key using OpenSSL (see Figure 9-1). First, create the root directory for the CA `C:\ROOT_CA` and run the OpenSSL command from the command prompt. The OpenSSL `genrsa` command will generate the RSA 4,096-bit key and encrypt it by Triple DES:

```
openssl genrsa -des3 -out C:\ROOT_CA\root_ca.key 4096
```

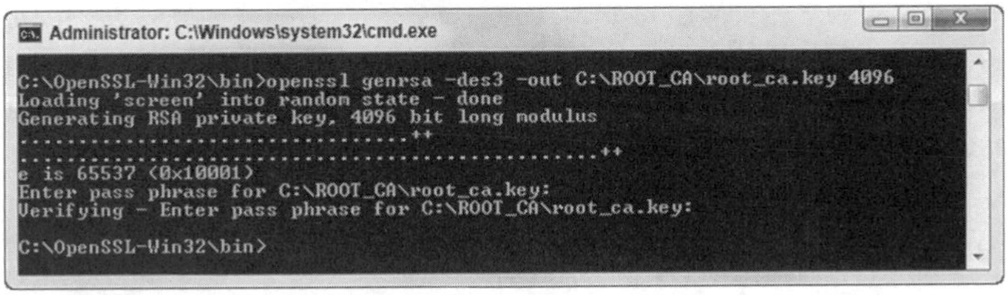

Figure 9-1: Generating test root CA private key using OpenSSL

In order to create the public key CA certificate, run the OpenSSL `req` command (Figure 9-2) with the arguments described in Table 9-1:

```
openssl req -new -x509 -days 3650 -key C:\ROOT_CA\root_ca.key
-out C:\ROOT_CA\root_ca.crt
```

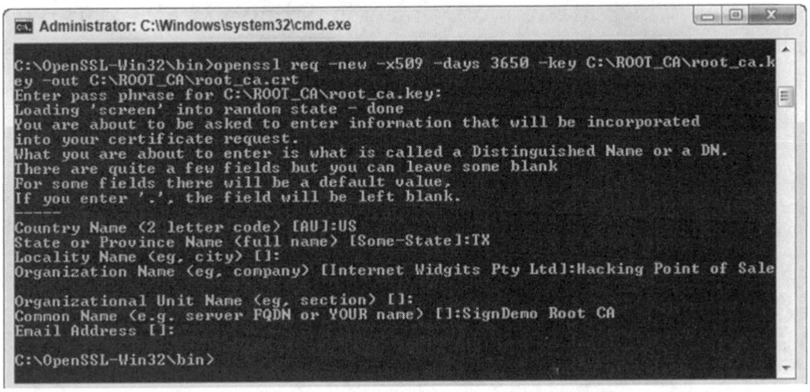

Figure 9-2: Generating the root CA public key certificate using OpenSSL

Table 9-1: OpenSSL Parameters for Generating the Root CA Certificate

PARAMETER	VALUE	DESCRIPTION
req	N/A	Create certificate signing request
-new	N/A	Create new request
-X509	N/A	Create the certificate instead of certificate request (see more details about certificate request in section "Creating Production-grade Code Signing Certificate"
-days	3650	Set expiration date in 10 years
-key	C:\ROOT_CA\root_ca.key	Location and name of the CA root private key
-out	C:\ROOT_CA\root_ca.crt	Location and name of the CA root public-key certificate that is being created

The last step is installing the root CA certificate into the Trusted Root Certification Authorities store by clicking the `root_ca.crt` file and following the same instructions presented in Chapter 8 for `SSLDemoRoot.cer` file.

Certificate Formats

As you may have noticed, MakeCert and OpenSSL commands operate with different public key certificate and private key file extensions: `.cer` and `.pvk` for MakeCert, and `.crt` and `.key` for OpenSSL. Although both tools use the same basic internal certificate format (X.509[8]), by default they recognize two different forms of data representation: *binary* and *Base-64* encoded. These formats are often referred as *DER* (Distinguished Encoding Rules) and *PEM* (Privacy-enhanced Electronic Mail) accordingly. The binary DER format is a little more compact because it uses all the possible byte values (Figure 9-3), while Base-64 encoded PEM uses 64 printable ASCII characters which makes it convenient for string and XML data type operations and transmissions (Figure 9-4). Base-64 certificate data starts with `-----BEGIN CERTIFICATE-----` and ends with `-----END CERTIFICATE-----` delimiters.

The same difference exists between the two private key containers: `.pvk` has binary format, while `.key` is a Base-64 encoded file.

Figure 9-3: Binary encoded DER (.cer) certificate format

Figure 9-4: Base-64 encoded PEM (.crt) certificate format

Creating a Production-grade Code Signing Certificate

As demonstrated in Chapters 7 and 8, the code signing certificate for development and testing could also be created by MakeCert. Here we will use OpenSSL, however, and not without reason. OpenSSL is able to create a *certificate signing request* which can be sent to a public CA for issuing a code signing certificate that can be used in the production code signing process.

Creation of a code signing certificate using OpenSSL includes the following steps.

Step 1: Generating the Code Signing Private Key

This command will generate a 2,048-bit (as recommended by NIST[9]) RSA private key and encrypt it using the Triple DES algorithm with the pass phrase which it prompts the user to enter (Figure 9-5):

```
openssl genrsa -des3 -out C:\CODE_SIGN\CodeSignDemo.key 2048
```

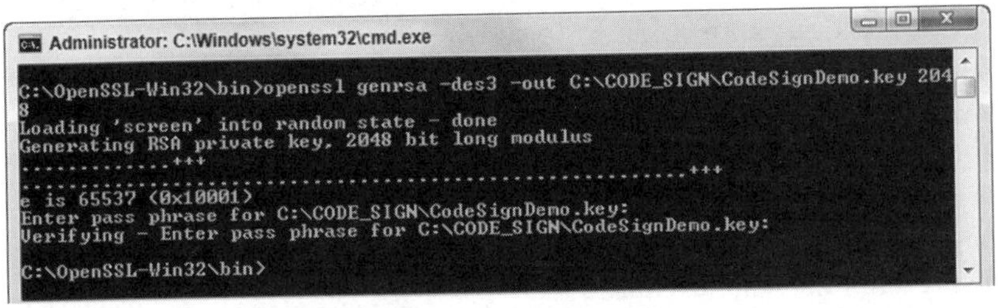

Figure 9-5: Generating RSA private key using OpenSSL

Step 2: Creating the Certificate Signing Request

The OpenSSL `req` command with the arguments described in Table 9-2 will create the certificate signing request (see Figure 9-6):

```
openssl req -new -key C:\CODE_SIGN\CodeSignDemo.key
-out c:\CODE_SIGN\CodeSignDemo.csr
```

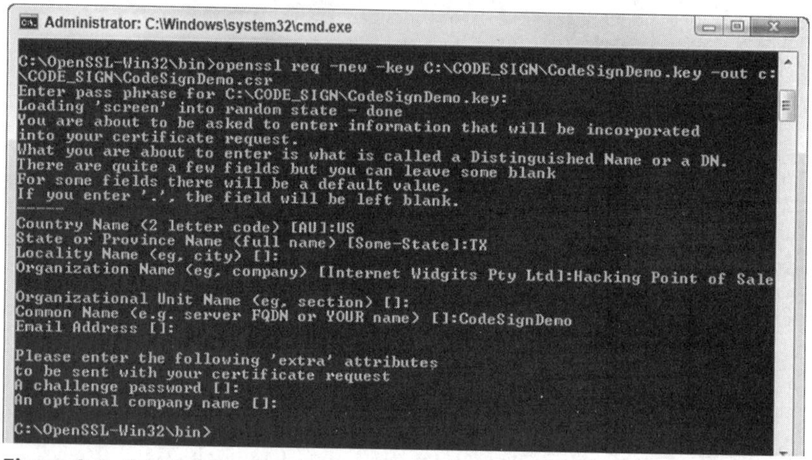

Figure 9-6: Creating Certificate Signing Request using OpenSSL

Table 9-2: OpenSSL Parameters for Generating the Certificate Signing Request Command

PARAMETER	VALUE	DESCRIPTION
req	N/A	Create certificate signing request
-new	N/A	Create new request
-days	3650	Set expiration date in 10 years
-key	C:\CODE_SIGN\CodeSignDemo.key	Location and name of the code signing private key
-out	C:\CODE_SIGN\CodeSignDemo.csr	Location and name of the certificate signing request that is being created. Note that the file extension is `.csr`.

At this point, the `CodeSignDemo.csr` can be sent to the public CA for signing in order to issue a production-grade code signing certificate.

> **NOTE** If you are planning to use HSM for certificate storage and code signing, which is strongly recommended since it provides the highest level of security for the entire code signing process, the first two steps would be performed by the HSM which would securely generate and store the private key using hardware protection, as well as generate the certificate signing request.

Step 3: Signing the Code Signing Certificate by Root CA

The next step is to create the code signing certificate from the certificate signing request and sign it by the Root CA. In a production environment, this step will most probably be performed by the public CA. For development and testing purposes, the OpenSSL x509 command (Table 9-3) can take the certificate signing request and sign the certificate with the test Root CA (Figure 9-7):

```
openssl x509 -req -days 3650 -in c:\CODE_SIGN\CodeSignDemo.csr
-CA C:\ROOT_CA\root_ca.crt -CAkey C:\ROOT_CA\root_ca.key
-set_serial 01 -out C:\CODE_SIGN\CodeSignDemo.crt
```

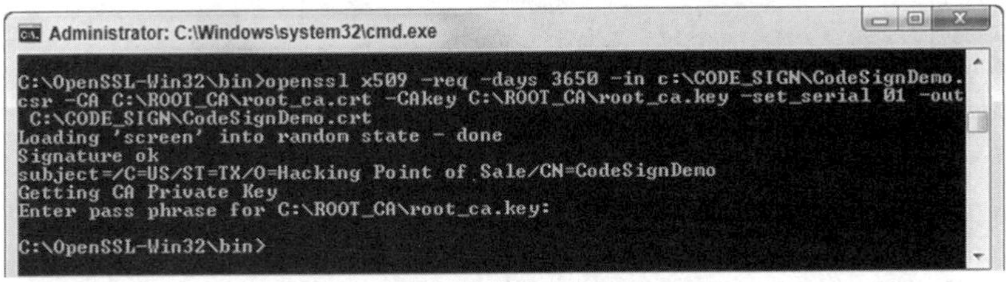

Figure 9-7: Signing the Code Signing Certificate by Root CA using OpenSSL

Table 9-3: OpenSSL Parameters for Signing the Code Signing Certificate by Root CA

PARAMETER	VALUE	DESCRIPTION
x509	N/A	X509 can perform different operations with certificates depending on following arguments
-req	N/A	Input is a certificate signing request
-days	3650	Set expiration date in 10 years
-in	C:\CODE_SIGN\CodeSignDemo.csr	The input file (certificate signing request)
-CA	C:\ROOT_CA\root_ca.crt	Root CA public-key certificate file
-CAkey	C:\ROOT_CA\root_ca.key	Root CA private-key file
-set_serial	01	Set serial number of the certificate
-out	C:\CODE_SIGN\CodeSignDemo.crt	Location and name of the output certificate file

Step 4: Compiling the PFX File

SignTool, which is going to be used for the signing, does not accept the signing certificate in the form of two separate files (public key certificate and private key), but rather requires a single PFX file be provided. So the last step is the PFX compilation which can also be done using the OpenSSL `pkcs12` command (Figure 9-8):

```
openssl pkcs12 -export -out c:\CODE_SIGN\CodeSignDemo.pfx
-inkey c:\CODE_SIGN\CodeSignDemo.key -in c:\CODE_SIGN\CodeSignDemo.crt
-certfile C:\ROOT_CA\root_ca.crt
```

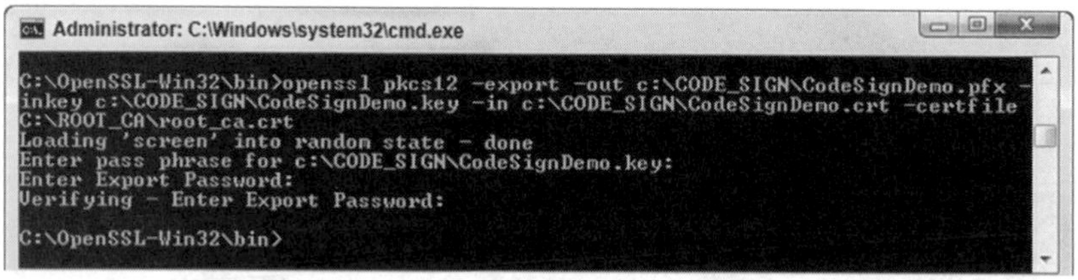

Figure 9-8: Creating PFX file using OpenSSL

Timestamp

Timestamp is required in order to prolong the validity of the signed software beyond the end of life of the code signing certificate (which is usually limited to 1–5 years).

The digital signature verification process consists of the following steps:

1. Validating the signature itself by calculating the hash of the file and comparing the result with the hash that was calculated during the signing process and encrypted with the signing certificate's private key.

2. Validating all the parameters of the signing certificate (which is usually packed along with the signature), *including its expiration date.*

3. Validating the chain of trust (all the certificates in the chain up to the root CA certificate).

The problem with digital signatures is that they may become invalid once the code signing certificate is expired. The timestamping takes care of the situation when the second validation step fails due to certificate expiration, but you still want to use the software if the results of all other checks are positive. The timestamp fixes the problem by demonstrating to the validation system that the file was signed at the time when the signing certificate was still valid (before it expired).

The timestamp is signed and verified in a way similar to how the code signature itself is done. Timestamping can be done by a proprietary or public timestamping service. There are free public timestamping services available for both testing and production code signing (Table 9-4). The /t parameter with the timestamping service URL should be added to the SignCode certificate issuing command in order to add the timestamp, for example:

```
/t "http://timestamp.verisign.com/scripts/timstamp.dll"
```

Table 9-4: Examples of Free Online Timestamping Services

PROVIDER	URL
Verisign	`http://timestamp.verisign.com/scripts/timstamp.dll`
Comodo	`http://timestamp.comodoca.com/authenticode`
Digicert	`http://timestamp.digicert.com`

Implementing Code Signing

The code signing process itself is very simple and can be done from a command line or application using command shell. The SignTool is included in Windows SDK which is available for download from the MSDN website.[10] The 32-bit version (which is recommended) of SignTool will be installed at `<SDK install location>\Windows Kits\8.0\bin\x86`.

The following command will sign the `EncryptionDemo.exe` file using the code signing certificate previously created (Figure 9-9):

```
signtool sign /f CodeSignDemo.pfx /p HackingPOS /v
/t "http://timestamp.verisign.com/scripts/timstamp.dll"
/d "Hacking POS" /a EncryptionDemo.exe
```

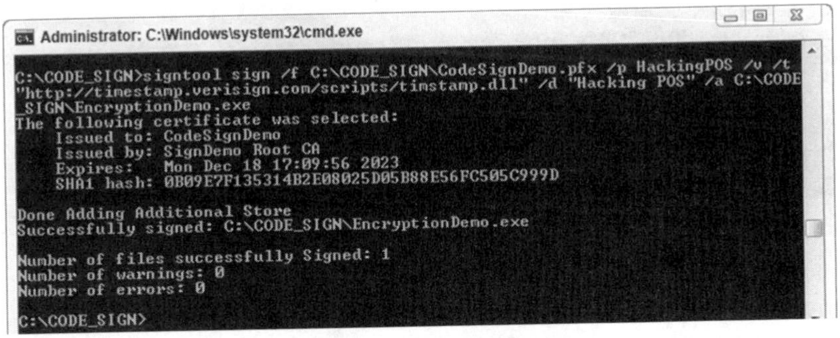

Figure 9-9: Signing the executable file using SignTool

Once the executable is signed, right-clicking the file will open the file properties screen where the new *Digital Signatures* tab now shows the digital signature and timestamp (Figure 9-10).

Figure 9-10: File properties dialog showing the digital signature and the timestamp

The signature can be validated using the same SignTool with the following parameters (Figure 9-11):

```
signtool verify /pa EncryptionDemo.exe
```

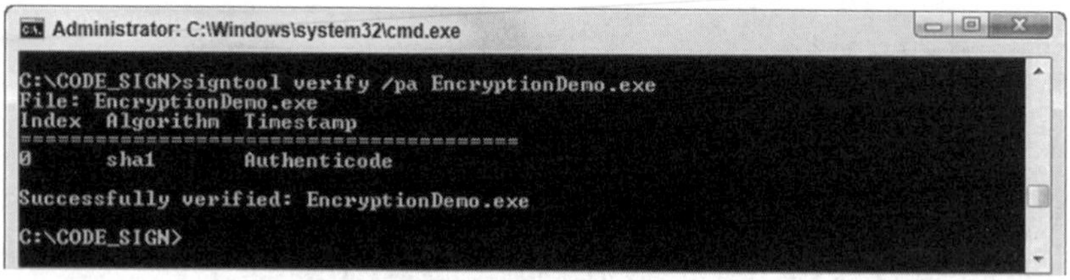

Figure 9-11: Verifying the code signature using SignTool

The SigningDemo application (Figure 9-12) simply calls the SignTool command using the .NET `Process` class:

```
ProcessStartInfo processStartInfo =
    new processStartInfo(textBoxSignToolLocation.Text, parameters);
Process process = new Process();
process.StartInfo = processStartInfo;
process.Start();
```

```
outputReader = process.StandardOutput;
errorReader = process.StandardError;
process.WaitForExit();
```

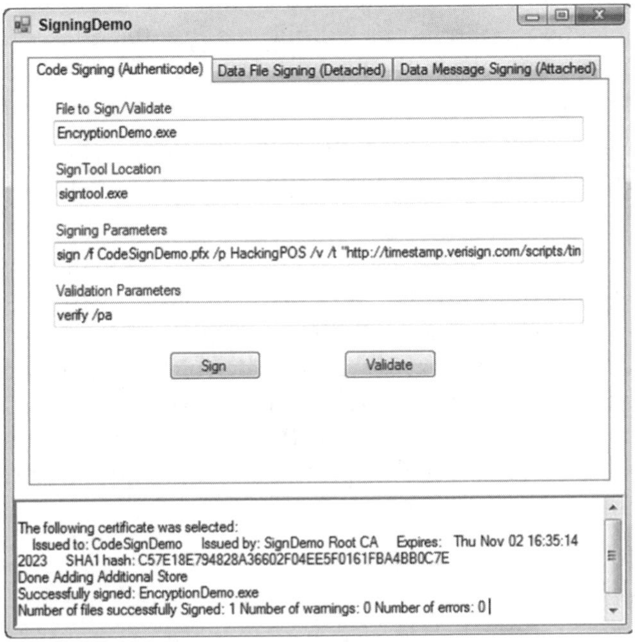

Figure 9-12: SigningDemo: Authenticode code signing

Signing Configuration and Data Files

Code signing is certainly the most important part of the code protection strategy. However, you should not forget the fact that software application behavior can be modified not only by alternating the code, but also through the configuration changes. For example, changing the database connection string may switch the payment application to a dummy database server, while a modified value of the IP address parameter may forward transactions to a bogus server installed for MITM attack. In order to avoid such situations, application configuration and data files can also be signed so their signatures can be verified by the application during the startup or even on every data read.

Attached or Detached?

The basic principles of data files and message signing stay the same as they are for the code signing: generating the digital signature after the data is written, and signature validation before the data is read. However, the technology behind the data signing is slightly different from Authenticode which was previously described in connection to the code signing.

Chapter 7 briefly reviewed two major groups of data signatures:

- An *attached*, or *enveloped*, signature is located in the same container as the content that is being signed. So in the case of file signing, the attached signature is located in the same file as the file content. Authenticode is an example of attached signature.

- A *detached* signature is separated from the object that is being signed. So in the case of file signing, the detached signature is located in a separate *signature file*.

These differences define the areas of application. If it is undesirable to modify the file or the message that is being signed, a detached signature is used. A detached signature provides the ability to sign virtually any digital object without affecting its existing format and the functionality around it, which is especially important when designing security enhancements for existing systems. Usually, this is the case for application configuration files and other application data files so they remain readable by older versions of the application that do not support the signature verification.

Data Signing Certificate

Once again, there are several options for signing certificate creation and deployment, depending on the use case and the target environment:

- Reuse the SSLDemoRoot test CA which was created for SSL testing in Chapter 8. The root CA certificate (SSLDemoRoot.cer file) should be installed to Trusted Root Certification Authorities store so it is available for both signing and validation of the digital signatures. The *MakeCert* and *Pvk2pfx* command arguments for signing certificate generation are similar to SSL client certificates. The only difference is that the purpose of the certificate (-sky parameter) should be set to signature:

```
makecert -a sha256 -len 2048 -n "CN=SigningDemo" -b 01/01/2013
-e 01/01/2023 -ic SSLDemoRoot.cer -iv SSLDemoRoot.pvk
-sky signature -sv SigningDemo.pvk SigningDemo.cer

pvk2pfx -pvk SigningDemo.pvk -spc SigningDemo.cer
-pfx SigningDemo.pfx -pi 1
```

This option can be used for development and testing only, and it's the one used by the SigningDemo application for configuration file signing.

- Reuse the root CA and the signing certificate that were previously created with OpenSSL for the code signing. This option is mostly for development and testing, but in theory it can be used for production.

- Create a certificate request and sign it by public CA as previously described for code signing. This option is suitable for production.

- Issue the signing certificate using a proprietary CA, which can be configured to use signing certificates using *certificate templates*[11] (Figure 9-13), which in turn define all the required characteristics of the signing certificate so the CA can automatically issue multiple certificates with the same parameters using the *certificate autoenrollment*[12] mechanism. This option is suitable for production inside isolated LAN or corporate WAN.

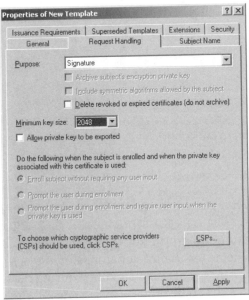

Figure 9-13: Example of Certificate Template Setup Dialog

Certificate Store

In all demo applications in this book, all the certificates except the root CA certificate are located in files because it is convenient for education, development, and testing, and in some cases even for production. Another option is installing the signing certificate into the certificate store. In this case, the private key is secured by the certificate store. It is still not ideal protection, but it is a little better than a certificate file which can be easily stolen. If you make the private key non-exportable, then theoretically the certificate (its private key part) cannot be copied to another computer. In order to install the certificate in the store, just click the PFX file and follow the *Certificate Import Wizard* instructions. Make sure the *"Mark this key as exportable"* option is unchecked (Figure 9-14).

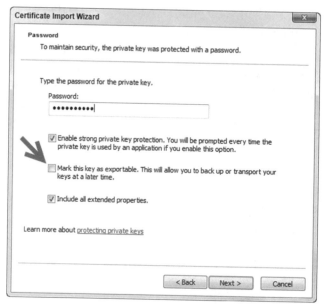

Figure 9-14: Importing signing certificate to certificate store

Implementing Detached Signature

The Data File Signing tab of the SigningDemo application demonstrates the implementation of a detached signature (Figure 9-15). `SigningDemo.config` (it can be any file) is signed using the certificate and private key from the `SigningDemo.pfx` file. The result of the signing is a detached digital signature stored in a separate `SigningDemo.config.p7s` file. The original file is not modified during the signing operation. However, if you change the content of the `SigningDemo.config` file and try to validate the signature, the following error message will be displayed:

```
Signature Validation Failed:
The hash value is not correct.
```

Signing Code

First, the *Sign* method of `DetachedSignature` class loads the data from the `SigningDemo.config` file and the singing certificate and private key from the `SigningDemo.pfx`:

```
byte[] fileContent = getFileContent(FileName);
string signatureFileName = FileName + ".p7s";
X509Certificate2 signerCertificate =
    new X509Certificate2(Certificate, Password);
```

Figure 9-15: SigningDemo: Signing configuration file using detached signature

Then, the instances of the CmsSigner and SignedCms classes (System.Security .Cryptography.Pkcs namespace) are used to calculate the digital signature:

```
Oid signatureFileContentType = new Oid(PKCS7_CONTENT_TYPE_SIGNED_DATA);
var contentInfo =
    new ContentInfo(signatureFileContentType, fileContent);
var signedCms = new SignedCms(contentInfo, true);
var cmsSigner = new CmsSigner(signerCertificate);
signedCms.ComputeSignature(cmsSigner);
```

The resulting signature buffer is written into the SigningDemo.config .p7s file:

```
byte[] signature = signedCms.Encode();
using (var binaryWriter =
    new BinaryWriter(File.Open(FileName, FileMode.Create)))
{
    binaryWriter.Write(signature);
    binaryWriter.Close();
}
```

Validation Code

The signature verification is just the opposite of the signing process. First, it loads the signature data from the signature file, and the signed data from the original .config file:

```
byte[] fileContent = getFileContent(FileName);
byte[] signatureFileContent = getFileContent(FileName + ".p7s");
```

The standard getFileContent method in the BaseSignature class just reads the entire binary content of any file:

```
using (var filestream =
    new FileStream(filename, FileMode.Open, FileAccess.Read))
{
    try
    {
        using (var binaryreader = new BinaryReader(filestream))
        {
            try
            {
                long count = new FileInfo(filename).Length;
                fileContent = binaryreader.ReadBytes((int)count);
            }
            finally
            {
                binaryreader.Close();
            }
        }
    }
    finally
    {
        filestream.Close();
    }
}
```

Then, using the same SignedCms class it checks the signature,

```
signedCms.CheckSignature(true);
```

and validates the signing certificate and its chain (only root CA certificate in our case):

```
var signingCertificate = signedCms.Certificates[0];
var chain = new X509Chain
{
    ChainPolicy =
    {
        RevocationFlag = X509RevocationFlag.EntireChain,
        RevocationMode = X509RevocationMode.NoCheck,
```

```
            UrlRetrievalTimeout = new TimeSpan(0, 0, 5),
            VerificationFlags = X509VerificationFlags.NoFlag
        }
    };
    chain.Build(signingCertificate);
    foreach (X509ChainStatus status in chain.ChainStatus)
    {
        throw new ApplicationException("Certificate validation error: " +
            status.Status.ToString());
    }
```

Attached Signatures

Detached signatures are universal because they do not modify the original file or message, and therefore can be applied virtually to any object. However, there are cases when attached signature is more suitable — for code signing, for example. Imagine that all the binary files are signed with detached signatures. Then you would have up to twice the number of application files on every computer. Data files, including configuration, can also be signed using attached signatures. The only limitation is that the resulting file can be read only by specialized code which knows to distinguish the data from its signature. Attached signatures can also be used for data in transit signing since the data in message can be handled the same way as the data in file.

Signing XML Files

The standard for XML attached signature is XMLDSIG[13] which defines the way XML documents can be signed. .NET has an implementation of XML signing[14, 15] which is based on XMLDSIG and can be used, for example, to sign the .NET `app.config` file. However, this implementation is limited to XML files only. The following method is suitable for signing the data content using attached signature and saving the result (the data and the signature) in a single file.

Implementing Attached Signature

There is no separate section about signing certificate for attached signature because the certificate generation process that was discussed previously for code signing and detached signatures is the same for attached signatures. You just reuse the same data signing certificate (`SigningDemo.pfx`). The SigningDemo application has a third tab which demonstrates the attached signature created for the custom configuration data entered in the Input Data text box (Figure 9-16). The result (the content, its signature, and the signing certificate combined together) is stored in the `Database.cfg` file (Figure 9-17).

Figure 9-16: SigningDemo: Signing configuration file using attached signature

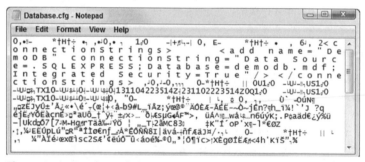

Figure 9-17: Database.cfg file: The output of the attached signature demo

Signing and Validation Code

The signing code (`AttachedSignature` class) is similar to detached signature implementation. The major difference is that it stores both the signed data and the signature in the same output file:

```
var contentInfo = new ContentInfo(
new Oid(PKCS7_CONTENT_TYPE_ENVELOPED_DATA), messageBuffer);
var signedCms = new SignedCms(contentInfo, false);
var cmsSigner = new CmsSigner(signerCertificate);
signedCms.ComputeSignature(cmsSigner);
byte[] messageAndSignature = signedCms.Encode();
writeToFile(OutputFile, messageAndSignature);
```

The validation code, accordingly, first reads the data buffer from the file and extracts the signature portion of it:

```
byte[] fileContent = getFileContent(FileName);
SignedCms signedCms = new SignedCms();
signedCms.Decode(fileContent);
```

Then it verifies the signature and the signing certificate,

```
signedCms.CheckSignature(true);
var signingCertificate = signedCms.Certificates[0];
validateCertificate(signingCertificate);
```

and finally, extracts the data:

```
byte[] resultBuffer = signedCms.ContentInfo.Content;
string result = Encoding.Unicode.GetString(resultBuffer);
```

Code Obfuscation

Simply put, *code obfuscation* is protection against *reverse engineering*. A brief explanation of reverse engineering will help to understand what code obfuscation is and why it is needed in the first place.

Reverse Engineering

Reverse engineering is a process of *decompiling*, or *disassembling* the compiled application binary files in order to re-create the original source code. Reverse engineering is used to understand the logic and details of implementation of the software application when there is no access to its source code. It can be done, for example, in order to study a competitor's product, understand and disable the application access controls, or learn about the application's encryption algorithms and hard-coded parameter values. Even though it is impossible in most cases to re-create the exact source code from the compiled binaries, in some language environments, such as .NET and Java, the result of decompiling can be very close to the original.

Let's conduct a small experiment with the encryption demo code from Chapter 7 to see how reverse engineering works. This is the fragment of the original .NET C# source code which creates the PAN token using salted hash function (the full demo source code can be downloaded from the Wiley website at www.wiley.com/go/hackingpos):

The Original Source Code

```
namespace HackingPOS.Cryptography.Encryption
{
    public class Hashing
```

```
    {
        private const string CONSTANT_SALT_COMPONENT =
            "PE67nf0hnHkd8Dx81SroA4PH7J1Z7HAUNe9g6a+8ml8";
        private string user_defined_salt_component;
        private const int ITERATIONS = 1024;
        private const int SALT_COMPONENT_SIZE = 32;

        public Hashing(string user_defined_salt_component)
        {
            this.user_defined_salt_component =
                user_defined_salt_component;
        }

        public string CreateToken(
            string PAN, string VariableSaltComponent)
        {
            Random random =
                new Random(VariableSaltComponent.GetHashCode());
            byte[] variable_salt_bytes = new byte[SALT_COMPONENT_SIZE];
            random.NextBytes(variable_salt_bytes);
            byte[] hash_result = hash(PAN, variable_salt_bytes);
            return Convert.ToBase64String(hash_result);
        }

        private byte[] hash(
            string plaintext, byte[] variable_salt_component)
        {
            Rfc2898DeriveBytes saltGenerator = new Rfc2898DeriveBytes(
                Encoding.ASCII.GetBytes(CONSTANT_SALT_COMPONENT +
                user_defined_salt_component),
                variable_salt_component,
                ITERATIONS);
            byte[] salt_bytes =
                saltGenerator.GetBytes(SALT_COMPONENT_SIZE);
            byte[] plaintext_bytes = Encoding.ASCII.GetBytes(plaintext);
            byte[] hash_input = new byte[SALT_COMPONENT_SIZE +
                plaintext_bytes.Length];
            Buffer.BlockCopy(
                salt_bytes, 0, hash_input, 0, SALT_COMPONENT_SIZE);
            Buffer.BlockCopy(
                plaintext_bytes, 0, hash_input, SALT_COMPONENT_SIZE,
                plaintext_bytes.Length);

            SHA256 sha256 = SHA256.Create();
            return sha256.ComputeHash(hash_input);
        }
    }
}
```

As a result of this source code compilation and build process, the .NET compiler creates an *assembly* (binary file) called HackingPOS.Cryptography.Encryption

.dll which contains *Common Intermediate Language* (*CIL*) code. Unlike regular executable or .dll files, which contain direct CPU instructions, CIL code requires a *virtual machine* (such as *.NET Framework* for Windows systems or *Mono*[16] for Linux, Android, or iOS) in order to be executed. The existence of the intermediate code explains the fact that the content of the .NET assembly file is partially readable. Even opening this assembly in simple text editor may give you a clue about what's going on in that code since some names of variables, classes, and methods are stored unmodified from the original source, although most parts of it still look like gibberish (Figure 9-18).

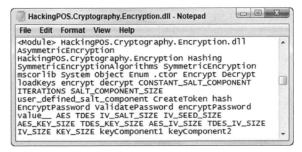

Figure 9-18: .NET assembly in text editor

However, when opened by the special tool *decompiler*[17], the assembly will look very close to the original source code:

Decompiled Code

```
namespace HackingPOS.Cryptography.Encryption
{
    public class Hashing
    {
        private const string CONSTANT_SALT_COMPONENT =
            "PE67nf0hnHkd8Dx8lSroA4PH7J1Z7HAUNe9g6a+8ml8";
        private const int ITERATIONS = 1024;
        private const int SALT_COMPONENT_SIZE = 32;
        private string user_defined_salt_component;

        public Hashing(string user_defined_salt_component)
        {
            this.user_defined_salt_component =
                user_defined_salt_component;
        }

        public string CreateToken(
            string PAN, string VariableSaltComponent)
        {
            Random random =
                new Random(VariableSaltComponent.GetHashCode());
```

```
            byte[] numArray = new byte[32];
            random.NextBytes(numArray);
            return Convert.ToBase64String(this.hash(PAN, numArray));
        }

        private byte[] hash(
            string plaintext, byte[] variable_salt_component)
        {
            Rfc2898DeriveBytes rfc2898DeriveByte =
                new Rfc2898DeriveBytes(
                Encoding.ASCII.GetBytes(string.Concat(
                "PE67nf0hnHkd8Dx81SroA4PH7J1Z7HAUNe9g6a+8ml8",
                this.user_defined_salt_component)),
                variable_salt_component, 1024);
            byte[] bytes = rfc2898DeriveByte.GetBytes(32);
            byte[] numArray = Encoding.ASCII.GetBytes(plaintext);
            byte[] numArray1 = new byte[32 + (int)numArray.Length];
            Buffer.BlockCopy(bytes, 0, numArray1, 0, 32);
            Buffer.BlockCopy(
                numArray, 0, numArray1, 32, (int)numArray.Length);
            return SHA256.Create().ComputeHash(numArray1);
        }
    }
}
```

In this reversed code, the logic of the PAN token generation and the hard-coded internal salt component value are clearly readable, which makes the tokens created by this code less secure. Another important point is that with the variety of available tools, decompiling can be done by anyone, even by a person with limited technical knowledge.

Obfuscating the Code

Code obfuscation is a technique — or more precisely, a set of various techniques (the more the better) — that allows preventing, or at least disturbing and slowing down, the reverse engineering. Code obfuscation not only hides the hard-coded sensitive data such as encryption key components and seed values from easy access, but also protects the intellectual property of the software manufacturer. In information security terms, code signing protects the integrity and the authenticity of the application code, while code obfuscation protects its confidentiality.

Nevertheless, it is important to understand that the security of software (and as in many other situations, payment application is no exception) should not solely rely on code obfuscation. Security through obscurity can deter an attacker and make an attack more difficult, but it still cannot provide a proper level of protection on its own. Obfuscation should be regarded as an extra barrier in an overall multilayer defense-in-depth strategy.

There are several obfuscation tools to choose from. My personal preference is *smartassembly*[18], but I still recommend trying several tools and making sure they really meet your expectations. Some vendors claim to provide the highest level of protection available, but in reality they do not all fulfill their promises.

Obfuscation is usually one of the last steps of the code-building process, since it must happen before the code signing because the digital signature must be calculated on the final, obfuscated version of the assembly. If you take one of the obfuscation tools and process the code from the previous example, some elements of the CIL will still be readable in the text editor, but they will no longer reveal the same level of detail (Figure 9-19).

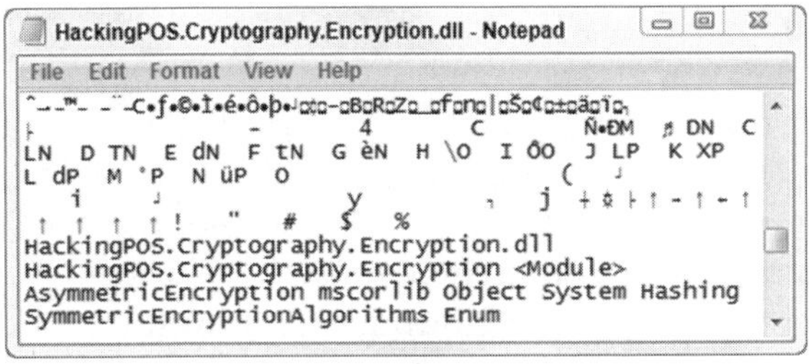

Figure 9-19: Obfuscated .NET assembly in text editor

The decompiler will be completely confused and the reversed code may look like this:

Decompiled Code after Obfuscation

```
namespace HackingPOS.Cryptography.Encryption
{
    public class Hashing
    {
        internal string  ;

        public Hashing(string user_defined_salt_component)
        {
            this. = user_defined_salt_component;
        }
        public string CreateToken(
            string PAN, string VariableSaltComponent)
        {
            Random random = new Random(.~(VariableSaltComponent));
            byte[] numArray = new byte[32];
            .~ (random, numArray);
            byte[] numArray1 = .(PAN, numArray, this);
            return .(numArray1);
        }
    }
}
```

Perhaps one may still realize the intention of the `CreateToken` method, and even understand the basic logic behind it. However, both the `CONSTANT_SALT_COMPONENT` variable name and value plus any reference to the internal `hash` method are completely gone, so the very fact of internal hard-coded salt component existence is fully hidden!

As with most other security controls, code obfuscation is not a panacea, and most likely a team of professionals will be able to crack your code. However, the obfuscation can still deter an average hacker, which might be worth some moderate efforts required to implement the obfuscation project.

Secure Coding Guidelines

A book about payment application security would not be complete if it did not mention the secure coding standards. On the one hand, it seems that PA-DSS took over standardization of payment application security development. On the other hand, this standard requires software vendors to "develop all payment applications (internal and external, and including web administrative access to product) based on secure coding guidelines,"[19] providing just generic recommendations and references. Let's review the available secure coding guidelines to see if they are compatible with the realm of payment application development.

OWASP Top 10

From all known secure coding prescriptions, the OWASP (Open Web Application Security Project) Top 10 Most Critical Web Application Security Risks[20] is perhaps the most famous due to the high popularity of web programming. OWASP Top 10 is a list of the 10 most painful web application vulnerabilities, accompanied by recommendations on how to mitigate them. Once every few years, OWASP reevaluates all known application vulnerabilities and sorts them in descending order by their severity. Basically, the same web application weaknesses are shifted up and down every year depending on trends. At this point we could end the OWASP review because at first glance web security threats are not directly relevant for most point-of-sale and payment applications running primarily on desktops and servers. However, this is not exactly true because web and desktop programming become closer as time passes. Web apps interact with desktops, and desktop software modules communicate with each other through web interfaces, such as Web Services, whether it is on an intranet or the Internet. In addition, put aside all the special web illnesses, such as *SQL injection* and *XSS (cross-site scripting)*, and you will see that there is information deserving attention (Table 9-5).

Table 9-5: OWASP Top 10 Most Critical Web Application Security Risks

RANK	RISK	COMMENT	DIRECTLY APPLICABLE TO POS/PA
1	Injection	OWASP is mostly focused on SQL Injections, which is applicable to WEB applications only, because it is still the biggest web security threat. However, code injection flaws in general can be dangerous to desktop payment applications as well.	Selectively
2	Broken Authentication and Session Management	Relevant to remote modules of distributed payment applications.	Yes
3	Cross-site Scripting (XSS)	Web only.	No
4	Insecure Direct Object References	Web only.	No
5	Security Misconfiguration	This is about configuration and updates which are relevant to any application.	Yes
6	Sensitive Data Exposure	This is the main subject of PCI DSS and PA-DSS.	Yes
7	Missing Function Level Access Control	Important for any type of application.	Yes
8	Cross-site Request Forgery (CSRF)	Web only.	No
9	Using Components with Known Vulnerabilities	Important for any type of application.	
10	Unvalidated Redirects and Forwards	Web only.	No

CWE/SANS Top 25

CWE (Common Weakness Enumeration)/SANS (SysAdmin, Audit, Networking, and Security) Top 25 Most Dangerous Software Errors is less famous compared to OWASP Top 10, and so it compensates by adding 15 extra vulnerabilities.[21] Unlike OWASP, the CWE/SANS list is not exclusively focused on web application sins, so it contains vulnerabilities that are in many situations relevant to POS software. There is helpful information that developers of payment applications can learn after weeding out most of the web-related issues. In order to do that, let's first remove all the strictly native web vulnerabilities from the list (Table 9-6):

Table 9-6: SANS Top 25 Software Errors Relevant to Web Applications Only

RANK	ERROR
1	Improper Neutralization of Special Elements used in an SQL Command ('SQL Injection')
4	Improper Neutralization of Input During Web Page Generation ('Cross-site Scripting')
9	Unrestricted Upload of File with Dangerous Type
12	Cross-Site Request Forgery (CSRF)
22	URL Redirection to Untrusted Site ('Open Redirect')

Assuming in the 21st century only brave and rich people still develop business applications using unmanaged code, even more illnesses can be removed from the final list (Table 9-7):

Table 9-7: SANS Top 25 Software Errors Relevant to Unmanaged Code Only

RANK	ERROR
3	Buffer Copy without Checking Size of Input ("Classic Buffer Overflow")
16	Inclusion of Functionality from Untrusted Control Sphere
18	Use of Potentially Dangerous Function
20	Incorrect Calculation of Buffer Size
23	Uncontrolled Format String

The next group that can be eliminated is the errors that could theoretically be found in payment application, but in practice would be difficult to use as attack vectors (Table 9-8):

Table 9-8: CWE/SANS Top 25 Software Errors Not Applicable to Payment Applications

RANK	ERROR
2	Improper Neutralization of Special Elements used in an OS Command ("OS Command Injection")
13	Improper Limitation of a Pathname to a Restricted Directory ("Path Traversal")
15	Incorrect Authorization

Now we are left with 12 issues that are directly relevant to payment application security, and I dare to sort them according to the level of potential risk. Table 9-9 contains the resulting list, which can be correlated with the real-world payment application threats discussed in previous chapters.

Table 9-9: Top 12 Payment Application Security Errors Derived from CWE/SANS Top 25

RANK	ORIGINAL RANK	ERROR
1	8	Missing Encryption of Sensitive Data
2	25	Use of a One-way Hash without a Salt
3	19	Use of a Broken or Risky Cryptographic Algorithm
4	7	Use of Hard-coded Credentials
5	14	Download of Code Without Integrity Check
6	11	Execution with Unnecessary Privileges
7	5	Missing Authentication for Critical Function
8	6	Missing Authorization
9	10	Reliance on Untrusted Inputs in a Security Decision
10	17	Incorrect Permission Assignment for Critical Resource
11	21	Improper Restriction of Excessive Authentication Attempts
12	24	Integer Overflow or Wraparound

Language-specific Guidelines

The OWASP Top 10 and CWE/SANS Top 25 lists contain generic descriptions of vulnerabilities and their mitigations, with sketchy code examples. Developers create applications using specific programming languages, so they look for more concrete instructions on how to prevent those vulnerabilities in particular development environments. Table 9-10 summarizes the available information about language-specific secure coding guidelines.

Table 9-10: Language-specific Secure Coding Guidelines and Standards

LANGUAGE	GUIDELINES OR STANDARD	PROVIDER
C	CERT C Coding Standard[22]	CERT
C++	The CERT C++ Secure Coding Standard[23]	CERT
C#	Secure Coding Guidelines[24]	Microsoft
Java	Secure Coding Guidelines for the Java Programming Language[25]	Oracle
Java	The CERT Oracle Secure Coding Standard for Java[26]	CERT

Summary

In addition to protection of explicit sensitive cardholder data, payment application code and configuration should be secured as well. Digital signatures confirm the integrity and authenticity of the application code, configuration, or data, while obfuscation protects the confidentiality of the source code.

There are two major types of digital signatures: attached (enveloped) and detached. Authenticode is a code signing technology that transparently implants an attached digital signature into any type of binary application file, such as .exe and .dll, so the end user can verify the authenticity and integrity of the software they run. Detached digital signatures are used to sign configuration and data files without modifying their internal structure.

Code obfuscation protects against disclosure of intellectual property and implementation details of cryptographic algorithms. However, the security of a payment application should not rely solely on obfuscation, which should be implemented only as part of an in-depth defense strategy.

The OWASP Top 10 and SWE/SANS Top 25 are lists of the most common software vulnerabilities. Language-specific secure coding guidelines and standards provide developers with more detailed instructions on how to write secure code within a particular development environment.

Notes

1. MSDN, "Authenticode," http://msdn.microsoft.com/en-us/library/ms537359.aspx

2. MSDN, "SignTool," http://msdn.microsoft.com/en-us/library/windows/desktop/aa387764.aspx

3. MSDN, "Creating and Using Strong-Named Assemblies," http://msdn.microsoft.com/en-us/library/xwb8f617.aspx

4. Symantec (VeriSign), "Symantec Code Signing Certificates," http://www.symantec.com/code-signing

5. Comodo, "Code Signing Certificates," http://www.comodo.com/business-security/code-signing-certificates/code-signing.php

6. OpenSSL, http://www.openssl.org/

7. Shining Light Productions, "Download Win32 OpenSSL for Windows," http://slproweb.com/products/Win32OpenSSL.html

8. IETF, "RFC 4158, Internet X.509 Public Key Infrastructure: Certification Path Building," http://tools.ietf.org/html/rfc4158

9. NIST, "Recommendation for Key Management – Part 1: General (Revision 3)," Special Publication 800-57, (July 2012), `http://csrc.nist.gov/publications/nistpubs/800-57/sp800-57_part1_rev3_general.pdf`

10. MSDN, "Downloads for developing desktop apps," `http://msdn.microsoft.com/en-us/windows/desktop/aa904949`

11. Microsoft TechNet, "Certificate Templates Overview," `http://technet.microsoft.com/en-us/library/cc730826.aspx`

12. Microsoft TechNet, "Set Up Automatic Certificate Enrollment," `http://technet.microsoft.com/en-us/library/cc770546.aspx`

13. W3C, "XML Signature Syntax and Processing (Second Edition)," `http://www.w3.org/TR/xmldsig-core/`

14. MSDN, "How to: Sign XML Documents with Digital Signatures," `http://msdn.microsoft.com/en-us/library/ms229745.aspx`

15. MSDN, "How to: Verify the Digital Signatures of XML Documents," `http://msdn.microsoft.com/en-us/library/ms229950.aspx`

16. Mono, `http://www.mono-project.com/`

17. Telerik, "The Free .NET Decompiler for Everyone," `http://www.telerik.com/products/decompiler.aspx`

18. Red Gate, "SmartAssembly 6, Robust .NET obfuscator," `http://www.red-gate.com/products/dotnet-development/smartassembly/`

19. PCI SSC, "PCI PA-DSS Requirements and Security Assessment Procedures Version 2.0" (October 2010), `https://www.pcisecuritystandards.org/documents/pa-dss_v2.pdf`

20. OWASP, "OWASP Top 10" (2013), `https://www.owasp.org/index.php/Top_10_2013-Top_10`

21. CWE/SANS, "2011 CWE/SANS Top 25 Most Dangerous Software Errors", `http://cwe.mitre.org/top25/`

22. CERT, "CERT C Coding Standard," `https://www.securecoding.cert.org/confluence/display/seccode/CERT+C+Coding+Standard`

23. CERT, "The CERT C++ Secure Coding Standard," `https://www.securecoding.cert.org/confluence/pages/viewpage.action?pageId=637`

24. MSDN, "Secure Coding Guidelines," `http://msdn.microsoft.com/en-us/library/8a3x2b7f.aspx`

25. Oracle, "Secure Coding Guidelines for the Java Programming Language, Version 4.0," `http://www.oracle.com/technetwork/java/seccodeguide-139067.html`

26. CERT, "The CERT Oracle Secure Coding Standard for Java," `https://www.securecoding.cert.org/confluence/display/java/The+CERT+Oracle+Secure+Coding+Standard+for+Java`

Conclusion

If he wrote it he could get rid of it. He had gotten rid of many things by writing them.
— Ernest Hemingway

This is the end of the book, but not the end of the story. For many payment security technologies, our time is just a beginning. So what's next? You now know that current POS systems are extremely vulnerable. You know how such vulnerabilities can be exploited, and how to prevent many such exploitations. You know that current security standards fail to help prevent exploitations. This is demonstrated by the fact that, despite huge investments in security, the number of data breaches is not declining but growing. Is there any way to stop it? Everything made by men can be broken by men. That's probably true, but at least we can try to build secure systems. Here is my opinion on what should be done.

Merchants' customer-facing environments, such as retail stores, should be freed of any obligation to implement PCI DSS controls and pass PCI DSS audits. Payment application providers should be exempted from PA-DSS validations. Instead, both merchants and software vendors should be required to implement P2PE solutions. Not just any P2PE, but Hardware P2PE. In lieu of wasting money on badly configured firewalls and useless log reviews, merchants should be investing in real, robust security technologies. Without hardware encryption, sensitive cardholder data should never touch the merchants' territory. In conjunction with EMV, tokenization, mobile payments, and other emerging technologies, P2PE is capable of providing adequate protection to cardholder data in customer-facing environments, without the need for PCI DSS and PA-DSS.

However, this does not mean that PCI DSS should be completely eliminated. The scope of its applicability should be limited to ensure the security of environments where it is still effective: data centers of payment gateways, processors, e-commerce, and acquirers. I know this is not a simple change, but it seems to be the only realistic way to deter the bad guys.

At the same time, it's quite obvious that existing payment technology—plastic cards with exposed account numbers, magnetic stripes, and even chips—while being extremely successful commercially, totally fail from a security point of view and must be replaced by some sort of digital equivalent. A change similar to what's happened in the music industry with tapes and then compact disks will eventually happen with plastic payment cards. There is no unified opinion on what such a technology will look like, but this is indeed something that will emerge very soon, and bring new security challenges with it.

POS Vulnerability Rank Calculator

From a drop of water a logician could predict an Atlantic or a Niagara.

— Arthur Conan Doyle

Security Questionnaire and Vulnerability Rank

The POS Vulnerability Rank Calculator is based on a security questionnaire that is intended to provide a brief risk assessment of the POS system and/or its associated payment application and hardware. The goal is to introduce a universal tool for initial evaluation of the POS/Payment application security posture which can then be followed by a more detailed risk assessment process. The result of the assessment is a numerical score ("vulnerability rank") ranging from 0 to 20, where 0 indicates ideal POS security, and 20 indicates a payment system without any security. Keep in mind that fewer than 10 years ago, almost any POS system would have received a rank of 20, while today some sophisticated products score closer to 0.

When merchants are in the process of selecting a new POS payment software and hardware, they can use the calculator to quickly review several products and determine the POS Vulnerability Rank of each solution. The results can then be used to further evaluate each product. In addition, vulnerability ranks calculated for specific implementations can be published by merchants, software vendors, or security assessors so that consumers (cardholders) are also able to compare different systems and become aware of the risks of swiping their cards at particular business locations.

The Scoring System

The calculation formula of the vulnerability rank is simple: each "Yes" answer gets 1 point, and the rank is the sum of all the points. Note that such a scoring system is not perfect because, in reality, not all the questions and their answers have the same weight, even though each positive answer adds 1 point to the score. For example, the presence of sensitive card data in memory in clear text (Questions 1–3) is more dangerous for sensitive card data than the lack of authentication (Questions 19 and 20). However, each question reflects a different kind of security threat to sensitive card data confidentiality or transaction integrity, so each one is counted as 1 point.

The suggested scoring system is not based on any standard simply because there are no existing standards for payment application risk assessment. The rank calculator can be easily customized if necessary by adjusting the weight of the answers for particular groups of questions.

Instructions

The calculator can be applied using the following steps:

1. Go through the security questionnaire and provide the appropriate answers for your system (1 point for "Yes," 0 points for either "No" or "N/A"). Note that, depending on the architecture and features of the particular payment system being evaluated, some questions might be not applicable. In such cases, the value of the answer would be the same as for a negative answer: 0.

2. Calculate the rank by adding up the values of all answered questions. Each "Yes" answer adds 1 point to the total score, while any "No" or "N/A" answer does not change the score.

3. Go to the Decoding the Results section at the end of the questionnaire to evaluate the overall level of security of the POS system and payment application based on the vulnerability rank. In general, the lower the rank value, the better the POS system security.

POS Security Questionnaire

The following table lists the questions used in the evaluation.

NO.	QUESTION	ANSWER (YES = 1, NO = 0, N/A = 0)
1	Does the POI/MSR device perform any operations (including but not limited to encryption) with unencrypted sensitive card data in memory (outside of TRSM)?	
2	Does the software on the POS machine perform any operations (including but not limited to encryption) with unencrypted sensitive card data in memory (outside of TRSM)?	
3	Does the store server perform any operations (including but not limited to encryption) with unencrypted sensitive card data in memory (outside of TRSM)?	
4	Does the POI/MSR device transmit unencrypted sensitive card data to the POS machine or store server?	
5	Does the POS machine transmit unencrypted sensitive card data to the store server?	
6	Does the POI/MSR, POS machine, or store server send unencrypted sensitive card data to the payment gateway/processor?	
7	Does the POI/MSR store unencrypted sensitive card data on permanent storage (outside of TRSM)?	
8	Does the software on the POS machine store unencrypted sensitive card data on a hard drive (outside of TRSM)?	
9	Does the store server store unencrypted sensitive card data on a hard drive (outside of TRSM)?	
10	Does the POI/MSR expose unencrypted DEK or KEK (or any components of DEK or KEK), which can be used for sensitive card data encryption and/or decryption, to memory or permanent storage (outside of TRSM)?	
11	Does the software on the POS machine expose unencrypted DEK or KEK (or any components of DEK or KEK), which can be used for sensitive card data encryption and/or decryption, to memory or permanent storage of the POS machine (outside of TRSM)?	

Continues

(continued)

NO.	QUESTION	ANSWER (YES = 1, NO = 0, N/A = 0)
12	Does the store server expose unencrypted DEK or KEK (or any components of DEK or KEK), which can be used for sensitive card data encryption and/or decryption, to memory or permanent storage (outside of TRSM)?	
13	Does any component of the POS system store, process, or transmit any tokens created using a hash function of sensitive card data?	
14	Does any component of the POS system store, process, or transmit any tokens created using a hash function of sensitive card data without dynamic (different for each token) salt?	
15	Does any component of the POS system store, process, or transmit the token mapping (token vault)?	
16	Does the POI/MSR device allow updating or loading of the software/firmware or configuration without validation of the software/hardware vendor's digital signatures?	
17	Does the POS machine allow updating or loading of software or configuration without validation of the software/hardware vendor's digital signatures?	
18	Does the store server allow updating or loading of software or configuration without validation of the software/hardware vendor's digital signatures?	
19	Do the POS/payment software and/or POI/MSR allow transaction processing without strong cryptographic authentication (for example, using server certificates) of the payment gateway/processor?	
20	Does the payment gateway/processor allow transaction processing without cryptographic authentication (for example, using client certificates) of the client POS/payment software and/or POI/MSR device?	
	Total Score (Vulnerability Rank):	

Decoding the Results

Evaluate the results of the assessment using the following information.

VULNERABILITY RANK	MEANING
0	Congratulations! This is a perfect payment system!
1	The system is highly secure.
2	The system is secure, but there are issues that must be addressed.
3–4	The system has vulnerabilities that must be fixed as soon as possible to reduce the risk of security breach.
5–9	The system is insecure and has a very high risk of security breach.
10–20	The system is vulnerable and can be breached at any moment. In fact, if this is a production environment, it is very possible that the system is already broken but the security breach is not recognized.

Glossary of Terms and Abbreviations

AES (Advanced Encryption Standard) — Symmetric encryption algorithm created by *NIST* based on the Rijndael encryption algorithm.

Attack Vector — Method of an attack on a computer system with a detailed description of how security controls have been broken.

AOC (Attestation of Compliance) — An application form submitted by a merchant or service provider to PCI SSC for PCI DSS assessment registration.

AOV (Attestation of Validation) — An application form submitted by a payment application vendor to PCI SSC for PA-DSS revalidation registration.

API (Application Programming Interface) — A set of functions exposed by an application in order to communicate with other applications. For example, payment application API exposed to POS application, or payment gateway API exposed to payment applications.

ATM Card (Automated Teller Machine Card) — The bank card intended for cash withdrawal that usually cannot be accepted for payment by merchants, unlike a debit card (see *debit card*).

Authorization — The first stage of a payment transaction when the payment processor checks that the account associated with the card has enough credit (for credit cards) or funds (for debit and gift cards) for the transaction.

Batch — A group of payment transactions that were processed by a payment application during a specific period of time (usually one business day) and are awaiting settlement.

BDK (Base Derivation Key) — In a DUKPT key management scheme, the base key used for generating the keys that are injected into the POI devices.

BIN (Bank Identification Number) — See *ISO Prefix*.

BOS (Back Office Server) — A computer, or group of computers, located at the "back" of the store (in small stores, often physically located in the "back office" of store manager), and often used as a store server.

Carders — People involved in a *carding* process.

Carding — Process of selling and buying stolen payment card data.

Card-not-present Transaction (or Card-absent Transaction) — Payment transaction processed either online or by phone, when a payment system does not physically read the magnetic stripe of the card.

Card-present Transaction — Payment transaction processed in a brick-and-mortar store when the POS system actually reads the magnetic stripe of the card, or the card data is entered manually and verified by cashier.

Chargeback — Rejected payment transaction.

CHD (Cardholder Data) — See *Sensitive Data*.

Completion — The second stage of payment transaction processing (after *authorization*) when the exact amount of the transaction is recorded (authorization amount can be more than actual transaction amount).

CVV (Card Verification Value) (also called CAV, CSC, CVC) — 3- or 4-digit code located at magnetic Tracks 1 and 2 of a payment card.

CVV2 (Card Verification Value 2) (also called CID, CAV2, CVC2) — 3-digit code located on the back or front of a plastic payment card.

Debit Card — Card used as both an *ATM* (bank) card for cash withdrawal and as a payment card accepted by merchants. Transactions with a debit card usually require two-factor authentication with a PIN number.

DEK (Data Encryption Key) — A cryptographic key used for data encryption (see also *KEK*).

DES (Data Encryption Standard) — Deprecated symmetric encryption algorithm (see also *Triple DES*).

DUKPT (Derived Unique Key Per Transaction) — Encryption and key management mechanism used for debit PIN protection and P2PE.

Encoding — The process of writing card data information into magnetic tracks of a plastic payment card.

Embossing — The process of stamping the PAN digits and other cardholder information onto a plastic card.

EPS (Electronic Payments Server) (also called Electronic Payments Service, Electronic Payments System) — A software and/or hardware application dedicated to processing electronic payments.

Failover — The ability of a payment application to switch to a different communication type or authorization host if the main connection or host is offline.

Fallback — Can mean Offline Fallback Processing (see *S&F*) or *Failover*.

FIPS (Federal Information Processing Standards) — A set of standards defining requirements for cryptographic algorithms and systems.

Host — Authorization server at the payment processor's data center.

Host to Host Protocol — Transaction protocol for data exchange between payment gateways, processors, and acquirers.

HSM (Hardware Security Module) — A device designed to process cryptographic operations (encryption, decryption, cryptographic key management) in a secure environment protected by physical security controls.

ICCR (Integrated Circuit Card Reader) — EMV (Chip & PIN) card reader device.

IIN (Issuer Identification Number) — See *ISO Prefix*.

ISO Prefix (also called IIN, BIN) — The first 6 digits of PAN that identify the card issuer.

KEK (Key Encryption Key) — A cryptographic key used for encrypting the *DEK*.

KIF (Key Injection Facility) — A place where *POI* containing *pinpad* and/or *MSR* devices are being injected with debit PIN or P2PE encryption keys.

KSN (Key Serial Number) — In a DUKPT key management scheme, the data that is being sent by the encrypting end (POI device) to the decrypting end in order to identify the BDK and session key used for data encryption.

MITM (Man-in-the-Middle) — An attack on a communication system (such as SSL-protected TCP/IP traffic) when an attacker is wedged between the client and the server.

MSR (Magnetic Stripe Reader) — A device (usually mounted on a POS or POI) that reads the magnetic stripe of a card when the card is swiped by the customer at the store.

NIST (National Institute of Standards and Technology) — Organization that creates and maintains various standards, including *FIPS*.

P2PE (Point-to-Point Encryption) (Synonym: End-to-End Encryption) — Technology that keeps sensitive cardholder data encrypted throughout the entire process of payment from its entry at the POI/MSR device to the data center of the payment gateway or processor.

PA (Payment Application) — Software application created for electronic payment processing. PA implements all functions associated with acceptance, processing, storage, and transmission of sensitive card data.

PA-DSS (Payment Application Data Security Standard) — Security standard for payment software providers.

PAN (Primary Account Number) — Identifies the cardholder; usually 16 digits long.

PA-QSA (Payment Application Qualified Security Assessor) — A company or individual who is authorized by PCI SSC to perform PA-DSS validation.

PA-QSA (P2PE) (Payment Application Qualified Security Assessor, Point-to-Point Encryption) — A company or individual who is authorized by PCI SSC to perform P2PE application validation.

Payment Gateway — Company-service provider that accepts transaction requests from multiple stores and routes them to different Payment Processors depending on merchant configuration.

Payment Processor (also called Authorizer) — Company that processes electronic payments for merchants. Payment Processor accepts authorization, completion, and settlement messages from stores and routes them to appropriate acquirers for approval and settlement.

Payment Switch (also called Switch) — Server or group of servers at the merchant's or Payment Gateway's data center which consolidate transaction messages from multiple stores and route them to appropriate Payment Processors based on merchant configuration.

PCI SSC (Payment Card Industry Security Standards Council) — Organization that creates and maintains PCI security standards, approves PCI DSS, PA-DSS, PTS, and P2PE assessments, and certifies the QSA. PCI SSC also maintains the list of validated payment applications, certified POI devices, and validated P2PE applications and solutions.

PCI DSS (Payment Card Industry Data Security Standard) — Security standard for merchants and service providers.

PED (PIN Entry Device) — See *POI*.

PIN (Personal Identification Number) — Numeric code (typically 4 digits) used as a second authentication factor ("something you know") in *two-factor authentication* of the cardholder.

POI (Point of Interaction) (also called PED, PIN pad, pinpad, payment terminal) — A device that combines several functions and subsystems, such as MSR, PIN Entry Keyboard, Customer Display, TRSM, and others.

POS (Point of Sale) (also called register, lane, point of service) — Software application and/or hardware device that processes and records transactions (including payments) between the merchant and its customers.

Post Void — Cancellation of payment that was processed after POS transaction is finalized.

PreAuth — The process of obtaining *authorization* so it can be stored and used later for transaction *completion*.

PTS (PIN Transaction Security) — Security standard and certification for POI and HSM device manufacturers.

QSA (P2PE) (Qualified Security Assessor, Point-to-Point Encryption) — A company or individual who is authorized by PCI SSC to perform P2PE assessments.

QSA (Qualified Security Assessor) — A company or individual authorized by PCI SSC to perform PCI DSS assessments.

RAM (Random Access Memory) — A device for temporary data storage (until the power to the machine is turned off).

Reconciliation — Part of the *settlement* process when two parts of the payment processing (for example, POS and payment processor) compare the number and amount of processed transactions.

Redemption — Payment with gift card.

Refund (also called return) — Crediting cardholder account, usually when previously purchased items are returned to the merchant.

Response Timeout — The maximum time allowed for a response to be returned by the server to the client (for example, payment gateway to POS). If the response timeout interval is exceeded, the payment application goes to error handling, *fallback*, or *failover* mode.

Return — See Refund.

ROC (Report on Compliance) — A document created by a PCI QSA as the result of a PCI DSS assessment.

ROV (Report of Validation) — A document created by a PA QSA as the result of a PA-DSS validation process.

RSA (Rivest, Shamir, Adleman) — Asymmetric encryption algorithm created in 1977 by Ron Rivest, Adi Shamir, and Leonard Adleman.

S&F (Store and Forward) (also called SAF, Fallback, Stand-in) — Mechanism that allows the store payment system to authorize and complete payment transactions with no communication with the payment processor (if the authorization network or host is down).

SCD (Secure Cryptographic Device) — PCI term for *TRSM* and *HSM*.

SCR (Secure Card Reader) — PCI term for secure (*PTS*-certified) *MSR* or *ICCR*. MSR must be PTS with *SRED* certified.

Sensitive Authentication Data — See Sensitive Data.

Sensitive Card Data, Sensitive Cardholder Data — See Sensitive Data.

Sensitive Data (also called Cardholder Data, Sensitive Authentication Data) — Information that identifies the cardholder and (if compromised) can be used to process fraudulent payment transactions. Sensitive Data includes Track 1, Track 2, PAN, Expiration Date, Service Code, PIN, and more. In general, the difference between Sensitive Authentication Data and Cardholder Data is that the former can be used "as is" in order to manufacture a duplicate of the original payment card, while the latter can be used as an input component for constructing the former. Sensitive Authentication Data includes Track 1 and 2, while Cardholder Data contains the PAN. Although it is much easier to counterfeit cards with Sensitive Authentication Data than Cardholder Data, both are a target for hackers. In most places throughout this book, Sensitive Authentication Data and Cardholder Data are not differentiated, so for the sake of simplicity they are combined in a single term: *Sensitive Data*.

Settlement — A process in which a payment transaction is *reconciled* between the issuer, acquirer, processor, and merchant.

SHA (Secure Hash Algorithm) — One-way encryption algorithm.

Split Dial — Ability of a payment application to *route* transactions to different payment processors based on BIN range, transaction type, or other parameters.

SRED (Secure Reading and Exchange of Data) — One of the modules of PCI PTS certification. An SRED-certified POI device is required for PCI HW P2PE certification.

Stand-in — See S&F.

Store Server — A computer or group of computers that serve as a central location for various store-level applications, including *back office server* and POS server.

Switch — See Payment Switch.

Tender — Payment method such as cash, credit, or check. POS transaction may contain more than one tender if a customer chooses to pay, for instance, by both cash and credit card.

Tipping — The process of painting the embossed numbers (see *Embossing*) and letters using gold or silver foil.

Token — Unique ID that identifies the PAN without compromising the actual cardholder data.

Tokenization — Technology that protects cardholder data by using a *token* instead of PAN. The token can be either a cryptographic function of the cardholder data (for example, hash) or a randomly generated value mapped using *token vault*.

TOR (Timeout Reversal) — A cancellation of the previous attempt to send a message in case of no response (response timeout) from the authorization host.

Track 1, Track 2 — Information about card issuer and cardholder encoded on the magnetic stripe of payment cards.

Triple DEA (Triple Data Encryption Algorithm) — See *Triple DES*.

Triple DES (also called Triple DEA, 3DES, TDES, TDEA) — Symmetric block cipher used as a standard algorithm for debit PIN encryption.

TRSM (Tamper-Resistant Security Module) — Cryptographic device (typically located inside POI) which physically protects the encryption keys and destroys them when an attempt is made to open its tamper-resistant case.

Two-Factor Authentication (also called multi-factor authentication) — Requires more than one factor to be used to authenticate the user. The two authentication factors must be from different types. There are three common types: "something you have," "something you know," and "something you are." Examples of two-factor authentication in payments are debit with PIN, chip & pin, and ATM cards where one authentication factor ("something you have") is the card itself and the second authentication factor ("something you know") is the PIN number.

Void — Cancellation of a payment tender during the same POS transaction.

Zero Day Attack — The sort of attack that exploits zero-day software vulnerability which was not discovered and/or publicly disclosed yet, and as a result was never fixed and patched by the software vendor.

Index